Teaching and Developing Reading Skills

Cambridge Handbooks for Language Teachers

This series, now with over 50 titles, offers practical ideas, techniques and activities for the teaching of English and other languages, providing inspiration for both teachers and trainers.

Recent titles in this series:

Teaching and Developing Reading Skills

Peter Watkins

Consultant and editor: Scott Thornbury

CAMBRIDGE
UNIVERSITY PRESS

CAMBRIDGE
UNIVERSITY PRESS

University Printing House, Cambridge CB2 8BS, United Kingdom

One Liberty Plaza, 20th Floor, New York, NY 10006, USA

477 Williamstown Road, Port Melbourne, VIC 3207, Australia

314–321, 3rd Floor, Plot 3, Splendor Forum, Jasola District Centre,
New Delhi – 110025, India

79 Anson Road, #06–04/06, Singapore 079906

Cambridge University Press is part of the University of Cambridge.

It furthers the University's mission by disseminating knowledge in the pursuit of
education, learning and research at the highest international levels of excellence.

www.cambridge.org
Information on this title: www.cambridge.org/9781316647318

© Cambridge University Press 2017

It is normally necessary for written permission for copying to be obtained
in advance from a publisher. The worksheets and role play cards
contained in this book are designed to be copied and distributed in class.
The normal requirements are waived here and it is not necessary to write to
Cambridge University Press for permission for an individual teacher to make copies
for use within his or her own classroom. Only those pages that carry the wording
'© Cambridge University Press' may be copied.

First published 2017

20 19 18 17 16 15 14 13 12 11 10 9 8 7 6 5 4 3

Printed in Great Britain by CPI Group (UK) Ltd, Croydon CR0 4YY

A catalogue record for this publication is available from the British Library

Library of Congress Cataloguing in Publication data

ISBN 978-1-316-64731-8 Paperback
ISBN 978-1-316-64735-6 Apple ibook
ISBN 978-1-316-64737-0 Google ebook
ISBN 978-1-316-64734-9 Kindle ebook
ISBN 978-1-316-64736-3 ebooks.com ebook

Additional resources for this publication at http://esource.cambridge.org

Cambridge University Press has no responsibility for the persistence or accuracy
of URLs for external or third-party internet websites referred to in this publication,
and does not guarantee that any content on such websites is, or will remain,
accurate or appropriate.

Contents

Thanks

I am grateful to Cambridge University Press for continuing to see the relevance and importance of books of this kind for practising teachers. In particular I would like to thank Karen Momber, Jo Timerick and Helen Forrest for their support for, input into, and editing of this book – their expertise and patience are greatly appreciated. My sincere thanks also go to Scott Thornbury for his ever-generous guidance and support.

I would also like to thank Robyn Brooks, Carmen Pasamar Márquez and Monika Grządka for their help with specific activities and texts.

For Sarah and Charlie.

Acknowledgements

The authors and publishers acknowledge the following sources of copyright material and are grateful for the permissions granted. While every effort has been made, it has not always been possible to identify the sources of all the material used, or to trace all copyright holders. If any omissions are brought to our notice, we will be happy to include the appropriate acknowledgements on reprinting and in the next update to the digital edition, as applicable.

Text:

BrainyQuote for the text on p. 106 from the BrainyQuote website, www.brainyquote.com. Copyright © 2017 BrainyQuote; Macmillan Education for the text on p. 109 from *Beyond the Sentence: Introducing Discourse Analysis* by Scott Thornbury. Copyright © 2005 Macmillan Education. Reproduced with permission; Atlantic Books for the text on p. 136 from *The Shallows: How the Internet is Changing the Way We Think, Read and Remember* by Nicholas Carr. Copyright © Atlantic Books; Delta Publishing for the text on p. 171 and p. 273 from *Learning to Teach English* by Peter Watkins. Copyright © 2014 Delta publishing. Reproduced with kind permission; National Geographic Society for the text on p. 177 and pp. 270–272 from 'It's Time to Accept That Elephants, Like Us, Are Empathetic Beings' by Virginia Morell, http://news.nationalgeographic.com/news/2014/02/140221-elephants-poaching-empathy-grief-extinction-science/. Copyright © 2014 National Geographic Society. Reproduced with permission; Text on p. 186 adapted from 'How technology disrupted the truth' by Katharine Viner, *The Guardian*, 12.07.12.

Photos:

The publishers are grateful to the following for permission to reproduce copyright photograph and material

Key: L = Left, R = Right, T = Top, B = Below.

p. 48 (L), p. 48 (R): Courtesy of Peter Watkins; p. 270: Gallo Images - Michael Poliza/Riser/Getty Images; p. 271: Pjmalsbury/E+/Getty Images; p. 273 (T): Courtesy of Robyn Brooks; p. 273 (B): Roger de la Harpe/Gallo Images/Getty Images; p. 277: SPL IMAGES/ Photographer's Choice/ Getty Images.

Introduction

The place of reading

Reading and writing are incredible human achievements, allowing us to communicate across both space and time. Amongst other things, the magic of reading allows us to witness history as it was being made, be transported to magical worlds, gain new knowledge and stay in touch with loved ones when we are thousands of miles apart. There can be no doubt that reading and writing are truly amazing accomplishments.

Unlike listening, reading is a skill learned through conscious effort and the process of learning usually starts in the first language (L1) sometime around the beginning of formal education, with a very high proportion of the population being successful in the task. Learning to read and write is vital for providing life chances and the transformative nature of these skills is indicated by the way in which the raising of literacy standards is frequently linked to the reduction of poverty (National Literacy Trust, 2011).

Being a proficient reader in just one language is enormously empowering, and having ability in more than one language increases this further. Moreover, in second language (L2) learning contexts, reading is not just a means of maintaining social interaction or gaining world knowledge but also important to the process of learning. While many would question Krashen's (1985, and elsewhere) claim that comprehensible input is *sufficient* for language learning, very few would question the *necessity* of learners being exposed to a huge amount of input in order to be successful, and reading is a crucial source of such input. More recently, the increasing internationalization of education (Altbach and Knight, 2007), and the use of L2s (primarily English) as mediums of instruction, has increased the need for many learners to develop a high level of reading proficiency in languages other than their L1.

How we understand text

Just as with the skills of listening, speaking and writing, there is a tendency to think of reading as a single skill. However, reading is complex, made up of a whole range of different processes happening very quickly and often simultaneously. When we read, we decode the combinations of letters quickly. In order to do this, we may need to 'sound out', at least in our heads, the sounds the letters represent (*th* can represent a /θ/ or a /ð/ sound, for example). We match the pattern that emerges from the decoding to our lexical knowledge. So, when we see the combination of letters *t-h-i-r-d* we recognize it as a word and that links to what we understand *third* to mean. Perhaps the biggest single difference between L1 and L2 reading is that the L1 reader has a much wider lexical store to draw on and the knowledge held on each item is likely to be richer and more detailed. We will discuss L1 and L2 reading differences more fully a little later.

As well as lexical knowledge, when reading we also use our knowledge of grammar to group words into phrases (*the third man*) and we make connections from one part of the text to another using our understanding of discourse. In addition, we infer anything that is not explicitly stated from what we have already understood, or our general background knowledge of the topic and text type. All of these knowledge bases are constantly being used as we process text and the deeper our lexical, phonological, grammatical and discourse awareness is, the easier the reading task becomes. These complex processes happen very quickly. When reading for understanding (that is constructing a mental summary version of the text), readers in their L1 process text at somewhere between 250 and 300 words per minute (Carrell and Grabe, 2010, p. 216). In order to be able to operate at such speeds, readers must be able to recognize the vast majority of words instantly and automatically, emphasizing the importance of lexical knowledge to reading.

The recognizing of letter–sound combinations, words and grammar patterns is often referred to as 'bottom-up processing'. This is usually contrasted with 'top-down processing' (Grabe and Stoller, 2011, pp. 285 and 295), which is characterized as sampling the text in order to confirm our expectations of content. Those expectations may be based on our background knowledge, awareness of the context, and also what we know of the discourse structure (or text type). As we read, we make use of both top-down and bottom-up processes, with failures in one potentially being compensated by the other. For example, a reader working in their L2 may increasingly rely on what they know about the context to try to make sense of a text if they fail to recognize a significant proportion of the words on the page.

The balance between bottom-up and top-down processing will vary in any given situation. This variation will depend on a whole host of factors, not least the type of text being read and the purpose for reading it (see below), along with the difficulty of the text, the reader's familiarity with the topic and the presence or absence of relevant contextual information. In addition, in L2 reading situations, the kind of task that has been set is also likely to influence the distribution of bottom-up and top-down processing.

These two types of processing work together and contribute to comprehension, which, Grabe (2009) argues, can also be seen as consisting of two parts. The first part is a 'text model of comprehension' and involves the reader processing words and grammar from the text and building them into a mental representation of meaning. This representation of meaning needs to be held in working memory so that new information from the text can be fitted into the developing picture. The text model, as the name suggests, deals very much with meaning derived from the text and therefore draws on bottom-up processing. Grabe's explanation of understanding texts also has a 'situation model of comprehension', which is much more reader-based. Here, the reader combines their own background knowledge with information derived from the text to arrive at a richer interpretation of what has been read. This layer of understanding will include our attitudes to the text, writer and situation. It explains how two readers can read the same text, agree on its content, but interpret it differently. Potentially the two layers of comprehension develop simultaneously as we read and they combine to produce a coherent message. We can see that we do not just decode information from the text, but also build that information into what we already know, or believe, about the topic, and in this sense, each reader constructs meaning as they read, rather than simply 'receiving' meaning.

While in the past reading has been characterised as a passive skill (Nunan, 2015), the situation model of comprehension implies that reading is much more than the passive decoding of the writer's message. It is 'an active – even interactive – process' (Thornbury, 2017, p. 238).

Much of the two-fold comprehension process described above happens without conscious thought in proficient readers. However, there will be times when we need to manage our mental resources and take deliberate actions to help when we find understanding difficult. This happens in both L1 and L2 and may take the form of such things as rereading sections of text, finding, or guessing, the meaning of unknown words, or consciously summarizing parts of a text. These are examples of reading strategies and successful readers not only use a range of strategies but also use strategies in combination (Anderson, 1991). These types of reading strategy are deployed to help us process texts, or parts of texts, that are otherwise difficult to understand.

Purposes of reading

One of the key characteristics of reading, at least in reading outside the classroom, is that we have a clear purpose for doing it. Grellet (1981, p. 4) identifies two main reasons for reading: reading for pleasure and reading for information. However, each of these categories is very broad and could be further subdivided. For example, reading for pleasure might include reading humorous posts on social media or reading a novel, as well as many things in between. Reading for information could also be broken down into related but separate areas, such as reading quickly to identify appropriate information, evaluating information, and integrating information from multiple sources.

Our reasons for reading a particular text and the level of detail we require from it will influence how we read that text, including, as we have seen, how we balance bottom-up and top-down processing. An undergraduate consulting a range of sources while writing a final dissertation is likely to read more carefully and extract more detail than someone flicking through a magazine while in a dentist's waiting area. The undergraduate is reading to learn and will need to both integrate information from multiple sources and evaluate the strengths and usefulness of each text. This will require detailed, careful reading. The dental patient, on the other hand, is reading for pleasure (or at least distraction) and is more likely to read quickly, paying less attention to details. So, the way in which we set about reading a text will depend very much on our purpose for reading it. The implication of this is that learners need to develop flexible reading skills so that they can be successful in a range of situations.

In L2 learning contexts we may be able to add a further category to those proposed by Grellet as learners may choose to read not primarily for pleasure nor to gain new information, but as a language learning strategy. In these cases the primary purpose for reading is to develop language knowledge (for example, building vocabulary range) and skills (such as reading fluency). In terms of developing language knowledge, this could involve consciously looking out for and exploiting the learning opportunities a text offers or may rely simply on the benefits of exposure to the target language.

Types of reading

As we have seen, different texts may be read in different ways and in order to take account of this, the general term 'reading' is often broken down into sub-categories. The following terms are frequently used in the literature:

- 'Scanning' is the very quick processing of text, as we look for a specific detail, such as the price of a product in an advertisement. It is important to note that scanning involves the recognition of form, rather than developing an understanding of the text as a whole, and this results in reading speeds of around 600 words per minute, much faster than where meaning is processed (Carrell and Grabe, 2010, p. 216).

- 'Skimming', or gist reading, is to read quickly for a general understanding, such as when we look quickly at an old document on our hard drive to see if it can be permanently deleted.
- 'Detailed reading' is to read carefully to understand as much of the content as possible, such as when we read instructions on a medicine bottle, or an academic text on which we will later base an argument.

In addition, in second language learning contexts, it is common to talk about a contrast between 'intensive' and 'extensive' reading. Intensive reading is essentially another term for detailed reading, as described above, and makes use of relatively short texts that are at the limit of comfortable intelligibility for learners. Extensive reading, on the other hand, is usually associated with the reading of longer texts outside the classroom and is principally for pleasure. The texts used for these purposes are generally within the range of comfortable understanding.

Another potential distinction is between silent reading and reading aloud. Much of the reading we do outside of learning situations is done silently and therefore there is a strong case that reading programmes should focus on this. Reading aloud, on the other hand, is relatively less used but can be effective in teaching situations (Cameron, 2001). One form of reading aloud is when the teacher reads to the class as a whole. This can be very helpful as a model of fluent reading, showing appropriate pausing and how texts need to be 'chunked'. It also exposes learners to particular genres, which can be helpful in their own reading, and can also aid classroom dynamics by providing a shared positive experience. Reading aloud in this way is most often associated with young learners, but others, particularly L2 beginners, may also benefit. Harmer (2001) points out the dramatic nature of this type of reading and therefore the performance skills required by the teacher.

A second type of reading aloud is when learners themselves read aloud, either on a one-to-one or small group basis, or to the whole class. When done on a one-to-one or small group basis, this can have good results, particularly when used as a remedial strategy (Geva and Ramírez, 2015). However, in many L2 teaching situations having learners read aloud is often advised against. This is because the mental processing required to articulate the text can prejudice understanding. Essentially, there is a focus on form over meaning. Added to this, learners can find it very stressful to read in front of others and also those called on to listen may soon become disengaged if the reading lacks the performance skills referred to by Harmer. Where reading aloud is used, it is probably wise not to allow it to dominate the reading programme, given that learners will generally need to use silent reading skills more often outside of class. Also, it can be useful to allow learners to prepare the text silently first, so that they can focus on meaning before reading aloud.

How reading is taught

The teaching of reading in L1 situations (which has impacted on L2 teaching) has been dominated by two opposing views.

The first of these is known as a 'phonics approach', in which readers are systematically taught how letters, and combinations of letters, equate to sounds. So we may sound out the letters *p*, *e* and *n* to make *pen*. Phonics instruction is most effective when it is explicit and systematic (Geva and Ramírez, 2015) and it gives readers the ability to decode words and this ability, in turn, leads to higher levels of reading comprehension (Stanovich, 2000). In a phonics approach, learners typically move from letters and sounds to simple words and traditionally worksheets may be used to practise particular letter–sound relationships (McBride, 2016). This may develop into reading simple stories that make use of only those words that contain the letter–sound combinations already learned.

The relatively weak relationship of sound and orthography in English means that some words, such as *two*, remain problematic and are probably best recognized as a whole rather than from component letters. However, a much stronger criticism of the phonics approach is made by proponents, such as Smith (1971), of a 'whole language' approach to the teaching of reading. Their argument is that the explicit attention paid to phonics promotes the mechanical decoding of words over meaning and as a result can be rather dull, and actually risks alienating young readers. Instead, a whole language approach stresses that a reader's objective should be to derive meaning from continuous text and that an awareness of phonics will develop automatically from plentiful, meaning-driven, exposure to texts.

The arguments for both sides have been put forcefully, but we should remember that classroom practice is just one element of learning to read. It is likely that other variables, such as the place of reading in the home environment, will also impact on a learner's success. More importantly, as Cameron (2001, p. 124) points out, the dichotomy between a strictly phonics approach and a strictly whole language approach is a false one, which does 'a disservice to learners, who need it all'. In other words, programmes for beginner readers need to achieve a balance between both approaches. This is probably the case in both L1 and L2 reading, at least for alphabet-based scripts.

Paran (1996) argues convincingly that the teaching of English as an L2 has embraced the top-down and whole language views of reading more enthusiastically than it has the basic decoding of words, despite the research evidence that efficient reading depends on efficient decoding. This position is perhaps a result of the focus on meaning being more aligned to the values of communicative language teaching, which also tends to prioritize meaning, and has been widely adopted in one form or another in many contexts.

Comparing L1 and L2 reading

There are clear differences in the twin challenges of learning to read in a first language and a second language. The most obvious of these is the amount of language knowledge available in each case. An L1 learner at around school starting age will already know several thousand words and will have an implicit understanding of how words are formed and strung together. On the other hand, an L2 learner will frequently be starting reading with a very limited knowledge of lexis and grammar. The lack of such basic linguistic knowledge as not knowing the meaning of a high proportion of the words in a text is a major obstacle to successful L2 reading.

Researchers disagree on the exact proportion of known to unknown words in a text that is necessary for comprehension. This is not surprising given that 'comprehension' is hard to define and measure precisely. However, there is agreement that the proportion of known words must be very high. Nation (2006), for example, argues that a reader needs to be familiar with around 98% of the words in a text to feel confident that they understand it. How many actual words that means a learner needs to know in total will depend on the types of text a learner needs to read, but Nation's study suggests that knowledge of around 8,000–9,000 word families would be required to read most texts independently. The number is likely to increase where more specialist texts are read, such as in academic situations. The inescapable implication of this is that developing vocabulary knowledge is an essential part of developing reading skills.

Another key difference between L1 and L2 reading is that the L2 reader has some knowledge of at least two languages. Particularly at lower proficiency levels, the L2 reader is likely to draw on knowledge from the first language, perhaps looking for similarities in word forms, or anticipating text structure. This is a resource that is not available to L1 readers and the success of such strategies will vary according to the language background of the learner. Where languages share a number of cognates, syntactic similarities and discourse conventions, such as English and French, it is more likely to be effective. On the other hand, in cases where a learner's L1 is very distant from the L2, including using a different orthography (Arabic or Cyrillic, for example), the strategy is unlikely to be useful and additional difficulties in processing are likely to be encountered (Carrell and Grabe, 2010). There are other strategies L2 readers may use that draw on their L1. For example, a learner may use the strategy of translating the text into their L1 in order to check the coherence of the message they are building.

As well as having L1 linguistic resources, an L2 reader will usually have developed strategies for reading in their L1 which might be accessed in L2 reading. For example, an L2 reader studying in an academic context may be able to transfer strategies for annotating and highlighting text that they already know are successful in supporting recall and understanding. This implies that, in some instances at least, L1 reading proficiency will predict L2 reading proficiency.

However, it seems that L1 skills and strategies are not always available to a reader when using an L2. One of the most discussed concepts in L2 reading is the so-called 'language threshold'. The essential tenet of the argument is that L2 readers must understand enough L2 vocabulary and grammar to be able to transfer L1 reading strategies successfully. If there is too much unknown material, the reader is forced to devote almost their entire effort to working out the potential meanings of unfamiliar content, rather than applying the processes they would use in L1 reading. Clearly, the point at which a threshold is crossed and learners understand nearly all the words in the text will depend on the learner, their L2 language proficiency and the text they are dealing with. It may be that a learner crosses the threshold one day because they already know the majority of words in a given text, but are unable to do so again the next day with a different text because more of that text is unknown to them.

Another key difference in developing L1 and L2 reading is the environment in which it happens. In many L2 settings, learners may have very limited opportunities to read in the L2, whereas L1 readers will typically be surrounded by text in their day-to-day lives. L1 readers will probably be very motivated to learn to read as it is a social expectation, key to life chances, and a stated government educational goal. As well as having fewer opportunities, L2 readers may see less reason to read and may perhaps be demotivated by the text types with which they are presented in classrooms, particularly where they are accompanied by anxiety-raising comprehension tests.

Having looked at how people read and the differences between L1 and L2 reading, we will consider how classroom practice tends to treat the development of reading skills.

Staging reading lessons

As Communicative Language Teaching (CLT) came to prominence in the 1970s, there was an increased interest in the teaching of the four skills. This is not surprising because if we assume that the purpose of learning is to communicate, there is a clear argument to develop the skills through which we do that: speaking, listening, reading and writing.

CLT is something of an umbrella term (Hall, 2011) and so it is not easy to generalize about how teaching takes place in different contexts. However, a glance at almost any coursebook written for a global market suggests that, across proficiency levels and across publishers, a fairly standard approach to reading is adopted (Cunningham and Moor, 2005; Soars and Soars, 2006; Tilbury, Hendra, Rea and Clementson, 2010; Dummet, Hughes and Stephenson, 2013). A norm has emerged which generally involves a fairly fixed sequence of stages, as listed in the table below:

Pre-reading	• The teacher builds interest in the topic of the text. • The teacher pre-teaches vocabulary that appears in the text.
While-reading	• The teacher sets a task and the learners read to complete it. • The teacher checks that this has been done accurately. • The teacher sets a second task and the learners read again to complete it. • The teacher checks that this has been done accurately.
Post-reading	• The teacher sets up an activity that follows on from the text, such as a discussion or a role play.

Building interest in the text is an opportunity to activate background knowledge. This is important in building expectations of the text and enabling top-down processing. It is also certainly true that learners need to be motivated to read and so building interest would seem a sensible teaching strategy.

Some of the stages outlined above may not be present in every reading lesson. For example, the pre-teaching of vocabulary, essentially a strategy for adjusting the level of the text by providing additional support for bottom-up processing, may be omitted, particularly where a teacher decides that their learners will not need such support to process the text successfully. In addition, after this sequence of stages which focuses on the meaning of the text, there may be further stages that use the text as an object of study. For example, a salient grammar point may be selected and studied, or a lexical set identified. There are great advantages for learners to see language in context in this way. Celce-Murcia and Olshtain (2000) amongst others, point out that language choices frequently depend on contextual demands. However, in the cases where this type of language study stage is included in coursebook material, we may question the extent to which the context is fully explored and exploited. In some cases it seems that the highlighting of a grammar point in a text is little more than a neat segue into a traditional sentence-level analysis and seldom fully considers how the context has impacted on the linguistic choices made.

Selecting reading texts

It seems axiomatic that the success of reading lessons will not just depend on their staging, but also on the choice of text itself. The use of so-called 'authentic' material has long been discussed in language teaching literature. Authentic material is conventionally glossed as being that material which was not originally written for language learning purposes (e.g. Watkins, 2014, p. 163). While this definition may be useful in some circumstances, we can easily see its limitations. First, it tends to present 'authenticity' as a binary concept – something is either authentic or it is not. However, in reality, coursebook writers or teachers may make slight changes to a text, such as removing a word likely to cause offence. Therefore authenticity is more usefully seen as a continuum. The difficulties of the concept do not end there. If I take a menu from a local restaurant and use it in a lesson, it would fit a conventional definition of authentic material. But as my learners start to study the menu at 9:00 on a Monday morning, the situation is not authentic. A menu is written to be read (and frequently discussed) in a restaurant or café, when people are hungry and want food. My 9:00 lesson does not provide an authentic context for using the text. In a sense, once the text is taken from the sphere for which it was intended, it loses its authenticity.

The debate between authentic and scripted material is perhaps not usefully characterized as one being superior to the other. Macaro (2003, p. 147) points out that there is very little research on what sorts of texts learners prefer using, or whether they are particularly sensitive to authenticity issues, and Swan argued over 30 years ago that the reality is that authentic, adapted, and specifically written texts can all be useful as long as they are appropriate for the learners who use them (Swan, 1985). Appropriacy may be hard to define but would include the level of the text, cultural sensitivities and, crucially, whether the text represents the discourse structures and styles that the learners will engage with outside the classroom. The likelihood is that learners at low levels of proficiency will be exposed to either specifically written material, or very heavily adapted material because of the difficulty of finding authentic material that is appropriate for their level. As learners become more proficient, so teachers are more likely to find appropriate authentic texts for them to use.

Just as we saw with the menu example above, as well as the reading materials themselves being realistic, it is important that the tasks that accompany them also reflect the purposes for which the text was originally written. In other words, it is important that learners have the opportunity of giving an authentic response to the text. For example, a text taken from a holiday brochure describing a holiday destination is written to persuade us that we would enjoy a holiday in that particular place and so authenticity suggests that we set a task that allows learners to express the extent to which they have been persuaded by it.

Having looked at both how lessons are staged and considered the selection of material, we will now move on to look at some of the issues in implementing reading lessons.

Implementing reading lessons

As we saw previously, the pre-reading, while-reading and post-reading stages of a reading lesson have an intuitive appeal. However, there are weaknesses too, particularly when the implementation of those three broad phases is considered. In many classrooms, the 'while-reading' sequence takes the form of comprehension checking, with extensive use of multiple choice questions, *True/False* type statements, and so on. These tests of comprehension may have a place in the development of reading skills because they encourage detailed reading, but it could be argued that they are used far too widely in many teaching contexts and bring with them a series of pedagogical difficulties. The questions necessarily focus on parts of the text that are unambiguous so that a 'correct' answer can be supplied, although directing the learner's attention to these parts may not be the best means of offering support to overall comprehension. These question formats foreground reading as a product (i.e. what information has been successfully extracted), but do little to focus on the process of reading, and therefore do not necessarily contribute to teaching learners how to read more effectively. Further, such tests of comprehension are artificial in the sense that texts outside the classroom do not have accompanying tests and they can restrict more authentic responses to the text used. These issues are discussed more fully in Chapter 2: *Moving beyond factual comprehension questions*.

The reliance on factually-based comprehension questions is not the only difficulty of the model as it is currently frequently implemented. The model most often operates by having a materials writer choose a text that they believe will be interesting and motivating for learners to read. This in itself is not easy, particularly where materials will be used globally and the sensitivities of many cultures have to be considered. The pressures of this can lead to the use of texts that cover a narrow range of apparently 'safe' topics and text types and this can negatively impact on learner motivation. Additionally, the selection of texts that are written and produced in English-speaking western countries will inevitably be imbued with the cultural values of those countries and may be seen as a form of cultural imperialism (Pennycook, 1994).

However, it is quite possible to teach reading in ways that do not rely on starting with the choice of a text and then the identification of information that can be extracted from it. In reality, people frequently read because we have questions we need answers to. Imagine a situation in which a person wants to apply for a visa to visit another country. They are likely to search online, find the relevant embassy information and read about how to apply for a visa. In other words, the need for a particular piece of knowledge leads to the selection of the text, rather than vice versa. It could be argued that identifying appropriate texts to solve particular problems is exactly the sort of reading skill that learners need to develop, particularly as the choice is now so vast, and yet it is not catered for in many teaching materials.

Towards a balanced reading programme

It can be argued that current teaching of reading relies over-heavily on testing and does not do enough to promote the teaching of reading. This does not mean that intensive reading and comprehension checks have nothing to offer but that they should be part, rather than the sum, of a reading programme. We can add to this limited strategy and achieve better-balanced programmes that are more likely to help learners become better L2 readers.

A key goal for any reading course should be to develop the learners' ability to transfer L1 reading skills to the L2. Fundamental to this is building an extensive L2 sight vocabulary, as crossing the language threshold depends on having a critical mass of L2 knowledge and that knowledge is primarily lexical in nature. There is a strong argument that one of the best ways to help learners read more effectively is to teach more vocabulary and so reading programmes need a strong lexical element.

As we look for alternatives to reading development based on comprehension exercises, the explicit, principled teaching of reading strategies offers another compelling option. Research evidence shows that successful readers are able to deploy combinations of strategies at appropriate times and there is also evidence that explicit instruction on strategies can lead to their uptake (Oxford, 2011). Helping learners develop into strategic readers, readers who have a range of options that they can use to overcome difficulties, is an important step in moving from a testing model of reading to a more teaching-focused approach.

Much classroom material and practice tends to focus on accuracy of understanding. While this is clearly crucial, the rapidity of reading is also important because models of comprehension are based on our having only limited working memory capacity. If too much attention needs to be paid to recognizing words, retrieving word meaning, and so on, there are unlikely to be sufficient resources available to build a coherent understanding of the text. Therefore a balanced reading course would also try to develop reading fluency, as well as accuracy, as we move from largely testing reading towards more teaching of reading.

As we noted above, classroom reading activities tend to focus on intensive reading. However, it is likely that we can only become successful readers through reading very large amounts of text (Eskey and Grabe, 1988) and some of that will need to be done outside class time. Extensive reading of this sort has several additional benefits, such as improved spelling, vocabulary and grammar, as well as supporting and enhancing reading fluency, and so the promotion of extensive reading would also form part of a well-balanced reading programme.

In some cases we may be able to predict very easily what kind of texts our learners will need and want to engage with outside the classroom. On other occasions, probably the majority of teaching situations, it is much harder to make assumptions and in those cases it is probably a good idea to use a range of texts from a variety of sources. Moreover, some of those texts need to be viewed in digital form, as reading from screens becomes ever more ubiquitous in the 21st century. The internet no doubt has many advantages but it also brings with it challenges, particularly for less experienced readers, because we constantly need to make judgements about what is, and what is not, trustworthy. As a result, critical reading skills are likely to become ever more important and their explicit development can form part of a reading programme.

Another option in developing reading skills is to situate reading within a broader task design, with learners needing to read in order to achieve some other outcome. That task may eventually take the form of a presentation, piece of writing, designing a hoarding, or any other thing that seems appropriate for a particular group of learners. They can be guided through the preparation steps, which have reading designed into them. The webquest model, developed principally by Bernie Dodge in 1995 (webquest.org), shows one way in which this can be achieved and has the added benefit of exploiting technology and encouraging online reading, and the particular skills that requires. This type of task design provides a strong reason for learners to read and they may need to integrate information from various texts, which is a necessary skill to develop, particularly at higher levels. In this paradigm, reading is no longer seen as an isolated skill, but instead is integrated into a rich communicative event.

As we can see, there are several ways in which we can teach our learners to become better readers through developing the skills and strategies they need. The rest of this book aims to provide principled and practical activities that can be used to achieve this.

Suggestions for using this book

This book aims to support teachers, and the successful teaching of reading, through providing practical classroom activities. However, these are not prescriptive activities, tied to specific texts, but instead are deliberately designed as activity frames which can be applied to a variety of written material. Many of the activities can be used at a range of levels and in a variety of teaching contexts: with young learners or adult learners, with small classes or large classes, where a teacher is using a coursebook, or where there is no coursebook. In this way it is hoped that a great many teachers will find the book useful and a very practical teaching resource.

Some activities will work better with certain types of text and where this is the case it is indicated in the activity description. Each activity also has an indication of the level (or levels), based on the Common European Framework of Reference, at which it is most likely to work successfully. Some activities are exemplified in order to provide clarity and where this is the case the example is, by necessity, based on a specific text. However, it should be remembered that this does not mean that the activity would not work perfectly well with other texts. Teachers tend to be very 'time-poor' and so suggested activities must work to support not just good teaching, but sustainably good teaching. To this end, some of the activities require no preparation at all, others require very small amounts, and only a few a little more.

Some users of this book may want to start at page 1 and read through each section in sequence. However, the book can equally be dipped in and out of as teachers look for an appealing idea that can be used immediately. This general introduction provides an overview of reading and how reading tends to be taught. In addition, each chapter has a short introductory section, highlighting the key issues relevant in that particular area. These brief theoretical outlines aim to support teachers in linking their own classroom experiences to relevant underlying theory.

Lastly, it is worth stressing that the activities here are not designed in a prescriptive tradition of steps that must be followed. Instead, they are ideas, and like all ideas, they can be developed by others and made more relevant for the particular situations to which they are applied. So while all of these activities are complete and do not require additions or adaptations to work effectively, it is anticipated that teachers may want to adapt them in order to fine tune them for the particular needs of their classes.

Most of the activities require little preparation, and where worksheets or role cards are needed, examples are given on separate photocopiable pages at the end of the activity. Many of the activities, including those with worksheets, role cards or instructions that teachers may wish to personalize, can also be downloaded from the dedicated website. Details of this can be found on the inside front cover. Material which is available to download is marked with the symbol ▶.

References

Altbach, P. and Knight, J. (2007) 'The internationalization of higher education: motivations and realities', *Journal of Studies in International Education*, 11, pp. 290–305.

Anderson, N. (1991) 'Individual differences in strategy use in second language reading and testing', *Modern Language Journal*, 75(4), pp. 460–472.

Cameron, L. (2001) *Teaching Languages to Young Learners*, Cambridge: Cambridge University Press.

Carrell, P. and Grabe, W. (2010) 'Reading' in N. Schmitt (ed.), *Introduction to Applied Linguistics*, pp. 215–231, Abingdon: Taylor & Francis.

Celce-Murcia, M. and Olshtain, E. (2000) *Discourse and Context in Language Teaching*, New York: Cambridge University Press.

Cunningham, S. and Moor, P. (2005) *New Cutting Edge Intermediate* (2nd ed.), Harlow: Pearson.

Dodge, B. (2017) 'What is a webquest?' in *Webquest*. Available online at: http://webquest.org/. [Last accessed 5 August 2017]

Dummet, P., Hughes, J. and Stephenson, H. (2013) *Life Upper Intermediate*, Andover: Cengage Learning.

Eskey, D. and Grabe, W. (1988) 'Interactive models for second language reading: perspectives on instruction' in P. Carrell, J. Devine and D. Eskey (eds.), *Interactive Approaches to Second Language Reading*, pp. 223–238, Cambridge: Cambridge University Press.

Geva, E. and Ramírez, G. (2015) *Focus on Reading*, Oxford: Oxford University Press.

Grabe, W. (2009) *Reading in a Second Language: Moving from Theory to Practice*, New York: Cambridge University Press.

Grabe, W. and Stoller, F. (2011) *Teaching and Researching Reading* (2nd ed.), Abingdon: Taylor & Francis.

Grellet, F. (1981) *Developing Reading Skills*, Cambridge: Cambridge University Press.

Hall, G. (2011) *Exploring English Language Teaching: Language in Action*, Abingdon: Taylor & Francis.

Harmer, J. (2001) *The Practice of English Language Teaching* (5th ed.), Harlow: Pearson.

Krashen, S. (1985) *The Input Hypothesis: Issues and Implications*, London: Longman.

Macaro, E. (2003) *Teaching and Learning a Second Language*, London: Continuum.

McBride, C. (2016) *Children's Literacy Development: A Cross-Cultural Perspective on Learning to Read and Write* (2nd ed.), Abingdon: Taylor & Francis.

Nation, I.S.P. (2006) 'How large a vocabulary is needed for reading and listening?', *Canadian Modern Languages Review*, 63(1), pp. 59–82.

National Literacy Trust (2011) 'Literacy: A route to addressing child poverty?' Available online at: http://www.literacytrust.org.uk/assets/0001/1032/Literacy__Child_Poverty_2011.pdf. [Last accessed 5 August 2017]

Nunan, D. (2015) *Teaching English to Speakers of Other Languages: An Introduction*, Abingdon: Taylor & Francis.

Oxford, R. (2011) *Teaching and Researching Language Learning Strategies*, Harlow: Pearson.

Paran, A. (1996) 'Reading in EFL: Facts and fictions', *ELT Journal*, 50(1), pp. 25–34.

Pennycook, A. (1994) *The Cultural Politics of English as an International Language*, Abingdon: Taylor & Francis.

Smith, F. (1971) *Understanding Reading*, New York: Holt Rinehart and Winston.

Soars, L. and Soars, J. (2006) *New Headway Elementary* (3rd ed.), Oxford: Oxford University Press.

Stanovich, K. (2000) *Progress in Understanding Reading: Scientific Foundations and New Frontiers*, New York: Guilford Press.

Swan, M. (1985) 'A critical look at the Communicative Approach', *ELT Journal*, 39(1), pp. 2–12.

Tilbury, A., Hendra, L., Rea, D. and Clementson, T. (2010) *English Unlimited Upper Intermediate*, Cambridge: Cambridge University Press.

Thornbury, S. (2017) *The New A–Z of ELT: A Dictionary of Terms and Concepts*, London: Macmillan.

Watkins, P. (2014) *Learning to Teach English* (2nd ed.), Peaslake: Delta Publishing.

1 Preparing learners for reading

Reading lessons

'Preparing learners for reading' sometimes refers to the way that non-readers can be helped to become readers, and in that sense would involve such things as recognizing script and establishing letter–sound correspondences. However, the focus of this chapter is on how we can support learners before they read specific texts in the classroom. It assumes that the learners can already read in L2 to some extent.

When reading is the focus of a language learning lesson, it is common practice to follow a three-stage procedure which comprises:
- pre-reading activities
- while-reading activities
- post-reading activities.

Examples of this pattern can be found in almost any major coursebook and is advocated in teaching manuals (e.g. Thornbury and Watkins, 2007; Harmer, 2015). However, within this framework there is a lot of flexibility because various activity types can be used in each of the stages. In this chapter we will look at pre-reading activities, the rationales behind them, and the options available to teachers.

Common types of pre-reading activity

Reading comprehension, as we discussed in the introduction, seems to be an interaction between both 'text-based' and 'situational' models of comprehension. In the text-based model, readers use the words and grammar of the text to build a representation of meaning. In the situational model, readers fit information from the text into what they already know and believe about the topic and text type. Understanding is derived from these two models of comprehension working together.

Given these theories of comprehension, we should not be surprised that common pre-reading activities often support one or other type of processing. Learners are often asked to consider what they know about a topic, or what content they expect the text to include (basing predictions on such things as the title, visual content, or vocabulary items extracted from the text). These types of activity support the situational model of processing as they activate background knowledge. Less common is asking learners to make predictions about the structure of the text, based on similar texts they have read, although this is another type of background knowledge that can support comprehension (Grabe and Stoller, 2011; Duffy, 2014). There is general agreement that an increase in background knowledge leads to an increase in reading efficiency (Grabe, 2009) and this provides a strong rationale for such activities. However, it should be noted that weak readers sometimes trust their background knowledge over information derived from the text and this can actually impede text comprehension if there is a divergence between the two (Hammadou, 1991, cited in Macaro, 2003). In these cases, teachers may need to build background knowledge, rather than simply eliciting what learners already think they know about a topic.

An extension of activating and building background knowledge is to move towards previewing the actual content of the text. This can be appropriate where texts and reading tasks are likely to be particularly demanding and can be achieved through, for example, reading (or hearing) a summary of the text before a close, detailed reading. Skimming and scanning (see pages 3–4) activities are common in many language classrooms and can also be types of preview activity, as they generally lead to a more intensive reading phase.

The activity types above tend to support the situational model of comprehension but the text-based model of comprehension can also be supported through pre-reading activities. Typically, this is achieved through pre-teaching important vocabulary items in the text, which in turn supports bottom-up processing (see page 2), as learners, in theory, rapidly recognize the words in the text that they have just been taught. This allows learners to process the text reasonably quickly, as they will not need to stop frequently to find word meanings, and this support for bottom-up processing provides the rationale for pre-teaching vocabulary before intensive reading activities. On the other hand, it could be argued that outside the classroom texts do not come with vocabulary preparation and learners need to develop strategies to deal with the difficulties that this presents.

From a practical classroom perspective, teachers need to assess both what kind of support their learners are likely to require, and also how much support will be needed in order to process a text successfully. For example, a text with a lot of unknown vocabulary would suggest the need to support bottom-up processing through explicit vocabulary teaching, while a text which is likely to expose big gaps in cultural awareness would require support in building background knowledge. Teachers also need to consider how many gaps in knowledge can be plugged through pre-teaching activities before they deem the text to be inappropriate for their group and look for an alternative.

More than cognitive preparation

However, successful reading lessons depend on more than supporting comprehension. Learners need to be motivated to read and be prepared to put in the necessary effort to process the texts used in class. There are several ways in which teachers can help build and sustain motivation, including those things that are relevant to all teaching, such as using a variety of task types and setting clear, achievable (yet challenging) goals. In addition, there are factors that are specific to the teaching of reading, such as ensuring that a range of text types is used and choosing texts that are likely to appeal to specific groups of learners, piquing their interest.

The pre-reading stage is important, therefore, for building learners' desire to read the text. This can be partly achieved through promoting affective, as well as cognitive, engagement with the material. Reading lessons are not only about the accurate decoding of words and messages, but are also opportunities for learners to respond – either positively or negatively – to the situations, characters and ideas found in the texts. Giving learners opportunities to engage with material at an affective level, expressing feelings and emotions, both before and after reading, is likely to support motivation.

The activities that follow in this chapter aim to give teachers ideas on how they can prepare learners for reading tasks. They draw on the principles outlined above.

References

Duffy, G. (2014) *Explaining Reading* (3rd ed.), New York: Guilford Press.

Grabe, W. (2009) *Reading in a Second Language: Moving from Theory to Practice*, New York: Cambridge University Press.

Grabe, W. and Stoller, F. (2011) *Teaching and Researching Reading* (2nd ed.), Abingdon: Taylor & Francis.

Hammadou, J. (1991) 'Interrelationships among prior knowledge, inference and language proficiency in foreign language teaching', *Modern Language Journal*, 75(1), pp. 27–38.

Harmer, J. (2015) *The Practice of English Language Teaching* (5th ed.), Harlow: Pearson.

Macaro, E. (2003) *Teaching and Learning a Second Language*, London: Continuum.

Thornbury, S. and Watkins, P. (2007) *The CELTA Course Trainee Book*, Cambridge: Cambridge University Press.

1.1 Visualization

Outline	Learners affectively engage with a selected text through visualization techniques.
Level	Any (see *Notes*)
Time	Up to 15 minutes depending on the length of the visualization and the amount of discussion afterwards
Focus	Promoting affective engagement with a text, making difficult texts more accessible through a preview
Preparation	Choose a piece of music that you feel will add to the atmosphere of a text you are working with. Plan a series of questions and/or instructions that relate to the text (see *Example*).

Procedure

1 Pre-teach any necessary vocabulary.

2 Ask the learners to close their eyes. Play a minute or so of music.

3 After a minute or so, reduce the volume of the music and ask the first question (or give the first instruction). Learners are not expected to speak at this point but think about the question raised.

4 Allow time for learners to think with the music playing, before again reducing the volume and asking the next question.

5 When you have led the learners through the text, ask them to share what they thought and imagined in small groups.

6 Elicit the ideas of those who seem willing to share before introducing the reading task.

Example

The text *A true story* on page 273 is appropriate for a B1 class, with some preparation before reading. The text is set on the Masai Mara game reserve in Kenya and a simple search on YouTube (or a similar video-sharing website) should produce several results with appropriately evocative pieces of music that could be used for this activity.

Below are some questions/instructions that I have used with this particular text. After the visualization, the first reading task is to compare the learners' emotions and reactions to those of the young woman in the text. Learners also read to find out how the story finished.

Notes

Visualizations are best conducted with the teacher speaking in a slow, calm voice. Use plenty of pauses so that the learners have time to think and, to some extent, experience the situation.

Closing your eyes in a group situation can be quite difficult, even threatening, for some people. It can be a good idea to start with very short examples and build up to fuller visualizations.

This technique is remarkably flexible, and can be used at any level, although at very low levels some L1 may be required to support the communication. It can be used to introduce texts about all kinds of travel (a frequent theme in many ELT coursebooks), adventures and even daily routines. The internet provides easy access to a huge variety of music.

Visualization

[music]

You are staying at a lodge on a game reserve in Africa. Your first time in Africa. [pause] How do you feel? [pause] Are you excited, nervous, anxious?

[music]

You are staying with a friend. You are relaxing on the first day of your visit. You are in the grounds of the lodge. You are sunbathing, lying on a towel. Picture yourself lying on the grass. [pause] Feel the sun on your back. [pause] What can you hear? What can you smell?

[music]

Your eyes are closed. You begin to fall into a light sleep.

[music]

You become aware of something moving over your leg. [pause] How do you feel? What should you do?

[music]

You think about brushing it away but decide to look first. [pause] You see a snake. [pause]. You jump up. The snake disappears under your towel.

[music]

You shout for help. You tell your friend what happened – there's a snake under the towel! [pause] But your friend doesn't believe you. She tells you it's nothing to worry about. [pause] She says that lots of people are scared the first time they are on the reserve. [pause] How does this make you feel?

[music]

What do you do next?

[music]

Now, we are back in the classroom. In a moment we will read about a young woman in the same situation as you just thought about. [pause] When you are ready, open your eyes and tell your partner what you imagined and what you would do next.

Rationale

The use of visualizations is firmly in the humanist tradition of language teaching, which emphasizes the engagement of the whole person in the learning process and affective engagement in activities (as well as cognitive engagement).

Visualizations can make even quite challenging texts more accessible to learners through previewing them. The learners can be led through the stages of the text, and even key moments in the text, before they read.

1.2 Previewing a text by its vocabulary

Outline	Learners predict the content of a text from key vocabulary.
Level	Any
Time	15 minutes
Focus	Previewing a text based on in-depth engagement with its key vocabulary
Preparation	Select some key words and phrases from the text. These are most likely to be nouns and noun phrases. The words should be important to the text and at least some of them should be known to the learners. 8–10 words would be appropriate for most texts.

Procedure

1 Give the learners the selected words. Teach the meanings of any new words.

2 Divide the class into groups of three or four. Ask the learners to work together to brainstorm all the associations they can think of for the given words. This may include thinking of words with similar meanings, the emotions that the words evoke, typical collocations, or the types of text the words are likely to appear in.

3 Learners report back their ideas.

4 Guide the discussion by focusing and expanding on the ideas that are most relevant to the text. Elicit further associations where necessary through asking questions.

5 Set a standard comprehension exercise, or select an appropriate activity from elsewhere in this book.

6 Learners read the text and complete the task set.

7 Conduct feedback in the usual way.

Notes

If time is short, each group could be given one or two words to work on.

If the words selected are likely to occur in future texts, or are morphologically complex, it may be worth studying them further after the reading sequence and ensuring that they are recycled in future lessons.

An alternative is to prepare a slide which displays the keywords exactly where they are in the text, with the rest of the text blanked out. This has the advantage that learners will see the key words in sequence, which is likely to help the accuracy of predictions. Also, the unusual appearance of the slide may add to the learners' motivation to read and generate interest in the text.

The term 'keyword' has a technical sense in linguistics, and particularly corpus linguistics. It is used to label an item that appears significantly more frequently in a particular text than it does in a larger corpus of texts (Thornbury, 2017). For example, we find the word *elephant* far more frequently in the text on page 270 than we would if we looked through a random collection of other news stories. Keywords are a reliable indicator of the topic of a text and as comprehension is likely to be compromised if learners do not understand them, they are often targeted in pre-teaching phases of reading lessons (Thornbury, 2017).

Rationale

This activity deepens learners' awareness of vocabulary, central to successful reading. As key ideas in the text will be encoded through vocabulary, this activity also previews key elements of the text, thus making it easier to read.

Reference

Thornbury, S. (2017) *The New A–Z of ELT: A Dictionary of Terms and Concepts,* London: Macmillan.

1.3 Previewing a text through role play

Outline	Learners perform a role play based on the story.
Level	Intermediate and above (B1+)
Time	30 minutes
Focus	Promoting affective engagement with a text, making difficult texts more accessible through a preview
Preparation	Develop a simple role play, based on the themes of the text. The role card descriptions could usefully explore the emotions of the characters, as well as what they actually think and do.

Procedure

1 Introduce the topic and briefly discuss it. Teach any essential vocabulary for the role play.

2 Assign roles for the role play and allow some preparation time.

3 Ask learners to perform the role play in small groups.

4 The first reading task could be to find the links between the role play and the text.

Notes

The activity will work particularly well for texts where there are opposing views expressed or some other form of conflict. Stories about urban development, conflicts between neighbours, minor breaches of the law, relationship break ups and many more topics could all be introduced using the activity.

A potential follow-up activity is to repeat the role play after reading, with the learners adding more ideas and details that have been gained from the reading.

Rationale

The role play allows the learners the chance to build an affective connection to the text, which will increase their motivation to read.

1.4 A quick glimpse

Outline	Learners guess the content of the text through briefly seeing words and pictures.
Level	Any
Time	15 minutes
Focus	Previewing a text through images and vocabulary
Preparation	Select words and pictures that relate to the text. Include four or five pictures and ten or more words. These words could come directly from the text. An online search for images should make it easy to select appropriate pictures.
	Paste the images and write the words into a single document ('information sheet') that can be easily displayed (or printed).

Procedure

1 Tell the learners you will show them words and pictures that relate to the text that they are about to read. They will only see the information for 15 seconds. They must try to remember as much as they can in that time.

2 Display the information sheet for 15 seconds.

3 After 15 seconds, divide the class into small groups to discuss what they remember from the sheet.

4 Ask learners to predict what they think the text will be about, based on what they recall.

5 If necessary, display the information again for a further 15 seconds.

6 Invite some of the groups to report their predictions to the class.

7 The first reading task should be to see how accurate the predictions were.

Notes

The activity works best if the information sheet can be projected onto a screen for the whole class to see. However, if this is not possible, learners can be give a printed sheet, which they turn over when told to do so.

If a lot of information is included on the information sheet, the time limit can be extended.

It can be a good idea to use different fonts and font sizes for the words to make some items more noticeable than others. This will enhance the discussion of the items (stage 3 above) as some items may be noticed by just one or two people in the group.

Rationale

The activity should give quite a lot of support for reading through previewing the text content. The very short time limit tends to build energy and excitement, which can be useful before the quieter, individual reading phase.

1.5 Simplified to authentic

Outline	Learners read an authentic text after reading a simplified version.
Level	Intermediate and above (B1+)
Time	30 minutes
Focus	Previewing an authentic text by first reading a simplified version
Preparation	Select an authentic text that is potentially relevant and interesting to the learners. Rewrite the text, simplifying it in terms of vocabulary choices and, where necessary, sentence structure (see *Example*). Prepare two different comprehension tasks to use during the activity. The second may be a revised version of the first, and could be, for example, writing a simple summary. See the activities in Chapter 2: *Moving beyond factual comprehension questions* for further ideas for tasks.

Procedure

1   Activate background knowledge and/or pre-teach necessary vocabulary in the usual way.

2   Set a comprehension task.

3   Give the simplified text to the learners and ask them to complete the task. They can compare ideas before reporting back.

4   Tell the learners that they will read an authentic version of the same text. Elicit predictions of the kinds of change they anticipate.

5   Set a revised (or different) comprehension task.

6   Give the authentic text to the learners and ask them to complete the task. They can compare ideas before reporting back.

7   If appropriate, ask the learners to identify some of the differences in the two texts.

Example

The following example is a rewriting of the opening of the text *It's time to accept that elephants, like us, are empathetic beings* on page 270.

Elephants can understand each other just as people can

Elephants are in danger. We humans are killing them because we want their ivory.

The West African country of Gabon has most of Africa's remaining forest elephants. Most of Gabon's elephants are in the Minkebe National Park and the protected area around it. In 2004 it was home to about 28,500 elephants. By 2012 the number had dropped to about 7,000 – a loss of over 20,000 elephants.

People are killing the elephants so quickly, and the population is now so small, that some scientists think that it is already too late to stop elephants disappearing completely in the wild.

Notes

The activity will be useful for any text that would otherwise be significantly above the level of the learners.

The readings of the simplified text and the authentic text could be in different lessons. When simplifying the text, some details can be completely omitted because if too much information is packed into a shorter text, it may become more difficult to read, rather than easier!

An alternative to rewriting the text is to prepare a bullet-point summary.

Rationale

This is a way of previewing an otherwise difficult text. Learners can feel a sense of progress and success, which in turn can lead to additional, so-called 'resultative', motivation after successfully understanding texts that they recognize as being authentic.

1.6 L1 to L2 reading

Outline	Learners read a summary of a text in their L1 before they read the full L2 version. The activity is most easily used with monolingual groups.
Level	Any
Time	10 minutes
Focus	Previewing a challenging text by reading a summary in L1
Preparation	Select an appropriate text for the learners. The activity will substantially support learners' reading and so the text can be quite challenging.
	Write a summary of the text in the learners' L1. If the learners have very different proficiency levels in L2 reading, more than one version of the summary could be prepared (see *Notes*). Prepare a task based on the L2 text for stage 4.

Procedure

1 Build interest in the text and invite predictions about the content based on the title and/or accompanying visuals.

2 Distribute the L1 summary to the learners and ask them to read it.

3 Ask learners to identify the key points of the summary and report them back to the class. The reporting back can be done in either L1 or L2, as appropriate for the group.

4 When the key points have been established, distribute the L2 text and an accompanying task and complete in the usual way.

Notes

The activity works particularly well with very low-level learners, or if a text is particularly difficult.

The activity can be differentiated so that it suits learners at different levels of reading proficiency in L2 by preparing different versions of the summary, with more information given to weaker readers.

Rationale

This activity provides a preview of a text and can therefore support readers in processing a text that may otherwise be beyond their level. This sense of achievement can be very motivating for learners.

1.7 Predicting from pictures

Outline	Learners predict a story from pictures, some of which are relevant and some that are not.
Level	Elementary and above (A2+)
Time	15 minutes
Focus	Previewing a text through images
Preparation	Print out, or arrange to display digitally, pictures that are relevant to the text. Four or five pictures generally work well for short stories. Also, select two pictures that are not related to the text.

Procedure

1 Give the learners all the pictures. Ask them to make up a story using four of the pictures, disregarding two.

2 Learners work in small groups to prepare narratives.

3 After an appropriate length of time, the groups report back their ideas to the class.

4 The first reading task should be to establish which group was closest to predicting the story in the text and which two pictures are not relevant to the text.

Example

For the text *A true story*, on page 273, the following could be used:
- pictures that are relevant to the story: a snake, a game reserve, a towel and a stick
- pictures to include as distractors: a plane and a water bottle.

Notes

The activity is likely to work best with narrative-based texts.

The activity can also be done using items of vocabulary, rather than pictures.

If appropriate, the phase where the pictures are discussed and the narratives prepared could be done in L1 with lower-level groups.

Rationale

Learners are likely to be more motivated to read if they have previously invested in the potential narrative possibilities. There is also a slightly competitive element to see who can guess the story most closely.

1.8 Analyzing pictures

Outline	Learners analyze pictures that accompany texts before reading.
Level	Elementary and above (A2+)
Time	10 minutes
Focus	Previewing a text through the analysis of images
Preparation	None

Procedure

1 Before reading the text, draw the learners' attention to any accompanying pictures or other graphics.

2 Support learners in analyzing the pictures through asking appropriate questions (see *Example*). Learners could work in small groups to discuss these questions.

3 Learners read the text.

4 The first reading task could be to decide how successful the images were in previewing and supporting the messages of the text.

Example

The following questions are examples of what could be asked but of course specific pictures may prompt other questions.

Pictures of …	Possible questions
people	• Do these people look happy, excited or sad? What can you understand from their expressions? • Are these pictures of people in the 21st century, or are they from the past? • Are they young or old? • Do they look well off? • If there is more than one person, how might they be related?
objects	• Are these objects modern or old-fashioned? • Where would you expect to find them? • Why might this particular image have been chosen to represent the object?
places	• Do you recognize this place? • Does it look attractive? Would you like to be in this place? • Does this place look exciting / relaxing / boring, etc.? • Is this place unusual in any way? • Is the image typical of this place and what you would expect to see?

Notes

Texts may also be accompanied by graphics (such as charts and tables) and the trends they depict are likely to be useful in understanding the text. These too can be analyzed before reading.

Rationale

Many stories in magazines and newspapers, in both print and digital form, are accompanied by images. This is also true of texts used in coursebooks. We often ignore the images, treating them as little more than decoration on the page. However, they will usually have been chosen carefully and will convey a great deal of meaning. Consider, for example, choosing a picture of a politician to accompany a political story. A picture can be chosen that makes that person look serious and capable, friendly, emotional, or silly. Learners can benefit from spending time thinking about the additional meanings that the pictures bring to the text.

For more ideas on how to exploit the images that accompany a text, see *Working with Images* by Ben Goldstein (2008).

Reference

Goldstein, B. (2008) *Working with Images*, Cambridge: Cambridge University Press.

1.9 Predicting from text type

Outline	Learners make predictions about the text, based on their experience of other similar texts.
Level	Intermediate and above (B1+)
Time	10 minutes
Focus	Making predictions about a text based on awareness of text type
Preparation	Ensure you have a comprehension task to accompany the detailed reading of the text (stage 5).

Procedure

1 Explain to the class the type of text that they are about to read. Give as much detail as possible. For example, if it is a narrative, tell learners whether it is a news report, a joke, a fairy tale, a folk story and so on. Where possible, give specific examples of other similar texts that the learners have read.

2 Ask the learners to predict the features they will find in the text and how it will be structured.

3 The learners read the text to see if their predictions are correct.

4 Learners report back their ideas.

5 Set a standard comprehension task and ask the learners to reread the text.

6 Learners report back their ideas in the usual way.

Notes

This activity works particularly well if the learners have studied generic features of text types, and is indeed an opportunity to reinforce this knowledge.

The first time the class does this activity, it may be useful to play a short trailer from a film with a strong generic form, such as a romantic comedy. (Trailers are available on YouTube and the Internet Movie Database.) After watching, ask the class how the movie will end. This is highly predictable in the case of romantic comedies. Point out that the learners were able to make reliable predictions because of their familiarity with similar stories. Explain that they can make the same kinds of prediction for reading texts, based on texts they have previously seen.

Rationale

Background knowledge of the text type has been shown to increase reading efficiency and yet text type knowledge is rarely explicitly drawn attention to in teaching material.

1.10 Predicting from the reactions of others

Outline	Learners make predictions about the text, based on the reactions of other readers.
Level	Intermediate and above (B1+)
Time	20 minutes
Focus	Previewing a text by considering the reactions of others who have read it
Preparation	Select an appropriate text. Ask people who have read it before to record brief comments about it. These could include whether they liked it, how it made them feel, who they would recommend it for and so on. Do not use any spoilers that explicitly give details about what the text is about (see *Example*).

Procedure

1 Tell the learners that they will hear a recording of people reacting to a text.

2 After each contribution on the recording, stop and ask learners for predictions about what sort of text they think is being discussed and what it might include.

3 After the recording has been listened to, draw together predictions.

4 Learners read the text.

5 The first reading task could be for learners to decide which recorded reactions to the text were closest to their own.

Example

The following comments are taken from a B2 class that read the text *It's time to accept that elephants, like us, are empathetic beings* on page 270. Spelling and grammar mistakes have been tidied up so that they do not distract from the central purpose.

- *I think people who do this to animals should go to prison for the rest of their lives. It's terrible.*
- *I had lots of toy elephants when I was young. I love them. This is so sad.*
- *I think it's incredible how they support each other.*
- *Some of the vocabulary – peril, endangered, ecological – was quite difficult but it was good to read this.*
- *I don't recommend this to anyone who is easily upset.*

Notes

If recording is difficult, written comments can be used. See Activity 6.6: *Predicting from others' reactions* for a variation on this using digital texts.

It can be very motivating to get one class to record their reactions immediately after reading a text, for another class to listen to. For example, if the same coursebook will be used next year, ask this year's class to record comments to be used with next year's.

Rationale

The recommendation of a text by others (particularly peers) can be very motivating. It is also likely that the preview material will introduce key vocabulary, making the text easier to read.

1.11 What I want to find out

Outline	Learners specify their goals before reading by stating what information they want to find out.
Level	Intermediate and above (B1+)
Focus	Setting goals for reading
Time	15 minutes
Preparation	None

Procedure

1 Tell learners the title of the text and a little of what the text is about.

2 Elicit what they know about the topic and what they would like to find out. Try to guide the discussion so that at least some of what they want to find out is covered by the text.

3 Draw the following table on the board and ask learners to copy it in their notebooks:

What I know about this topic	What I think is true about this topic	What I want to find out about this topic

4 Give learners time to complete the table. When this has been done individually, learners compare ideas in small groups.

5 The first reading task could be to check:
  • whether the information in the first column is correct
  • whether the ideas in the second column are confirmed
  • whether there are answers to the questions in the third column.

Notes
The activity is likely to work best with information-based texts.

Rationale
Setting goals for reading is a key reading skill and this activity explicitly encourages this. Also, if learners have the opportunity to find out things they actually want to know, motivation is likely to increase.

1.12 What we believe

Outline	Learners specify what they believe about a topic before reading and read to see if the text supports their views.
Level	Intermediate and above (B1+)
Time	20 minutes
Focus	Using background knowledge to support comprehension, using the text as a means of building on existing knowledge
Preparation	None

Procedure

1 Tell the learners the topic of the text.

2 Elicit at least five beliefs about the topic of the text from the group. These could be facts that the learners believe to be true, but opinions connected to the topic also tend to work well, particularly with higher-level learners.

3 Write the list of beliefs on the board.

4 Learners read to see if the text supports (or contradicts) the opinions and beliefs listed.

5 Learners compare their ideas in small groups, telling each other the evidence from the text they based their judgements on.

6 Encourage learners to report back their ideas.

Notes
The initial discussion of beliefs could be done in small groups if preferred.

Rationale

This activity explicitly activates background knowledge and encourages readers to check if the text supports their beliefs. This is important because some weaker readers have been shown to rely more on background knowledge than information derived from the text.

Moving beyond factual questions

Traditional 'while-reading' questions

As we saw in Chapter 1, a three-phase model for reading lessons, involving pre-reading activities, while-reading activities, and post-reading activities is very common. In this chapter, we will focus on the while-reading component of the lesson, which is probably the most important of the phases (Paran, 2003). Activities used at this stage of the lesson can provide learners with a reason for reading and also guide them towards the most important parts of the text, pushing them to focus resources on understanding its key messages. In addition, the degree of success in completing the activities can also be used to gauge the level of the learners' understanding.

While theoretically there are a great many things that teachers could ask learners to do during the while-reading phase of a lesson, the reality is that materials designed to promote reading tend to be dominated by question types that test factual comprehension. They typically centre on information that can be found explicitly in the text and have a single correct response. The following are common examples:

- answering multiple choice questions
- answering *True/False* questions
- answering *Yes/No* questions
- answering *Who, What, When, Where, How* type questions (where the answer is clearly stated in the text)
- putting pictures into a sequence
- inserting sentences/paragraphs into gaps in the text from which they were previously removed
- matching pictures to parts of a text
- matching sub-headings to parts of a text
- correcting errors in a summary of a text.

All of these types of exercise can be potentially useful in the classroom because they are likely to promote a need for detailed processing of the text. However, while these activities may have a place in the development of reading skills, they do not, in themselves, teach reading. They are actually testing devices and their use inevitably leads to learners being tested on their comprehension of a text and the replacement of teaching with testing can have some unfortunate consequences.

Testing versus teaching

Testing situations place a value on there being a single 'correct' answer but such answers can limit authentic responses to the text, which may not be so neatly characterized. For example, if we read a funny text, an authentic response might be to comment on the parts we find the most funny, but such subjective responses cannot be easily captured by the types of exercise outlined above.

Indeed, comprehension testing exercises are marked by their lack of authenticity – no newspaper article comes with a set of multiple choice questions to check we have understood details from the text. Furthermore, while the exercise format favours a focus on detail, those details are not always crucial to a deep understanding of the writer's message and may actually distract readers from more important information. Brown (1990, p. 147) states, 'In real life we don't process discourse as if it were equally interesting or worthy of being remembered' and therefore, where factual questions are used, it is important that they support understanding of the text as a whole by focusing on the most important parts, rather than distracting readers by diverting their attention towards insignificant details. The qualitative difference between those questions that test and are product-oriented, and those that support and are more process-oriented, has led Thornbury (2017) to suggest differentiating the labels applied to them. He proposes using the term 'comprehension questions' to refer to those that primarily test, while the term 'comprehending questions' is used to refer to more process-oriented questions, capturing the way in which such questions can be used to support the understanding process.

While comprehension tests can signal that communication is imperfect, incomplete or simply wrong, they do not help us to identify the cause of difficulties. In order to develop reading skills, learners need to be engaged with, and reflective on, the process of reading, but, as we have seen, comprehension exercises are often product-oriented in nature (Watkins, 2011) and do little to encourage a process approach to classroom reading. Another drawback of the extensive use of testing techniques is that, as with all tests, they can be anxiety-provoking and remove any joy from reading. A crucial aspect of learning to read is to read as much as possible and it is fair to assume that this is more likely to be the case when it is associated with being a pleasurable, rather than stressful, experience.

Alternatives to factual reading comprehension questions

There are various alternatives to the use of the sort of factual comprehension questions described above. For example, we can set up activities that allow learners to engage with the text at an affective level, and which promote the description of the emotions and feelings that the text evokes. We can also encourage learners to use what they have read to inform other communication, such as by retelling a story or using texts as a starting point for a presentation, both authentic uses of reading. It is also very useful to use activities that encourage learners to make summaries of what they have read as this is an important reading skill, which is frequently needed outside the classroom and also helps to build comprehension. In addition, where course material provides questions that test a fairly surface level decoding of text, what Schacter (2006, cited by Anderson, 2012) terms 'thin' questions, 'thicker' ones can also be provided. These thicker questions push the learners to integrate information from various parts of the text, or to make inferences based on the text and so foster deeper understanding.

These alternatives tend to promote more authentic responses to texts and can also encourage the development of key reading skills and strategies.

The aim of this chapter is to give teachers some practical ideas for how they can extend the while-reading phases of reading lessons beyond simple tests of comprehension to include more engaging, and process-oriented, activity types.

References

Anderson, N. (2012) 'Reading instruction' in A. Burns and J.C. Richards (eds.), *The Cambridge Guide to Pedagogy and Practice in Second Language Teaching*, pp. 218–215, New York: Cambridge University Press.

Brown, G. (1990) *Listening to Spoken English* (2nd ed.), Abingdon: Taylor & Francis.

Paran, A. (2003) 'Intensive reading', *English Teaching Professional*, 28.

Schacter, J. (2006). *The master teacher series: Reading comprehension.* Sanford, CA: Teaching Doctors.

Thornbury, S. (2017) *The New A–Z of ELT: A Dictionary of Terms and Concepts*, London: Macmillan.

Watkins, P. (2011) 'Making the most of it', *English Teaching Professional*, 74.

2.1 Using symbols

Outline	Learners use symbols to record their responses to a text.
Level	Any, dependent on the text
Time	30 minutes, depending on the text used
Focus	Recording reactions to a text
Preparation	Plan a series of symbols that learners could use to express their reactions to the text, e.g.:

    ✓ = I agree with this.
    ✗ = I disagree with this.
    ? = I don't understand fully.
    Λ = I need/want more explanation.
    ↔ = Compare this to …
    ! = This is surprising / shocking.
    lol = This is funny.

Procedure

1 Explain the symbols to the learners.

2 If possible, display the symbols on the classroom wall, so that learners can refer to them whenever they are needed and in future lessons if the activity is repeated.

3 Lead in to the text in the usual way.

4 Ask the learners to annotate the text using the symbols.

5 Learners compare and explain their responses in small groups.

6 Develop a whole class discussion, comparing how learners responded.

Notes

The activity works well with texts that are likely to elicit a range of opinions and attitudes. Where learners use the Λ symbol, they can be encouraged to follow this up and find the information from alternative sources. Reading in a computer lab makes this particularly easy to do.

The activity can be used in conjunction with more standard tests of factual comprehension, if required.

Rationale

The learners have the opportunity to express their own reactions and emotions. This is likely to foster affective engagement in the activity. The Λ and ? symbols allow readers to consider inadequacies in the writing as the cause of communication breakdown, rather than always assuming that their own language resources are the cause of any difficulties in communication. The ↔ symbol allows learners to explicitly make links to existing knowledge or alternative views. This is a key part of the comprehension process.

2.2 Following instructions

Outline	Learners read in detail to follow a set of instructions.
Level	Elementary and above (A2+)
Time	15–20 minutes, depending on the number of instructions given
Focus	Reading for detail
Preparation	Write a set of instructions (see *Example*). Ensure that the majority of the vocabulary is already known to the learners. Any unknown vocabulary could be taught before the activity.

Procedure

1   Explain that the learners must read the instructions and follow them.

2   Distribute the instructions to the learners.

3   Monitor and support as necessary.

4   When the learners have completed the task, ask them to compare their responses.

Example

The following is a brief example appropriate for young learners. More instructions could be added. Here it is assumed that the learners know the vocabulary of shapes, and vocabulary such as *top, bottom, right* and *left*.

• Draw a circle in the centre of your paper.
• Write your name in the circle.
• Draw another circle in the bottom right corner of your paper. What is your favourite food? Write it in this circle.
• Draw a square in the top left of your paper. What is your favourite animal? Write it in the square.
• Draw a triangle in the bottom left of your paper. What is your favourite colour? Write it in the triangle.
• Next to the triangle write three things that are your favourite colour.
• Draw your favourite animal next to the square.

Variation

Write the instructions as a connected text for learners who are at a higher level, forcing them to pay attention to linking devices in particular. For example: *Start by drawing a circle in the centre of your paper and writing your name in it. After that, draw a …*

Notes

The instructions can be framed so that young learners can express themselves through drawing and colouring, rather than be pushed to produce language if they are not ready.

   If appropriate, the activity could be extended by having learners ask questions to a partner and adding that information to what they have written.

   Learners could also write sets of instructions for other members of the group to follow.

Rationale

The activity demands a detailed understanding of the text and allows learners to respond with their own personal preferences, making the activity potentially very engaging. In addition, the instructions can be used to recycle previously learned vocabulary.

2.3 Draw it

Outline	Young learners draw a picture in response to a text.
Level	Any – appropriate for young learners
Time	30 minutes
Focus	Responding creatively to a text
Preparation	Select an appropriate text for the group. If desirable, different learners could work with different texts (for example, if there is a very big range of reading level within the group).

Procedure

1 Lead in to the text in the usual way.

2 If appropriate set a standard comprehension exercise, or select an appropriate activity from elsewhere in this book.

3 Ask the learners to read (or reread) the text and choose a section of the story they like.

4 Ask the learners to draw a scene from the story.

5 As the learners work, circulate, asking them what they are drawing and why they chose that part of the story and so on. These conversations could take place in L1 or L2, as appropriate.

Notes

If the story comes with illustrations, it may be useful to withhold these, at least until after the activity, so that the learners' imaginations are not constrained.

The activity works particularly well with narrative texts.

Some of the pictures could form part of a wall display, depicting parts of the story.

Rationale

The activity requires the learners to identify an important part of the story and allows for a creative response to the text.

2.4 Retelling a text

Outline	Learners retell a story that they have read.
Level	Intermediate and above (B1+)
Time	45 minutes
Focus	Combining reading, speaking and listening skills
Preparation	Select two or more texts that you feel are appropriate for your learners. The texts should be related in some way. For example, short biographies of famous people who are likely to be of interest to the learners could be used.

Procedure

1 Allocate each learner a text and ask them to read it. Explain that they will have to tell the story to other learners later in the lesson.

2 Give time for the learners to read the text and make any notes that they want.

3 Group the learners who have the same text and allow them to compare their ideas about what to include in the retelling.

4 Create new groups, comprising learners who have read the different texts. So, if three texts are used, three people in a group would be ideal.

5 The learners should now take turns to retell their stories. Ensure that learners tell their stories at this point, rather than read the text to others. This can be achieved by insisting that the texts are turned over, for example.

6 Lead a reporting back phase, where learners report what they found interesting about each story that they heard (but did not read). Learners who actually read the story should be encouraged to correct any factual inaccuracies or to add details, where appropriate.

Notes

Emphasizing that all the learners will have to retell the story they read, encourages attention to processing at the reading stage. Also, allowing learners to make notes about the text can help them remember details and perform a better retelling. However, they should be discouraged from writing a script.

Rationale

This is an example of a jigsaw activity. This activity type creates a genuine need for communication because one learner has information which is withheld from another.

This particular task allows for a very authentic response, as we often retell stories to others that we have read (for example, summaries of books, news stories and so on).

The ability to summarize and identify key points is an important reading skill.

2.5 Finding the right phrase

Outline	Learners complete phrases about sections of the text and in so doing analyze the text.
Level	Intermediate and above (B1+)
Time	30 minutes, depending on the length of the text
Focus	Analyzing both the structure and content of a text
Preparation	Write (or select from *Example* below) a series of sentence stems that are appropriate for the text.

Procedure

1　Lead in to the text in the usual way.

2　Ask learners to read the text.

3　After the learners have read the text, ensure they understand the sentence stems.

4　The learners complete the relevant sentence stems by:
   - selecting relevant sentences (and/or sections) of text
   - highlighting the sentence in the text (or the longer section of text) they wish to comment on and numbering it
   - completing the appropriate stem in their notebooks and giving it the same number as the part of the text they have commented on.

5　The learners will now have a series of numbered sentences which correspond to the highlighted sections of the text.

6　Learners compare their ideas in small groups.

7　Learners report back their ideas to the whole class.

Example
Here are examples of possible sentence stems:

This sentence/section introduces …
This sentence/section summarizes …
This sentence/section links to …
This sentence/section is very important because …
This sentence/section does not seem very important because …
This sentence/section is confusing because …
This sentence/section reminds me of …
This sentence/section surprises me because …
This sentence/section is hard to believe because …

Notes
If appropriate, learners can complete the stems in pairs or small groups.

Learners do not necessarily have to complete all the stems, and they could use each stem more than once.

Learners can be encouraged to write their own sentences in a similar style if the stems given do not allow them to express what they wish to.

If the learners need additional support, the teacher can begin by guiding them on parts of the text to highlight.

Rationale

The activity can lead to an affective response to the text and can therefore be engaging for the learners. The stems lead learners to consider the function of different parts of the text and how they relate to each other.

2.6 Preparing a multimedia text

Outline	Learners suggest how a text could be enhanced if it were made digital.
Level	Intermediate and above (B1+)
Time	45 minutes
Focus	Discussing both content and stylistic features of a text
Preparation	Select a text for learners to use. The text must be a printed hard copy and could be from a coursebook, for example.

Procedure

1   Lead in to the text in the usual way. Set a standard comprehension task (or choose an alternative activity from elsewhere in this book) and ask learners to read and complete the task.

2   Discuss the responses to the task.

3   Brainstorm the potential features of multimedia texts. If possible, show an example or two. Features may include links to multimedia sources (such as related videos), links to the definition of words, links to related articles, interactive maps or other images, opportunities for readers to comment, and so on.

4   Ask the learners to reread the text and briefly make notes about the additions and changes they would make if it were a multimedia text. If the text is already accompanied by pictures, these could be evaluated and alternatives suggested where appropriate.

5   Divide the class into small groups to share and expand their ideas. At this point, they should make their suggestions as specific as possible. For example, if they have suggested providing links to the definition of words then they should specify the words to be linked to those definitions. Encourage learners to discuss the benefits of making the changes they suggest and how they would help readers.

6   Learners report back their ideas to the whole class.

Variation

Use a digital text with several multimedia features. Copy only the words of the text for each learner. When the learners have finished (following the procedure above) they can compare their ideas with the original digital version.

Notes

The activity works particularly well with information-based texts.

Rationale

Multimedia features are often used to make difficult sections of text clearer, or to give greater impact to a news story, for example. The learners will need to identify potential difficulties in order to suggest where multimedia sources could offer greater clarity, or would make the text more attractive.

2.7 Shallow to deep

Outline	Learners respond to questions that demand an interpretation of the text, in addition to those that require answers lifted directly from it.
Level	Intermediate and above (B1+)
Time	30 minutes
Focus	Making inferences, demonstrating a deeper understanding of a text
Preparation	If a coursebook text has a series of factual comprehension (or 'shallow') questions that can be answered directly from the text, write more open ('deeper') questions to accompany them. These should require the learners to interpret what they are reading (see *Example*).

Procedure

1 Lead in to the text in the usual way.

2 Set the task (answering both original and additional questions).

3 Learners read the text and answer the questions. When the learners have finished they can compare answers with a partner.

4 Learners report back their ideas.

Example

This example accompanies the text *An unusual meeting* on page 269.

Original questions	Additional questions
1a Where did they meet? (A café in Paris, *Café des Deux Magots*)	1b Why was the meeting unusual? (He didn't know her, but she knew him. He originally noticed her because of her self-harming behaviour.)
2a What was she wearing? (gloves)	2b Why are the gloves important to the story? (They partly absorb and conceal the blood. Picasso also kept them as a reminder of that occasion.)
3a What did the man do as she played her 'game'? (He watched.)	3b Imagine being in the café. What would you have done? (Various answers are possible but learners are most likely to suggest variations on asking about the woman's welfare.)
4a What language did she use to speak to the man? (Spanish)	4b Why did she use Spanish, when he had used French? (Probably because she recognized him and knew he was Spanish. Perhaps she also wanted to create a link between them – both Spanish speakers.)
5a What was her profession? (photographer)	5b Why is her profession important? (It establishes her as an independent artist in her own right and sets up a link (both artists) between her and Picasso.)

Notes

More probing (deeper) questions often focus on *why* or *how* things happen. Also, learners can be prompted to consider why details in the text are important to the story (as in question 5b, above).

The learners can be involved in devising deeper questions with the guidance of the teacher. This could be done as a whole class activity, with the learners suggesting alternative questions after reading.

Rationale

Questions that can be answered directly from the text often focus on small, sometimes insignificant details. However, a true understanding of the text requires learners to know why those details are significant (e.g. *Why did she answer in Spanish?*).

2.8 Editing a text

Outline	Learners edit a text, taking out irrelevant or unnecessarily repetitive parts.
Level	Elementary and above (A2+)
Time	30 minutes
Focus	Identifying unnecessary information
Preparation	Select a text that is appropriate for the group. Rewrite the text, adding information which is redundant or unnecessary (see *Example*). A text from a coursebook could be used as a way of previewing (or reviewing) it.

Procedure

1   Lead in to the text in the usual way. Explain to the learners that they must edit the text, removing redundant or unnecessary information.

2   After initial reading, put the learners into pairs or small groups to work on the text together.

3   Encourage the learners to report back their ideas and also to explain their reasons for deleting certain parts of the text. Remember that there may be good arguments for retaining some of the additions, or removing parts that were included in the original.

Example
The following is an example based on part of *An email of complaint* on page 276. The highlighted parts are the additions to the text.

> I am writing with regard to the order that I placed for the vintage poster of *Casablanca*, produced from an original promotional photograph, featuring Humphrey Bogart sat at a table with Ingrid Bergman which was taken at the time that the film was shot, 1942.
>
> First of all, I had to wait over two months for the delivery, although your website claimed it would be dispatched 'within days'. I did not get any explanation for the delay of over two months despite several emails and a phone call. This was very inconvenient as the poster had been purchased as a birthday gift for my partner and I had to apologize for not having a present to give. Moreover, when the product, a poster of *Casablanca*, arrived, it was packed only in a soft roll of light blue paper and this resulted in it being damaged and creased in transit.

Notes
The first time the learners do this activity, it is useful to go through one or two example additions to the text with the whole class first, so that they fully understand what is required.

As a homework assignment, the learners could be asked to look back at previously studied texts, type out a section and make additions. As a further homework task, these could then be swapped with other learners whose task is to edit them.

Rationale
Learners will benefit from being able to separate key information from trivial, unimportant information. Their discussions will also help them understand text structure, which can have a beneficial effect on both future reading and writing.

2.9 Writing a summary in bullet points

Outline	Learners summarize a text using bullet points.
Level	Elementary and above (A2+)
Time	30 minutes
Focus	Identifying the most important information
Preparation	Ensure an appropriate activity is available for stage 2, if required. This could be the activity that accompanies a coursebook text, for example.

Procedure

1 Lead in to the text in the usual way.

2 If appropriate, set a standard comprehension exercise, or select an appropriate activity from elsewhere in this book.

3 Ask the learners to summarize the text by writing three bullet points (or whatever number seems appropriate for the text).

4 Learners report back their summaries to the class.

5 Conduct feedback on the summaries.

Notes

When using bullet-point summaries, it can be useful to have learners work individually at first and then combine in pairs to agree on a list of three points. The pairs could form groups of four, and again come to a consensus on the three most important points.

Longer texts could be broken into sections, with learners creating summaries of each.

Rationale

An ability to summarize texts and sections of text is a key reading skill, demonstrating the ability to identify key points.

2.10 Writing a summary in 21 words

Outline	Learners summarize a text using a precise number of words.
Level	Elementary and above (A2+)
Time	30 minutes
Focus	Identifying key information
Preparation	Ensure an appropriate activity is available for stage 2, if required. This could be the activity that accompanies a coursebook text, for example.

Procedure

1 Lead in to the text in the usual way.

2 If appropriate, set a standard comprehension exercise, or select an appropriate activity from elsewhere in this book.

3 Ask the learners to summarize the text using precisely 21 words. Ensure they understand that a summary of either 20 or 22 words is not acceptable for this activity – it should be precisely 21.

4 Invite some learners to report back their summaries to the class.

5 Conduct feedback on the summaries.

Notes

Using a precise number of words gives learners an indication of the amount of detail that is expected. Additionally, the need to use a precise number of words provides grammar practice, as there is a need to manipulate the text in order to arrive at the correct word count.

If the text is quite long, the activity could be repeated for different sections.

Rationale

An ability to summarize texts and sections of text is a key reading skill, demonstrating the ability to identify key points. The word limit helps focus learners on selecting the most important parts of the text.

2.11 Read a handful

Outline	Learners read and recall what they have read before retelling it to others.
Level	Intermediate and above (B1+)
Time	30 minutes
Focus	Creating ongoing summaries of a text in order to support comprehension
Preparation	None

Procedure

1 Lead in to the text in the usual way, perhaps with learners making predictions based on the title, or accompanying images.

2 Explain to learners that they should place both hands over the text, with their fingers horizontal to the text. The first hand should cover the beginning of the text and the second hand should cover the next section of text (Picture 1).

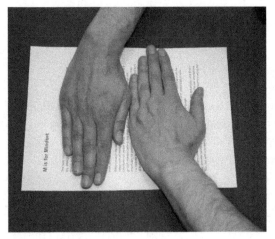

Picture 1

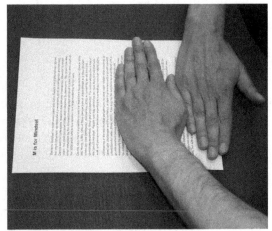

Picture 2

3 Learners should remove their top hand and read what is uncovered. When that piece of text has been read they should stop and place that hand below the second hand to cover the next section of text (Picture 2).

4 Learners think for a few moments about what they have read, before telling a partner what they can remember. Together they piece together as many details as possible.

5 Learners continue working in pairs to predict how they think the text will continue.

6 Now ask learners to read the second section of text, which had been covered by their second hand. Again, they stop when that section has been read and move their hand to cover another section of text as before. Again, they work with a partner to build a summary.

7 The learners continue covering and uncovering sections of the text until the text has been completed.

Notes

It is possible that the learners will not all stop at precisely the same point as they are likely to uncover slightly different amounts of text as they raise their hands. This can be an advantage as learners will not have precisely the same information and can discuss how the additional information affects their prediction of the next part of the text.

If you feel that the use of hands is too haphazard (or perhaps covers too much text for lower-level learners) you could cut strips of paper which learners place over the text and gradually remove.

Rationale

This activity encourages summary-building while reading, which is a key skill in proficient reading. The partial covering of longer texts can also make them less daunting for underconfident readers.

2.12 Making notes

Outline	Learners are given headings and make notes under each, based on their reading.
Level	Higher intermediate and above (B2+)
Time	30 minutes
Focus	Grouping information from a text and creating notes
Preparation	Select an appropriate text for the group (see *Notes*). Decide appropriate headings under which learners can take notes (see *Example*).

Procedure

1 Lead in to the text in the usual way.

2 Write the headings to be used on the board. These headings could also be used to prompt predictions about the text.

3 Give learners time to read and then write their notes.

4 After an appropriate length of time, ask learners to compare their ideas before reporting back.

5 If appropriate, the learners could use their notes as the basis of a piece of writing.

Example

The following headings could be used with the text *It's time to accept that elephants, like us, are empathetic beings* on page 270:

- The problem and the size of the problem
- What elephants do for each other
- The experiment.

Variation 1

If several headings are used, the activity could be done as a jigsaw activity, with some learners making notes on some topics while other learners work on different areas, before sharing information.

Variation 2

Higher-level learners could be given more than one text on the same subject but a common set of headings as this will make the task more challenging.

Notes

The activity works particularly well with longer texts and where learners have to take information from different parts of the text to complete notes for each heading. This ability to synthesize information is an important reading skill.

Rationale

Learners will benefit from practising integrating information from different parts of a text, or from multiple texts. This is a particularly useful task, for those learners learning English for academic purposes, or who need to write reports of some kind.

2.13 This text is ... because ...

Outline	Learners choose a text and explain the reason for their choices.
Level	Higher intermediate and above (B2+)
Time	30 minutes
Focus	Combining reading, speaking and listening skills
Preparation	Ensure learners have access to a number of appropriate texts (see *Notes*).

Procedure

1   Tell learners that they will read a number of texts and that they should choose the most interesting. (This criterion can, of course, be changed to the most exciting, useful, boring, surprising, funny, or whatever seems appropriate.) Explain that they will be expected to justify their choices.

2   Give learners time to read the texts. This could be done as a homework task/project.

3   Give learners time to prepare what they wish to say about the text, encouraging them to give as much detail as possible.

4   Ask learners to share their ideas in small groups before reporting back.

Notes

If preferred, learners can choose their own criterion for selecting a text. Other learners could then guess the criterion, based on what the learner says about the text, e.g. *I think Carmen thinks this text is exciting because she said ...*

The activity also works with much lower-level learners if an appropriate bank of texts can be found. For example, if the learners have access to an anthology of short, graded texts, they can select from that source.

If there are a number of reading texts in the course material, learners could review these and make a selection from previously read material. If this is the case, emphasize the need to include detail when talking about the text, so that they have a reason for rereading the text.

Rationale

The learners are encouraged to react to the text in an authentic way (i.e. as they would if they read the text outside of the learning context, in their daily lives). They judge whether it is interesting, for example, and in order to justify their decisions they will be pushed to both summarize the text and select key details from it.

2.14 Perhaps ... maybe

Outline	Learners categorize sections of a text according to what they are sure of, what they think may be true and what they do not know.
Level	Intermediate and above (B1+)
Time	30 minutes
Focus	Monitoring understanding
Preparation	None

Procedure

1 Lead in to the text in the usual way.

2 Draw the following table on the board and ask learners to copy it in their notebooks:

What I know	What is perhaps true	Things I don't know

3 Explain that the first column can be used to record information either from the text or things that the learner knows about the topic but are not referred to directly. The second column can be used for information that the learner finds ambiguous in the text, or is implied. The final column could be used for either things that are missing from the text but the learner would like to know, or things that the learner cannot understand from the text.

4 Learners read the text and complete the table.

5 Encourage learners to compare ideas in pairs or small groups before reporting back.

Variation

The activity can also be used as a pre-reading activity, with the learners adding to and amending the chart as they read.

Notes

The activity will work with a variety of texts because texts are very unlikely to include all possible information. At least with challenging texts, learners are likely to have doubts about their understanding and so will add these to column 2. However, it is also possible to select a text that is more open to interpretation (many poems have this characteristic, for example) and this will give learners plenty of opportunities to speculate on what may or may not be true.

Rationale

The activity encourages learners to identify parts of the text that they find challenging and they can therefore be supported in developing strategies to help overcome this. See Chapter 3: *Teaching reading strategies* for more on developing these. Reading is seen as a process and the teacher can offer additional support at the points that meaning breaks down for the reader (i.e. the things listed in the final column).

2.15 Role play

Outline	Learners perform a role play, based on a text that they have read.
Level	Intermediate and above (B1+)
Time	30 minutes
Focus	Combining reading, speaking and listening skills
Preparation	Choose an appropriate role play scenario based on a text (see *Notes*). Prepare a comprehension task, if required for stage 2.

Procedure

1   Lead in to the text in the usual way.

2   Set a standard comprehension exercise, or select an appropriate activity from elsewhere in this book.

3   Explain the role play and give learners time to prepare for their roles. This could be done with learners who will play the same role preparing together.

4   Learners perform the role play in pairs, or small groups, as appropriate.

5   If appropriate, invite some groups to perform for the class.

6   Offer feedback on the language used in the role plays and how well the learners drew on the information in the text.

Notes

The role plays could recreate an exchange in the selected text. For example, if the text *An unusual meeting* (page 269) was used, the learners could role play the conversation between Picasso and Dora Maar (using the target language rather than French/Spanish). However, for other texts an interview could be set up between a reporter and an 'expert'. An appropriate role play for the text *It's time to accept that elephants, like us, are empathetic beings* (page 270), for example, would be to have one learner interview another (in the role of expert) about what is happening to elephants and what we know about their behaviour.

Rationale

Role plays allow learners opportunities to engage affectively with texts. Role plays also require learners to understand the text in a detailed way in order to be able to frame and answer questions, support arguments and so on. In addition, role plays integrate reading with speaking and listening skills development.

2.16 Reading as preparation for speaking or writing

Outline	Learners integrate reading with speaking or writing.
Level	Intermediate and above (B1+)
Time	Allow 5–10 minutes per learner for the individual presentations. The preparation time is open-ended.
Focus	Using reading as a source of information for a task
Preparation	Devise a task which is appropriate for the learners and which will require some research to do effectively. For example, business English students could be asked to describe and analyze the history of a given company.
	Ensure that there are relevant texts available for the learners to read. In the case of the above example, company websites will probably provide some (but not unbiased) information.
	Explain to the learners that they must read the appropriate articles and then prepare a short presentation for the class. This presentation could be prepared in small groups.

Procedure

Learners take turns to give their presentations. Encourage other learners to ask questions.

Notes

Not all the presentations need be done in one lesson.

Alternatively, a written task can be set, such as writing a report or essay.

If the learners are sufficiently independent, they can be asked to find appropriate texts for themselves, with minimal help from the teacher.

Rationale

This is a very authentic task in the sense that we often read outside the classroom in order to find information which has to be reported back in some form. Learners are required to identify key information and construct arguments around it.

3 Teaching reading strategies

Strategies and skills

Strategies are often contrasted with skills. Oxford (2011, p.12) explains that 'Skills are automatic and out of awareness, whereas strategies are intentional and deliberate.' It is this conscious use of a strategy to achieve either a communicative or learning goal that sets it apart from a skill and the fact that strategies are marked by their 'intentional' and 'deliberate' use makes them open to explicit teaching.

However, as Grabe (2009) points out, the distinction between strategies and skills may not be as clear cut as at first appears. To take an example from reading, while the recognition of words may be automatic (and therefore considered a reading skill) it is likely that at the beginning stages of reading conscious attention is paid to morphemes in order to facilitate that recognition. Grabe also argues that we may apply certain strategies so frequently and so successfully that they become reading habits of which we are no longer conscious.

In short, we should be aware that what may start as a conscious strategy may, through repetition and success, eventually become a skill that is applied without conscious effort.

Do we need to teach reading strategies?

Successful reading in both L1 and L2 requires the reader to develop a range of skills and strategies and the research literature is clear and consistent on the fact that explicit teaching of strategies can be very effective in promoting efficient reading and comprehension (Carrell, 1985; Grabe, 2009; Grabe and Stoller, 2011).

However, it is also often argued that the teaching of reading strategies is unnecessary on the basis that most learners can already read in their L1 and that therefore L1 strategies will be automatically accessed in L2. While it may be true that strategies will sometimes be transferred it is certainly not always the case because learners may have to cross the so-called 'language threshold' for it to happen (Grabe and Stoller, 2011, p. 43). That is to say that L2 readers must understand enough L2 vocabulary and grammar to be able to activate L1 reading strategies successfully. If there is too much unknown material, the reader is forced to devote almost their entire effort to working out potential meanings, rather than applying the more global, higher-level, strategy processes they would use in L1 reading. Therefore, whether L1 reading strategies are available will depend on the L2 proficiency of the learner and the level of difficulty inherent in the text.

Research evidence is fairly conclusive that automatic access to L1 strategies while reading in the L2 cannot be relied upon, and that strategy instruction should have a central role in the teaching of reading (Grabe, 2009; Oxford, 2011).

What strategies can be taught?

Strategies are often divided into two types: metacognitive and cognitive. In terms of reading, metacognitive strategies largely focus on monitoring comprehension and may include the learner asking themselves questions such as *Do I understand this text? Can I identify the central argument of the text?* and *Can I summarize this text?*. If a learner can sense when they are beginning to lose understanding they can adopt specific (cognitive) strategies to rectify the situation. For example, they may go back a paragraph or two to where they last felt confident and reread. They could also decide to use a dictionary to check word meanings, or mentally translate difficult parts of the text.

However, other groupings of reading strategies have been suggested. Grabe and Stoller (2011, p. 226) draw on Mokhtari and Sheorey (2008) to propose three broad categories: global, monitoring and support reading strategies, and they provide examples of each. The following lists are adapted from Grabe and Stoller's work.

Typical global reading strategies include:
- setting goals before reading and reading selectively to achieve those goals
- activating prior knowledge
- previewing the text
- forming predictions
- monitoring the accuracy of those predictions and modifying them where necessary
- making summaries
- connecting knowledge gained from the text to background knowledge
- identifying central arguments
- forming appropriate questions about the text
- using text structure to predict direction of the text
- inferring meaning from context.

Typical monitoring reading strategies include:
- monitoring understanding
- taking steps to repair misunderstanding (through, for example, rereading, pausing to check other available information, such as graphics, and subvocalizing the main ideas)
- identifying difficulties in reading
- rereading
- judging how well goals/objectives are met
- reflecting on what has been learned from the text.

Typical reading support strategies include:
- using a dictionary (or translating device)
- taking notes
- paraphrasing the text
- using mental translation
- underlining, or highlighting, parts of the text
- using graphic organizers.

These are not exhaustive lists. For example, support reading strategies could also include breaking unfamiliar words into morphemes and 'sounding them out' (see *Introduction*, page 1) out to see if they match a word in our lexicons.

How can we teach strategies?

These strategies can all be helpful and of course there are many others that may be taught. However, the teacher is still left with the tricky task of how they should be introduced in a pedagogically principled way. One option is for the teacher to model strategies by explaining what processes they are going through as they read to the class (Janzen, 2002) – see Activity 3.2: *Look into my mind*, as an example. Alternatively, potential strategy options can be discussed in lessons as difficulties arise with reading comprehension. In this way strategy instruction is embedded within the immediate reading context, rather than being seen as something separate and distant. Given that we also know that successful readers not only use a range of strategies but also use strategies in combination (Anderson, 1991) it makes sense to promote those combinations in lessons.

The aim of this chapter is to give teachers some practical ideas for how they can go about teaching reading strategies in the classroom.

References

Anderson, N. (1991) 'Individual differences in strategy use in second language reading and testing', *Modern Language Journal,* 75(4), pp. 460–472.

Carrell, P. (1985) 'Facilitating ESL reading by teaching text structure', *TESOL Quarterly,* 19(4), pp. 727–752.

Grabe, W. (2009) *Reading in a Second Language: Moving from Theory to Practice,* New York: Cambridge University Press.

Grabe, W. and Stoller, F. (2011) *Teaching and Researching Reading* (2nd ed.), Harlow: Pearson.

Janzen, J. (2002) 'Teaching strategic reading' in J.C. Richards and W. Renandya (eds.), *Methodology in Language Teaching*, pp. 287–294, New York: Cambridge University Press.

Mokhtari, K. and Sheorey, R. (eds.) (2008) *Reading Strategies of First and Second-Language Learners,* Norwood, MA: Christopher-Gordon.

Oxford, R. (2011) *Teaching and Researching Language Learning Strategies*, Harlow: Pearson.

3.1 I sometimes ...

Outline	Learners discuss the reading strategies they use.
Level	Intermediate and above (B1+)
Time	20 minutes
Focus	Discussing strategy use
Preparation	Prepare a questionnaire such as the one below (see *Example*). Prioritize any strategies that you have discussed in class.

Procedure

1   Go through the questionnaire, explaining any problematic terms.

2   Ask the learners to indicate the strategies they use by circling the most appropriate word.

3   Discuss the responses with the learners as a group, taking the opportunity to share good strategy use.

Example
The questionnaire opposite can be copied or adapted for learners.

Notes
This discussion activity will work best when done shortly after a reading activity, so that learners can give specific examples of strategy use from a specific text. When explaining the questionnaire, examples could be taken from the text. For example, *before you read the text on page 273, did you look at the picture of the snake and the lodge and think what the story would be about?*

Learners could discuss their responses to the questionnaire in small groups before reporting back, if preferred.

Rationale
Strategies are consciously operated and therefore open to explicit teaching. It is likely that the sharing of strategy use will help weaker learners to develop not just specific strategies but how to use strategies in clusters to maximize their opportunities to understand texts.

▶ Reading strategies

What reading strategies do you use? Circle the most appropriate word in each sentence.

1 I *always / often / sometimes / never* set goals before reading.

2 I *always / often / sometimes / never* review whether I achieved my goals.

3 I *always / often / sometimes / never* ask myself what I know about the topic before reading.

4 I *always / often / sometimes / never* make predictions about what will be in the text before reading.

5 I *always / often / sometimes / never* check the predictions I make.

6 I *always / often / sometimes / never* ask myself if I understand the text as I read.

7 I *always / often / sometimes / never* guess meaning from context.

8 I *always / often / sometimes / never* try to separate the main points from supporting detail.

9 I *always / often / sometimes / never* ask myself questions about the text I am reading.

10 I *always / often / sometimes / never* ask myself if the text is similar in structure to others I have read.

11 I *always / often / sometimes / never* reread sections of the text that are difficult.

12 I *always / often / sometimes / never* translate sections of the text that are difficult.

3.2 Look into my mind

Outline	The teacher models strategies that can be used by readers when a text is difficult and the learners then also read and think aloud.
Level	Intermediate and above (B1+)
Time	30 minutes
Focus	Combining reading strategies to support comprehension of a text
Preparation	Choose a text that will be challenging for your learners. Practise reading it aloud if necessary. Think about which strategies the learners might be able to use while reading the text. Build these into your reading aloud (see *Example*). If necessary, make copies of the text for the learners, although a coursebook text could be used.

Procedure

1 Tell the learners that you will read to them and that you will also voice your thoughts as you do so. They should follow the text and also listen to what you are thinking as you read.

2 Read a paragraph or so, voicing the strategies you wish to model.

3 Ask learners to work in pairs to remember your thoughts (strategies).

4 Invite learners to report back their discussions. Highlight the strategies used.

5 Ask learners to silently read the next part of the text and to think carefully about the strategies they use.

6 Ask learners to read the same part of the text again. This time they should read in a low whisper and they should voice the thoughts they had the first time, just as in the model.

7 Invite a learner to read the paragraph, again voicing their thoughts, for the class.

8 Praise and highlight the strategies used.

Example

This is an example of a C1 level learner reading the start of *M is for Mindset* on page 274 with a key to the strategies used.

OK so *M is for Mindset* – that's a bit strange. I don't know what *mindset* means but I can see the word *mind* [1] so it must be something to do with the brain and with thinking. *It attempts to capture the 'implicit theories'* – Wow. Who knows? But if I read on [2] I see *intelligence* and *learning* and that fits with what I thought about *mind* [3] so all good, I think. [4] OK. The last sentence of that paragraph is difficult – really – but I see *huge readership* so I guess a lot of people read this [5]. It means 'popular'. I don't think that sentence is too important anyway [6]. *Dweck says that it is possible to see the 'world from two perspectives'* – OK, that's easy – two views or something like that? We have the same word *perspectiva* in my language[7]. So fixed mindset is what we are born with, I guess, our natural sort of intelligence. OK, growth is grow [8], right? So it gets bigger, gets more.

Key

[1] breaking the word into parts to find core meaning
[2] reading ahead to gain more context on which to base an inference
[3] monitoring understanding, checking that new information fits with previous information
[4] evaluating progress
[5] inferring the meaning of the sentence based on known parts
[6] separating key information from less important detail
[7] using L1 knowledge
[8] breaking the word into parts to find core meaning

Notes

If the learners are uncomfortable reading in front of the whole group, they could read (and explain their thoughts) to each other in pairs.

In the model you give, try to highlight the strategies that you have recently discussed with the class.

Rationale

Strategies are most effective when they are used in combinations. This activity allows learners to use strategies in combination and also to hear the strategies used by more proficient readers.

3.3 Annotating a text

Outline	Learners annotate a text as they read, recording the reading strategies they use.
Level	Intermediate and above (B1+)
Time	30 minutes, depending on the length and complexity of the text
Focus	Sharing strategy use
Preparation	Select an appropriate text for the group. If desirable, different learners could work with different texts (for example, if there is a very big range of reading level within the group).

Procedure

1 Focus the learners on the text(s) you have chosen. Try to avoid preparing the learners too much for what they will read as there is likely to be more conscious use of strategies if the learners find the text quite challenging.

2 Explain to the learners that they should annotate the text as they read. Annotations could, among other things, take the form of:
   - ticking the parts where they are confident they have understood
   - writing questions, such as *Does this mean …?*
   - translating words and phrases from the text
   - writing definitions of words and phrases
   - underlining new and/or difficult words
   - writing brief summaries of sections
   - indicating anything that seems inconsistent within the text
   - making a note of any particular strategy used (e.g. finding definitions in an online dictionary)
   - relating what they read to what they already know or believe.

3 Ensure that learners understand that the more annotations they make the better.

4 When the learners have finished, put them in small groups to discuss both what they understood from the text and the strategies they used. If more than one text was used, group learners who read the same text.

5 Monitor the groups carefully to get a sense of the strategies used.

6 When the groups have discussed the reading, lead a whole class discussion on which strategies were used and how effective they were.

Notes

You could usefully model the activity at the start by sharing a text with the learners that you yourself have annotated.

   Once modelled in class, the annotating of the text could be done as homework if time is short.

Rationale

There is research evidence that stronger readers use a wider range of strategies than weaker readers. This activity encourages learners to share strategies and see what others do when faced with reading challenges.

3.4 Traffic lights

Outline	Learners monitor their understanding of a text by using a traffic light scheme.
Level	Any
Time	30–60 minutes, depending on the text chosen
Focus	Monitoring comprehension
Preparation	Choose a text that is appropriate for your learners. Ensure learners have access to some coloured pens or highlighters, ideally green, orange and red, but other colours could substitute.

Procedure

1 Focus the learners on the text you have chosen.

2 Ask learners to use the pens to indicate on the text how easy they find different sections to understand:
   - green = confident they can understand
   - orange = some understanding
   - red = difficult to understand.

3 Monitor the activity carefully.

4 After the activity, lead a discussion on the sections that were relatively easy and which were relatively more difficult. Perhaps analyze a short but difficult section, explaining vocabulary, linking devices, or any area that has caused difficulty. Focus particularly on additional strategies that learners used during reading to overcome problems (such as rereading the text, using a dictionary and so on).

Notes

If coloured pens are not easily available, learners could use appropriate symbols such as:

✓ = confident they can understand

? = some understanding

✗ = difficult to understand.

This activity can be used in conjunction with traditional reading tasks.

Rationale

One of the most important strategies for learners to adopt is the monitoring of their comprehension. This may trigger other strategy use (such as rereading problematic sections of text). This activity promotes this monitoring of comprehension and offers the teacher the opportunity to see the parts of the text that learners find problematic. This in turn can lead to a discussion of strategies used to overcome difficulty.

3.5 Group reading

Outline	Learners work together to read a text and share strategy use.
Level	Higher intermediate and above (B2+)
Time	30 minutes
Focus	Reading collaboratively and sharing ideas for strategy use
Preparation	Copy a role card for each member of the group (see page 67). Look at the text and decide how long you think learners will need for each section of the group work.

Procedure

1   Divide the class into groups of four. Give each member of the group a different card. If numbers do not allow for groups of four, have some groups of five and give the same card to two people in the group.

2   Check everyone understands the instructions on their card.

3   Stress to the class that they need to work together and follow the instructions on the card exactly.

4   Tell learners how long they have for each section.

5   Learners work together in groups.

6   Monitor and support as much as possible.

7   When the reading has finished, invite learners to report back on each stage of the lesson and what their group did.

8   Spend some time highlighting the strategies used.

Notes
Think carefully which learners would benefit from which roles, as they are not all equally demanding.

   This activity demands a degree of maturity on the part of learners and an ability to work independently of the teacher. Therefore it may not be appropriate for all classes.

Rationale
Learners who use a smaller range of strategies, and also combine strategies less, can learn to be more strategic readers through working with more effective strategy users. This activity gives them the opportunity to do this.

Role cards

Person 1

Before reading, ask your group what they know about the topic. Encourage everyone to speak.

Tell the other members of the group to look at the title, pictures or other clues. Ask them: *What do you think the text will be about?*

Hand over to Person 2.

Person 2

Tell the group to quickly read the text (your teacher will tell you the exact time limit).

Ask the group: *Were our predictions (from stage 1) correct?*

Tell the group to read again more carefully.

When the group has finished, work together to write a few bullet points, highlighting the key points in the text. Encourage everyone to help.

Hand over to Person 3.

Person 3

Tell the group to look back at the text. Each person should take a minute or two to identify a part of the text that they found difficult to understand. When they have done that, ask:

What did you do? Did you stop and reread?

Did you guess the meaning? Did you use a dictionary or translator?

Hand over to person 4.

Person 4

Ask: *Do we have any other questions about the text? If the writer was sat with us, what questions would you like to ask the writer?*

Make a list of questions.

3.6 Questioning the text and author

Outline	Learners critique a text and in so doing practise various reading strategies.
Level	Intermediate and above (B1+)
Time	35 minutes
Focus	Analyzing the structure and content of a text
Preparation	Choose a text that is appropriate for the learners. The example below is designed to work with discursive and/or factual texts (see *Example*).

Procedure

1 Build interest in the text.

2 Display the questions below. Ensure that the learners understand the questions.

3 Learners work together in small groups to answer the questions before reporting back.

4 Allow plenty of time for the reporting back stage as this will inevitably lead to discussions about the text and the purposes for it being written. These discussions will build and demonstrate comprehension.

Example

1 *What are the main ideas in the text?*

2 *Does the author explain the points clearly?*

3 *Which parts of the text are difficult to understand?*

4 *Could the author help your understanding more? If so, in what ways?*

5 *Is the structure of the text easy to follow?*

6 *Could the author have done more to help you follow the text (for example, by using more, or different, linking devices)?*

7 *How does the information in this text connect to what you already know?*

8 *Do you think the author is a reliable source, or do they unreasonably favour one point of view?*

9 *How interesting and/or useful is this text?*

10 *What was the writer's reason for writing this text?*

Notes

If this activity is used several times with different texts, encourage learners to formulate the questions for themselves. This will help the progression from the classroom to using the strategy of interrogating the text outside the classroom.

Rationale

The activity encourages the learners not only to question their own comprehension (a vital strategy in itself) but also to analyze the structure of the text and techniques writers can use to make texts easier to read. They also critique the writing, which supports the development of critical reading skills.

3.7 Breaking it into bits

Outline	Learners study common word roots to support the inferring of meaning of unknown words.
Level	Elementary and above (A2+)
Time	15 minutes
Focus	Using existing knowledge about words to work out the meaning of new items
Preparation	Prepare examples of words that share a common root (see *Example*).

Procedure

1   Display one set of words you have selected (e.g. *multiplex, multiple, multiply*). Ask learners to identify the common part of the words – the root – and what it means.

2   Ask learners if they can work out the meaning of each word. If necessary, put the word into a sentence: *We went to the multiplex to see the new Spiderman film*. Ask if anyone can think of further example words which use the same root.

3   Divide the class into pairs and display the remaining sets of words. In pairs, learners discuss them before reporting back.

Example

cents	per cent	century	*(cent = one hundred)*
multiplex	multiple	multiply	*(multi = many)*
spectator	spectacles	inspection	*(spect = look)*
portable	porter	transportation	*(port = carry)*
biology	antibiotic	biography	*(bio = life)*
microscope	microscopic	microfilm	*(micro = small)*

Variation

This activity can be adapted to focus on prefixes, such as:

preview	pretest	prepare	*(pre = before)*
rewrite	retest	regain	*(re = again)*

The activity can also be used to teach suffixes, although they tend to have more of a grammatical orientation (indicating word class, for example).

Notes

This activity is probably best done regularly for short periods of time, rather than teaching too many items all at the same time.

The activity is particularly useful if some of the examples are taken from upcoming texts that the learners will study. This not only ensures that the vocabulary will be recycled, but also that the learners will have the opportunity to apply the strategy being focused on (breaking words into constituent parts) in the context of reading a new text.

Some learners will have similar roots in their own languages, particularly if those languages are Latin- or Greek-based.

Rationale

A key strategy in inferring the meaning of words is to break the words down into constituent parts (morphemes), looking for what is familiar and making inferences based on that information.

If learners are familiar with word parts, their vocabularies will grow and make this process easier.

3.8 Made-up words

Outline	Learners practise the strategy of inferring the meaning of unknown words from context.
Level	Higher intermediate and above (B2+)
Time	25 minutes
Focus	Inferring the meaning of words from context
Preparation	Choose a text which features some made-up language (such as *A Clockwork Orange* by Anthony Burgess) and that you think the class will be interested in. A simple internet search for 'books with made-up languages' will produce some results and excerpts of the books. Choose a short excerpt which has some made-up words in it.

Procedure

1   Build interest in the text. If possible explain a little about the book from which it is taken and how the excerpt fits into the story.

2   Pre-teach any non-made-up words necessary (see *Note*).

3   Explain to the class that the text features some made-up words. Tell the learners to read the text and try to work out what the words may mean. This could be done individually or in small groups.

4   Ask learners to report back their ideas, including a discussion of the clues used in inferring meaning.

Notes

It is exceptionally difficult to infer meaning of words if the vast majority of surrounding text is not understood, so some of the non-made-up words may need to be pre-taught.

It is likely that the meaning of the made-up words can be inferred because the author was no doubt anticipating that their readers would do this, and so will have provided sufficient clues within the text.

Rationale

Inferring the meaning of unknown words is a widely promoted strategy in language teaching. The use of a literary text makes it likely that sufficient context will be provided and also ensures an appropriate text for inferring meaning. It is not an appropriate strategy for all text types (for example, it would be unwise to infer the meaning of unknown words in instructions for how to use a medicine) and nor is it an easy strategy to use unless the bulk of the words in the surrounding text are already known to the learner.

3.9 The next word

Outline	Learners see a text a few words at a time and try to predict the next word or phrase.
Level	Any
Time	25 minutes
Focus	Making predictions about lexical and grammatical choices
Preparation	Choose an appropriate text (or part of a text) for the learners and ensure it can be displayed. This should be very easy in a classroom with digital facilities. However, if necessary, it can be written on the board.

Procedure

1   Tell learners the title of the text.

2   Display the first line or two of the text. Elicit suggestions from the learners as to how the text will continue. The learners may start with broad suggestions focusing on the overall message. This can be encouraged but eventually return to the very local level of what the next word or phrase will be.

3   Reveal the word/phrase and again elicit suggestions as to the next part.

4   Continue in this way, eliciting and then revealing the text in very small stages. At regular intervals, review earlier predictions about the overall content of the text and see if learners would like to change their predictions.

5   When the text has been completed, lead a short discussion on what learners can take away and apply to their own reading.

Notes

This activity works very well with classes that enjoy working in lockstep (i.e. all the learners working together on the same thing at the same time).

The teacher can guide or reject predictions by urging learners to take into account grammatical and collocational considerations, as well as the overall coherence of the text.

Rationale

This activity encourages learners to make predictions and also to review them. Learners will use grammatical, lexical and discourse knowledge to inform their predictions at the local level and all of these knowledge bases are essential to efficient reading.

3.10 Three words

Outline	Learners are allowed to look up a maximum of three words as they read a text.
Level	Elementary and above (A2+)
Time	25 minutes
Focus	Deciding when to infer meaning and when to investigate meaning
Preparation	You will need a comprehension task to use at stage 2. This could be an existing task that you regularly use with this text.

Procedure

1 Lead into the text that is being studied in the usual way but do not pre-teach any vocabulary.

2 Set a standard comprehension task.

3 Before learners read intensively to complete the task, tell them that they can look up a maximum of three words as they read (using dictionaries, translating devices, etc.).

4 Put learners into pairs to compare their answers to the comprehension task. Confirm the answers.

5 Ask learners to compare the three words they chose to look up. They should consider how useful they were and whether, in retrospect, any others might have been more useful.

6 Lead a discussion with the whole class of how the words were selected. For example, were they in a section of text that included a key point (rather than supporting detail)? Or were they words that were difficult to infer because there were few supporting clues in the context?

Notes

The number of words can be altered to suit the needs of the learners and the demands of the text.

A different maximum number of words can be given to different learners, allowing the teacher to differentiate the material. For example, weaker readers could be allowed to look up five or six words.

An alternative approach is to have individuals list their three words (before looking them up) and then compare these in pairs or small groups. They must then reach a consensus on just three words to look up as a group. If other people in the group know and can explain a word it can be eliminated from the list. Potentially, the small groups can merge to form bigger groups and again they must agree on their three words. This can continue until the whole class is involved in deciding just three words to look up.

Rationale

A key reading strategy is to be able to infer meaning from the supporting context. By allowing the learners to only look up relatively few words, learners are pushed to infer the meaning of others. By having to justify the choice of words to look up, learners are forced to consider the criteria they use for making a choice between inferring meaning and investigating meaning.

3.11 What I know …

Outline	Learners set goals and monitor their comprehension through dividing the text into what they know, are not sure about, and what they don't know.
Level	Intermediate and above (B1+)
Time	30 minutes
Focus	Setting goals and monitoring comprehension
Preparation	Choose an appropriate text for the learners.

Procedure

1   Introduce the text.

2   Encourage the learners to set goals for reading, particularly what they want to find out from the text. List the potential goals on the board.

3   Draw the following table on the board and ask learners to copy it in their notebooks:

What I know …	What I'm not sure about …	What I don't know …

4   Learners should read the text and then complete the table. Encourage learners to compare their responses before reporting back.

5   Focus particularly on the final two columns and help learners to develop their understanding of the text by applying a variety of strategies to difficult parts of the text.

6   If desired information (or goal) is not included in the text, encourage learners to consider where they could find it.

Notes

If two similar texts on the same topic are used (for example, two newspaper reports of the same event) the activity can be used in a 'jigsaw style', with the learner who has read one text working with another who has read the other text, to share information and therefore to fulfil more of the goals.

Rationale

The setting of goals and the monitoring of understanding are considered vital reading strategies. Further strategies can be applied in a meaningful way to work on information that is unclear, allowing those strategies to be practised in a meaningful, situated way.

3.12 Add the box

Outline	Learners summarize sections of text and make predictions of the content of the next section.
Level	Intermediate and above (B1+)
Time	30 minutes
Focus	Summarizing and predicting the content of sections of a text
Preparation	Choose an appropriate text for the learners and consider how it could be divided into sections. It may be that the text is already divided (using headings, subheadings, etc.).

Procedure

1 Focus the learners on the text.

2 Ask the learners to draw a small box at the end of each section you have identified. They number the first box as 1 and so on.

3 Draw the following box on the board and ask learners to copy it in their notebooks:

My one-line summary:
What will come next:

4 Tell the learners that they must complete this box after each section of the text (i.e. where they have drawn small boxes). They do this by writing in their notebooks. So, every time they come to a small box in the text, they must stop and complete the box in their notebooks.

5 After reading, ask learners to compare their summaries and also their predictions.

6 Encourage learners to report back on what they have done.

Notes

Encourage learners to write the summaries in largely their own words as this is likely to increase the engagement with the text. Stress that the summaries can be very brief.

If the necessary technology is available, learners could annotate the text on screen.

Rationale

Summarizing and making predictions on upcoming material are both vital reading strategies and through the conscious focus on the strategies here, learners will become more likely to apply the strategies to other texts.

4   Helping learners develop reading fluency

Fluency and reading fluency

'Fluency' is a widely used term in language teaching, although its use is not always consistent and precise. For some it stands in opposition to accuracy, and implies that a learner will focus on the communicative event, and getting their meaning across, rather than the formal accuracy of the language they use. While it is undoubtedly useful for a teacher to provide activities that focus on communicative effectiveness and also activities that focus on accuracy, the term 'fluency' is probably best separated from 'communication focus'.

Instead, fluency is best seen as the processing of language in real time, and the ability to operate successfully without undue, prolonged hesitations. In terms of reading, fluency would therefore mean 'the ability to read rapidly with ease and accuracy' (Grabe, 2009, p. 291). This definition implies reading without undue pausing or rereading and that requires accuracy. If the processing of text is not accurate, leading to the text being misunderstood, the reader is forced to back-track, which means that fluency will be put at risk.

Levels of reading fluency

In terms of reading, fluency can be measured at different levels. The first is word level, where the reader has to link the forms on the page to their bank of vocabulary knowledge. This may include recognizing prefixes and suffixes, as well as activating phonological and grammatical information about the word. Given that efficient readers read at somewhere between 250 and 300 words per minute in their L1 (Carrell and Grabe, 2010) it is clear that word recognition must be instant and automatic. It is worth noting that even proficient L2 readers tend to be around 30% slower than this (Walter, 2015) as they have fewer automatic processes to draw on.

As well as the automatic processing of words, readers also have to process grammatical information as they read. There is a clear difference in meaning between *the cat chased the squirrel* and *the cat was chased by the squirrel*. Again, this syntactic processing needs to be done automatically to allow for rapid, fluent reading.

Readers, of course, do not only read isolated words and sentences, but generally read complete texts. This requires the processing of words and grammar to be sustained over a period of time, leading to a further measure of fluency – passage level fluency. At the beginning stages of reading, and for young learners, this is sometimes measured by considering a learner's ability to read aloud while maintaining appropriate speed and expression. In L2 contexts, the value of reading aloud has frequently been questioned, with Scrivener (2011, p. 269) saying 'round-the-class reading tends to be a slow, tedious turn-off rather than a rouser of enthusiasm'. Thornbury and Watkins (2007) express similar views and point out that this may be because it often leads to a focus on form rather than meaning, with learners only concerning themselves with the pronunciation (form) of the next word, rather than the overall meaning of the passage. Where reading aloud is used, these potential problems need to be anticipated and mitigated, through, for example, pushing learners to read silently for meaning before reading aloud.

The importance of reading fluency

Developing reading fluency is not only important because it increases speed of processing: there is strong evidence that links word, syntax, and passage level fluency to comprehension. Grabe and Stoller (2011) cite research by Klauda and Guthrie (2008) in which students with high comprehension scores demonstrated fast recognition of isolated words, an ability to process phrases and sentences as syntactic units while reading, and passage level fluency. In other words, the researchers found a clear link between each fluency measure and comprehension.

It is likely that fluency is important to comprehension because we can only have limited amounts of our memory bank active at any one time (our so-called 'working memory'), meaning that automaticity of decoding is vital if we are to have sufficient resources available to build our understanding as the text unfolds. Research into L1 reading has consistently supported this model since it was described by LaBerge and Samuels in 1974. Indeed, in many contexts, fluency (often measured by 'words correct per minute' (WCPM) when reading aloud) is taken as a proxy for overall reading ability. There is evidence to support this assumption (Fuchs, Fuchs, Hosp and Jenkins, 2001) although as Scanlon, Anderson and Sweeney point out it is far from infallible (2017, p. 303). This is because learners may have the ability to decode words and then produce them orally without fully comprehending the message of the text. This makes WCPM an inappropriate measure on which to base high-stakes decisions, with these so-called 'word callers' potentially missing out on support from which they could benefit (Quirk and Beem, 2012).

The significance of this for L2 teachers is that developing reading fluency is essential but it is essential because it supports comprehension. Rapid reading aloud may be an indicator of general reading skills development, but it should not become an end in itself.

The aim of this chapter is to give teachers some ideas for how they can promote reading fluency, given that the research evidence indicates that it is essential for efficient reading and comprehension. It should be remembered that readers will only become fluent with plenty of reading practice and so extensive reading (see Chapter 10: *Encouraging extensive reading*) also plays a vital part in developing fluency.

References

Carrell, P. and Grabe, W. (2010) 'Reading' in N. Schmitt (ed.), *Introduction to Applied Linguistics*, pp. 215–231, London: Taylor & Francis.

Fuchs, L., Fuchs, D., Hosp, M. and Jenkins, J. (2001) 'Oral reading fluency as an indicator of reading competence: A theoretical, empirical and historical analysis', *Scientific Studies of Reading*, 5, pp. 239–256.

Grabe, W. (2009) *Reading in a Second Language: Moving from Theory to Practice*, New York: Cambridge University Press.

Grabe, W. and Stoller, F. (2011) *Teaching and Researching Reading*, Harlow: Pearson.

Klauda, S.L. and Guthrie, J.T. (2008) 'Relationships of three components of reading fluency to reading comprehension', *Journal of Educational Psychology*, 100, pp. 310–321.

LaBerge, D. and Samuels, S. (1974) 'Toward a theory of automatic information processing in reading', *Cognitive Psychology*, 6, pp. 293–323.

Quirk, M. and Beem, S. (2012) 'Examining the relations between reading fluency and reading comprehension for English language learners', *Psychology in the Schools*, 49(6), pp. 539–553.

Scanlon, D., Anderson, K. and Sweeney, J. (2017) *Early Intervention for Reading Difficulties*, New York: The Guilford Press.

Scrivener, J. (2011) *Learning Teaching* (3rd ed.), Oxford: Macmillan.

Thornbury, S. and Watkins, P. (2007) *The CELTA Course Trainer's Manual*, Cambridge: Cambridge University Press.

Walter, C. (2015) 'Reading in a second language', Centre for Languages, Linguistics and Area Studies. Available online at: https://www.llas.ac.uk//resources/gpg/1420. [Last accessed 5 August 2017]

4.1 Snap

Outline	Learners play a simple card game to practise the instant recognition of common words.
Level	Beginner–Elementary (A1–A2)
Time	10 minutes
Focus	Rapidly recognizing common words
Preparation	Prepare a set of cards for each small group (see *Example*). The learners should already be familiar with any function words used and know the meaning of any lexical words. The words should all have a similarity in form to at least some other words used, e.g. they may start with the same letter.

Procedure

1   Divide the class into small groups.

2   Demonstrate or explain the rules of the game:
   • The game is played in pairs or small groups.
   • Cards are shuffled and placed face down.
   • One card is turned over so that it is face up.
   • The next card is turned over. If it matches the card already showing, the first player to call *Snap!* wins that pair, keeping the two cards.
   • If the card does not match, it is placed on top of the showing card and another card is turned over.
   • The winner is the player with the most pairs of cards at the end.

3   The learners work in small groups to play the game.

Example
This example opposite is appropriate for an A1 group of learners.

Notes
The use of different fonts on the cards, as in the example, will make the game more challenging. This can be adapted according to the learners' needs.

   Some learners may prefer to play as a part of team and this could be achieved by, for example, having two pairs of learners play against each other.

   It is important to ensure that everyone can see the word easily. This may necessitate writing the word twice on each card, once upside down, so that everyone can see the word easily. Most word processing software will allow you to rotate text in this way.

   It is a good idea to use between 9 and 12 words as this will ensure a good ratio of matches to non-matches.

Rationale
The instant recognition of the most common words is essential to developing fluent reading. The competition element of the activity ensures the need for speed of processing. The similarity of the forms ensures that the word needs to be looked at carefully.

Snap! cards

for	for	for	FOR
or	or	or	OR
one	one	one	ONE
are	are	are	ARE
and	and	and	AND
but	but	but	BUT
be	be	be	BE
because	because	because	BECAUSE
have	have	have	HAVE
has	has	has	HAS

From *Teaching and Developing Reading Skills* © Cambridge University Press 2017   PHOTOCOPIABLE

4.2 Pelmanism

Outline	Learners play a simple game to practise the instant recognition of common words.
Level	Beginner–Elementary (A1–A2)
Time	15 minutes
Focus	Rapidly recognizing common words
Preparation	Produce a set of cards for each small group (see *Example*).

Procedure

1 Divide the class into small groups of three or four.

2 Explain the rules of the game:
  - Mix the cards and place them randomly face down.
  - The first player turns over one card and then another, with the aim of finding a matching pair.
  - If no pair is found, both cards are replaced, face down, and the next player takes a turn.
  - If a pair is found, the player continues their turn by trying to find another pair.
  - The winner is the player who accumulates most pairs.

3 The learners work in small groups to play the game.

Example
This example opposite uses 16 words that are often cited to be in the most common 50 words in written language.

Notes
A quick demonstration may be the most efficient way of explaining the rules if your learners are unfamiliar with the game.

The words used can be changed to suit the class but words which the learners will see frequently in written texts will prove the most beneficial for reading development.

When making the cards, ensure everyone can see the words easily. This may require the word being written twice on each card, once upside down, so that everyone can see the word easily. Most word processing software will allow you to rotate text in this way.

Ensure the learners understand the words and their uses before playing.

Rationale
Effective readers recognize common words automatically and instantly. This game gives frequent exposure to common words and so facilitates fluent reading.

Pelmanism cards

we	we	were	were
when	when	was	was
what	what	word	word
that	that	said	said
they	they	this	this
there	there	it	it
his	his	is	is
her	her	if	if

4.3 Reading Bingo

Outline	Learners play a game of Bingo to practise fluent reading at word level.
Level	Beginner–Elementary (A1–A2)
Time	15 minutes
Focus	Rapidly recognizing common words
Preparation	Copy a set of Bingo cards for the class so that each learner can have one card (see *Example*). Use words that have been learned previously.

Procedure

1 Explain the rules of the game:
   - Learners must tick off the words they hear on their card.
   - The winner is the first person to correctly tick all the words and shout *Bingo!*

2 Read the words to the class. Read quite quickly, so that learners are forced to identify words rapidly. If no one shouts *Bingo!* after all the words have been read, read the list again.

Example

The example opposite is appropriate for a class that has been taught numbers 1–10, some colour adjectives and days of the week. Read the words in the following order:

orange Thursday six blue one Monday two three eight Tuesday Friday brown ten nine yellow five grey green black Sunday four Wednesday (at this point the card with *three* in the top left corner should win) *Saturday seven.*

Notes

If you prefer, you could display the words on a screen for a second or two (rather than read) so that learners process the written form twice.

If learners are confident speaking in front of the class, you could ask one of them to read the list.

Rationale

The time pressure to tick words off before the next one is revealed pushes learners to process the words very quickly and therefore promotes fluent reading at word level.

Bingo cards

one	black	Monday
blue	nine	five
Saturday	eight	orange

✂--

two	brown	grey
blue	Tuesday	five
seven	four	Thursday

✂--

three	green	ten
blue	six	Sunday
Wednesday	yellow	Friday

4.4 Find the pairs

Outline	Learners practise the fast, automatic recognition of words by finding pairs in a grid.
Level	Beginner and above (A1+)
Time	10 minutes
Focus	Rapidly recognizing common words
Preparation	Prepare a grid with around 40 spaces. Fill the spaces with words known to the learners. Write some words twice and include one word which is similar in form. For example, fill three spaces with *bread*, *bread* and *break* (see *Example*). Make enough copies for each learner to have one.

Procedure

1 Tell the learners that they need to find the pairs of words. When they find pairs, they should circle both words, or highlight them in some other way. Tell the learners how many pairs there are.

2 Distribute the copies.

3 Set a time limit. As the aim is to practise very fast recognition of words this should be short. It can be extended if necessary but it is important to encourage learners to work quickly.

4 When the time is up, display the words and confirm the answers.

Example

The example opposite should take around three minutes. The paired words in this grid are:

bath   bread   buy   cafe   fast   gave   park   read   spend   safe   said   say   went

Variation

Alternatively, the activity can be set up as a race. For higher levels, phrases could also be included (e.g. *well paid / well played*).

Rationale

The fast, automatic recognition of words is essential to fluent reading and this activity pushes learners to do this.

Pairs

spend	by	paid	say	red
gave	baby	suspend	read	park
buy	spend	bath	café	bend
went	fast	well	bread	went
bread	game	said	park	bark
café	break	coffee	safe	fast
read	safe	gave	bath	said
last	pay	save	buy	say

4.5 Rogue words

Outline	Learners separate words they have learned from made-up words.
Level	Any
Time	10 minutes
Focus	Rapidly recognizing words
Preparation	Create a list of words and phrases that you have covered in class and that you expect the learners to know. Within the list put some made-up words. If you prefer, use words from a higher level that you would not expect your learners to know (see *Example*). The number of items may be affected by level slightly, but around 30–40 generally works well. Copy a list for each learner.

Procedure

1 Explain that the list contains both known and unknown words. The learners' task is to identify the unknown/made-up words as quickly as possible. They should circle the 'rogue' words as they find them.

2 Stress the need for the learners to work quickly, giving them only a minute or so for the task. Alternatively set the task up as a race, with the first learner to finish with all correct answers being the winner.

3 Confirm the answers when the learners have finished.

Example

The example opposite is for an A2–B1 class. In this example the made-up words are:

> *indide   struff   severate   lasy   grome   shoor   troaster   brody*

Notes

The activity can easily be repeated. In this case the learners can compete against themselves rather than each other. Ask learners to time themselves in identifying the unknown/made-up words. The next day, change the unknown words and the sequence of the other words. Ask learners to time themselves again to see if they can improve.

The activity can be designed to focus on prefixes and suffixes, the instant recognition of which is very important to fluent reading.

The activity can be made slightly easier by telling learners how many made-up words have been included.

Rationale

The activity encourages the instant recognition of known words. Unknown words will be identified as such through not being instantly recognized. The stressing of the need for speed promotes fluency at word recognition level.

The activity also gives an opportunity to review vocabulary previously taught.

⬚ Rogue words

manager	machine	student	stamp	exciting
country	struff	course	invite	wonder
toast	midnight	separated	grome	repair
indide	have a look	couple	boring	fruit juice
false	bad luck	ice cream	relax	troaster
jacket	severate	stuff	shoor	ourselves
body	should	born	page	brody
wallet	lasy	message	colour	lazy

4.6 PowerPoint pandemonium

Outline	Learners have to decide if affixes are used correctly while under a time pressure.
Level	Any
Time	10 minutes
Focus	Rapidly recognizing words
Preparation	Prepare a PowerPoint presentation with each slide consisting of one word. You will need 10–20 slides. The words used should be familiar to learners and contain prefixes and/or suffixes (see *Notes* for variations). Around 20–30% of the words used should be made up and not regularly used in standard English. So, you may use examples such as *imbalance*, *prochoice*, *prepaid*, *unchain*, and *undefeated* as 'correct' words and examples such as *unrecord*, *unstain* and *ungain* as made-up words.
	Programme the presentation so that each slide is only displayed for a second or two. (This can be done through clicking on the 'transitions' tab and then using the 'advance slide after' function in PowerPoint.)

Procedure

1 Explain to the learners that they will see words on the screen for a very short length of time. Stress that you can no longer control how long the words will be displayed.

2 Divide the class into two teams.

3 The teams must take turns to shout out *Yes* (= it is a word) or *No* (= it isn't a word) for each item. Anyone in the team can answer.

4 Explain that the game will progress very quickly and that there will be no break between items.

5 Once you start the PowerPoint presentation try to say nothing and let the learners shout out answers. Answers can be confirmed after the activity.

6 Try to keep score and a note of correct and incorrect responses.

Variation 1
Give additional bonus points for answers where a lot of members of one team all shout out the correct answer.

Variation 2
If you wish to avoid competitive games, simply allow the whole class to answer each question.

Variation 3
The same activity can be used without focusing on prefixes and suffixes. For example, at very low levels 'correct' words might include *and*, *but*, *because*, and *for*, while *thrit* would be an example of an incorrect word.

Variation 4
Essentially the same activity could be used to practise sentence level reading (although an additional second or two would need to be added to the transition time.

Notes

The game usually produces a lot of fun and energy as the learners realize that no one, not even the teacher, can control the relentless changing of the slides. The speed will often lead to members of the wrong team answering, or different answers from the same team. This creates a sense of fun and is not generally a problem, although tighter management may be required for big or boisterous classes, or those where learners expect a high degree of teacher control.

You may want to create a second PowerPoint presentation without automatic transitions so that you can go through the words after the activity, checking that learners understand the function of each prefix and suffix.

Rationale

The time pressure inherent in the activity pushes learners to read the words very quickly. Research evidence shows that the instant decoding of prefixes and suffixes contributes to fluent reading and therefore comprehension.

4.7 Quick flash

Outline	Learners decode words quickly and remember them.
Level	Any
Time	10 minutes
Focus	Rapidly recognizing words
Preparation	Prepare a PowerPoint presentation slide (or something similar), containing 15–20 words (although that can vary with level). Include words that are known to the learners and some distractors (see *Example* and *Notes*). Different fonts, font sizes and colours can be used to add attractiveness and draw attention to some words more than others.

Procedure

1 Tell the learners that they will see a slide with (for example) 15 L2 words they know. Tell them there are also some words they can ignore – they just need to focus on the L2 words.

2 Tell learners that they will only see the slide very briefly.

3 Flash the slide on the screen for a few seconds and then remove it.

4 Learners work in pairs to write down the words they remember.

5 If necessary, display the slide again and allow learners more time to complete their lists.

6 Confirm the answers.

Example
The following slide was prepared for an A2 level group of Spanish learners of English. Three Spanish words are included.

wardrobe   libro   chair

coat

shoes   lamp   guitarra

cupboard

television   cooker

saucepan

picture   door

laptop   plates

umbrella   cama   window

Notes

The distractor words can add a sense of fun to the activity. They can be made up words, or could be words from the learners' L1, assuming they share the same language.

Rationale

Rapid decoding of individual words is essential to fluent reading. This activity uses known words and so also recycles vocabulary previously learned.

4.8 Odd one out race

Outline	Learners identify correct and incorrect collocations and other word relationships.
Level	Elementary and above (A2 +)
Time	15 minutes
Focus	Developing sight vocabulary
Preparation	Prepare a number of questions (up to about 20) using vocabulary your learners have studied. Each question comprises a key word, two or three words that are related to the key word (for example they collocate with it, or are related in meaning) and one word that does not relate to the key word – the odd one out (see *Example* for questions designed for a B1 class).

Procedure

1 Explain that the learners must find the odd one out in each set of words. Use an example if necessary.

2 Set an 'average', or benchmark, time. Learners should aim to complete the activity within this time. This is known vocabulary so learners should be able to work quite quickly. Around four minutes for 20 questions should be enough but longer may be required, depending on the degree of familiarity of the words.

3 Learners work individually. Time the activity.

4 Learners score a bonus point for every 10 seconds they finish before the set time. They lose a point for every 10 seconds after the set time. So, for example, someone who gets 17 out of 20 answers correct and finishes 10 seconds under the time limit, scores a total of 18. A learner who scores 17 out of 20 but finishes 10 seconds over the time limit scores 16.

5 Confirm the answers with the learners. They score their own work and their total score is the combination of correct answers and points gained or lost through time.

Example

Here are three example questions, with *money*, *crime* and *jewellery* as the key words.

money	lose	make	play	give
crime	make	do	commit	solve
jewellery	necklace	glass	earring	ring

The odd ones out in these examples are: *play*, *make* and *glass*.

Notes

The activity works well when repeated as learners can see progress over time. It is not necessary to rewrite the activity completely but it is a good idea to add one or two items (and remove one or two). It is also useful to put the key words in a different order and change the sequence of the related words / odd one out.

Once they have completed this activity, learners could be encouraged to write their own questions of the type above for other learners to answer. This reduces the burden on the teacher.

Rationale

The activity focuses on reading and vocabulary. The development of a large, rich vocabulary cannot be underestimated in the development of reading. Without a large sight vocabulary in L2, L1 reading strategies cannot be accessed.

4.9 Find the changes

Outline	Learners reread a previously studied text and find changes in it.
Level	Any, dependent on the text
Time	20–30 minutes, depending on the length of the text and the number of changes made
Focus	Developing fluency through rereading a text
Preparation	Select a text that your learners have studied previously. Choose a section of the text and make some changes to it (see *Example,* which is short but could be extended, if appropriate).

Procedure

1 Ask the learners what they remember of the original text. If necessary ask them to reread the text quickly.

2 Give the learners the revised version of the text. Ask them to identify the changes and what effect the changes have.

3 If necessary, learners could look at both the original and revised versions as they find changes.

4 Learners could be asked to make changes in a similar way to other previously read texts, which they then share with the class.

Example

The following example is appropriate for a B2 level group of learners. The highlighted changes make the text more personal and less distanced.

Original text	Altered text
My work involves working with young people and helping them to get on the career ladder. Sometimes it helps to see a role model so I may introduce them to other young people who have been successful in finding work. Of course, not everyone can accept help easily. They may not be emotionally ready, for example, or the world of work may seem quite an alien place. In those cases it's important to remain patient because conveying frustration never helps in my experience. However, that can be hard. There was one case I recall where the person concerned simply did the opposite of whatever guidance I gave.	I work with young people and help them to get jobs. Sometimes it helps to see a role model so I often introduce them to other young people I have helped in the past. Of course, not everyone wants to be helped. They are not able to control their emotions, for example, or the workplace is just alien to them. In those cases I really have to remain patient because showing my frustration never helps. But that's not always easy. I remember one case where the person concerned always did the opposite of whatever guidance I gave.

Notes

This activity is very easy to prepare and can be used with very low level classes as the number and nature of the changes are easily adjusted.

Rationale

The need for learners to develop fluency in reading is clear in the literature and one way of achieving this is to reread texts. However, there is a reluctance to do this in most classes for fear that learners will not see any benefit as they are not doing anything 'new'. However, a task such as this gives a purpose to the rereading. In addition, in this example, there is the opportunity to discuss the writer's stance and the devices used to convey that.

4.10 Read that again

Outline	Learners are given a fixed time period to read a text and then the same time to reread the same text.
Level	Elementary and above (A2 +)
Time	10 minutes
Focus	Developing fluency through the rereading of texts
Preparation	Choose a text that is appropriate for your learners. The text should take longer than a few minutes to read in normal circumstances.

Procedure

1   If possible display a stop clock in the classroom. If you have an internet connection, a simple search will produce one.

2   Tell the learners that they should read the text at whatever speed they find comfortable but that they need not worry about every single word – an overall understanding is fine. Reassure the learners that they are not being tested. They do not need to finish the text.

3   Set the clock to a reasonably short time, such as two minutes. Stress that you are not necessarily expecting the learners to finish reading the text. They should read at their normal speed.

4   The learners should read for two minutes, or whatever time has been set and then make a note of where they had reached when the time finished. They should also grade their own understanding. This could be done with a numerical score (e.g. out of 10) or using smiling/frowning faces. They do not need to share this with anyone.

5   Reset the clock. The learners go back to the beginning of the text and reread it. They should not stop, however, until the two minutes have elapsed, making it possible to read more of the text. Again, after reading they should make a note of where they reached and give another grade for understanding.

6   Reset the clock. The learners should go back to the beginning and read again. Tell the learners that this is the last time they will read the text. Again, after reading they should make a note of where they reached and give a final grade for understanding.

7   Ask the learners if they can think of any advantages to rereading the same text (typically that more is understood and reading is quicker). Can they think of situations where they would need to reread a text? An example might be where detailed understanding was important and they were not sure of the meaning after the first read. Learners may well offer examples from the activity but do not pressure them to say how much they read or understood, as this may embarrass them and put them off future reading.

8   If viable, the learners can read to the end of the text, or do this for homework.

Notes

It is possible that the presence of the clock in the room will put undue pressure on the learners to read quickly, and this may impact on their ability to focus on meaning. If preferred, the teacher can simply tell the learners when to start and stop reading.

The learners do not all need to read the same text and they could choose the text themselves.

Learners can be encouraged to repeat the activity at home with a text of their choice.

Rationale

The research literature on reading is clear that fluent reading (often achieved through rereading) is of benefit in developing reading skills. It would be assumed that learners would read quicker on each rereading because they will automatically recognize words that they have recently seen. The literature would predict that this will also increase understanding, giving gains in both speed and comprehension.

4.11 Upgrade

Outline	Learners read and reread sections of text before moving on to different texts.
Level	Elementary and above (A2 +)
Time	10–15 minutes (repeated regularly)
Focus	Developing reading fluency through rereading texts
Preparation	Choose a selection of texts that are appropriate for your learners. They should be reasonably self-contained but could come from the opening pages of a graded reader, for example. If appropriate for your class, grade the texts from easy to relatively more difficult.

Procedure

1 Give each learner an appropriate text.

2 Explain that learners should read reasonably quickly, not worrying about each individual word, but must try to understand the overall meaning of the text.

3 The learners read the text. They time themselves reading and give a grade which self-assesses their understanding (such as a score out of 10).

4 Learners reread the same text. Again, they time themselves and grade their understanding.

5 Repeat this process.

6 When a learner improves in terms of speed and understanding three times running, they change text. If appropriate, suggest they move to a slightly more difficult one. If a learner gives the highest score for understanding on the first or second reading, they should match it in subsequent readings.

Notes

The first time you do the activity, you may like to devote more time to it so that you can firmly establish how it works.

Learners should be encouraged to take as long as they need to progress from one text to another. The only competitive element is with oneself, not other learners.

Try to monitor each learner's progress as far as possible.

Rationale

Rereading texts is an excellent way of developing reading fluency. The challenge to improve understanding and speed of reading is a good way of encouraging rereading.

4.12 All together

Outline	Learners prepare and then read chorally.
Level	Beginner–Intermediate (A1–B1)
Time	25 minutes
Focus	Helping weaker readers develop fluency by following stronger readers
Preparation	Choose a text that consists of a conversation between two people. This may come from a coursebook, or some other source. See *Football conversation* on page 278 as an example from an authentic source. Make one copy for each student or ensure that it can be displayed.

Procedure

1   Introduce the text you choose. For the text mentioned above this might include discussing the passions that people may feel when they watch their own team play. You may also need to pre-teach a small amount of vocabulary.

2   Split the class into two groups. Assign each group one side of the conversation. Give the learners time to prepare in their respective groups. They can discuss how the conversation should sound and should practise their performance.

3   Bring the class back together and have them perform the conversation chorally.

Notes

The activity can be developed by breaking the larger groups into smaller ones. For example, after the procedure above, create groups of four, comprising two people from each original group.

Rationale

The practising stage here is crucial. It means that weaker learners will follow along and be forced to speed up their reading to go at the pace of stronger learners. This should support fluency and not compromise understanding if the learners have been prepared for the activity.

4.13 Follow me

Outline	Learners follow a text as it is read to them.
Level	Beginner–Elementary (A1–A2)
Time	10 minutes
Focus	Developing reading fluency by following a text
Preparation	Choose an extended text that you think will be appropriate for your class. This could come from a graded reader. Many graded readers come with audio recordings, making it unnecessary to make a further recording (see below), but, if necessary, make a recording of yourself reading the text. Try to read at a natural pace and rhythm. Make copies of the text for your learners.

Procedure

Ask the learners to follow the text as you play the recording. If appropriate, set a brief comprehension task.

Notes

If you prefer, you could ask someone else to record the text so that the learners get used to hearing different speakers of English.

The advantage of making a recording before the lesson is that it can then be distributed electronically to learners for them to practise further at home. It also allows you to be free in the lesson to monitor and observe as the learners read, rather than having to focus on the text yourself. However, reading 'live' to the learners is also an option and can make the performance more personal and dramatic.

This activity is particularly useful for learners who are getting used to a new script and therefore need help in matching sounds to letters and letter combinations.

The activity can also be used to quieten a boisterous class. An alternative is to put the text on to PowerPoint slides and set a time limit after which the slideshow will automatically move on. The time limits can be gradually reduced, pushing learners to read faster and faster.

Variation 1

A variation on this activity is to stop the recording occasionally and ask the learners what the next word is. This checks whether they are indeed able to read with the recording.

Variation 2

Another variation is to ask the learners to bang their desks as soon as they get lost, confused, or have any sort of question. The banging of the desk is usually seen as funny by the learners and therefore removes the embarrassment often associated with asking questions. It simply becomes a way of making the rest of the class laugh, while signalling difficulty.

Rationale

The learners are pushed to read at the pace of the recording and this should improve the fluency of their reading.

4.14 The looking back quiz

Outline	Learners reread texts from their coursebook in order to win a quiz.
Level	Any
Time	30 minutes
Focus	Developing fluency through rereading texts
Preparation	Look back through the coursebook that your learners are using, focusing on the reading texts. Write a quiz using information from the texts. Use a selection of texts and tell learners which text/page each question relates to.

If possible, personalize the questions for the class, so you could write questions such as *Page 17 – Find what really annoyed Rabia when we read this text in class*. You could also focus on vocabulary that was studied, with questions such as *Page 29 – Find a word that means something similar to …*

Make copies of the quiz for each group.

Procedure

1   Divide the class into groups of four to six learners. They should work together to answer the questions.

2   Give each group a copy of the quiz.

3   Monitor and support as necessary.

4   When the first group has finished, ask them to talk through their answers, confirming or correcting as necessary.

Variation

The activity can be differentiated for different levels within a group by creating two (or more) quizzes, putting different questions on each quiz. For example, one version could focus on relatively easier texts than the other.

Rationale

The quiz acts as an enjoyable stimulus to rereading the texts and therefore promotes reading fluency.

4.15 The magazine quiz

Outline	Learners write short quizzes for each other from authentic material.
Level	Intermediate and above (B2+)
Time	30 minutes
Focus	Developing fluency with authentic material
Preparation	Collect a variety of magazines. These magazines need to include at least some articles that are of appropriate length and complexity for the group.

Procedure

1 Divide the class into pairs.

2 Distribute the magazines, one to each pair.

3 Each pair should quickly find an article and write three or four comprehension questions about it, making a separate note of the answers.

4 After an appropriate length of time, learners swap their magazines, along with the questions with the pair to the left.

5 Each pair now has to skim though the magazine to find the article and then scan the article to find the answers to the questions. They should write the answers and pass them back to the original pair for checking.

6 Repeat stages 4 and 5 above, with learners swapping with the pair to the right.

Notes

It can be helpful to remind learners of the types of question they could write. As the aim is to develop fluent reading, teachers may want to impose time limits for each stage of the lesson, pushing learners to read quickly.

Rationale

This activity exploits authentic material and in particular pushes the learners to read quickly to first select a text and then identify opportunities for questions.

4.16 What I remember

Outline	Learners recall what they remember from a text and then reread to add details.
Level	Elementary and above (A2+)
Time	30 minutes
Focus	Developing fluency through rereading texts
Preparation	Choose a text that has been read by the class previously. It should be from some time ago.

Procedure

1   Give learners the title of a text they have read previously. Do not let them look at the text at this point.

2   Divide the class into small groups to discuss what they remember from the text. These might be factual details, opinions/reactions to the text, or indeed individual words and phrases that were studied.

3   The learners briefly report back their discussions.

4   Try to avoid confirming or challenging what they recall.

5   Ask learners to read the text to confirm their recall and also to add further details.

6   Encourage learners to report back important points they had forgotten.

Variation

One variation is to split the rereading of the text. First the learners reread very quickly, skimming the text (see *Introduction*, page 4). They then hide the text and discuss what they now recall. They then read more slowly and carefully to add further detail.

Rationale

The activity promotes the rereading of text, which in turn promotes fluent reading and comprehension. Rereading is a very common practice, particularly in EAP contexts where the same textbooks and articles may be accessed frequently.

4.17 Who said that?

Outline	Learners read a series of short quotations and match them to the people who said them.
Level	Elementary and above (A2+) depending on the quotations chosen
Time	5–10 minutes
Focus	Building exposure to the L2 script
Preparation	Collect a series of quotations from famous people (i.e. people your learners will know). Ensure that the quotations are reasonably easy to understand.

Procedure

1 Learners try to match the quotes with who said them. They can work individually, or in pairs/groups.

2 The teacher confirms the answers.

3 The teacher conducts a discussion with the class, asking the learners which quotes they identify with, agree with, and so on.

4 For homework, the learners can be asked to choose three (or more) famous people and find a quote from each of them in English. They use these to produce a similar exercise. This will almost certainly necessitate the reading of many quotations. A selection of the exercises produced can be used in future lessons.

Example

1	Maya Angelou	A	'Everything you can imagine is real.'
2	Sigmund Freud	B	'We don't need to share the same opinions as others, but we do need to be respectful.'
3	Marilyn Monroe	C	'It is time for parents to teach young people early on that in diversity there is beauty and there is strength.'
4	Picasso	D	'I am not a victim of emotional conflicts. I am human.'
5	Taylor Swift	E	'The first human who hurled an insult instead of a stone was the founder of civilization.'

Key
1 C   2 E   3 D   4 A   5 B

Notes
The example is only to demonstrate how the activity works. Teachers can select people that they think their learners would identify with. This could include, for example, quotes, sayings or catchphrases from cartoon characters for younger learners.

Rationale

Teachers often find that a short activity at the start, middle or end of a lesson can be a useful device for a variety of reasons. Learners in countries that use the target language are surrounded by snippets of text every day that they notice and process to some extent. For example, they see advertising billboards, graffiti and shop signs. In countries where the target language is not commonly used there will almost certainly be less casual exposure of this kind. Teachers can therefore usefully supplement exposure by introducing short texts to lessons. This gives a purposeful activity while waiting for latecomers to arrive at the beginning of a lesson, or at the end when other activities have been concluded. Such activities as this one help to create a richer reading environment. Quotations make useful short texts because of their self-contained nature.

5 Exploiting literary texts

What is 'literature'?

For many people the word 'literature' comes with connotations of 'classic' texts – those texts which transcend the stories they tell to form part of the cultural capital of a society. Chaucer, Shakespeare, Austen, Brontë, Dickens and Hardy are all examples of English authors whose works form part of the cultural heritage of England, for example. Their names are well known and their works are held in high esteem, even if many people do not actually read the books themselves.

Not only do these classic texts not appeal to everyone, some people may find them off-putting, even excluding, associating them with difficulty and being old-fashioned. This is not to say that these texts are not well loved by others, and some learners may aspire to reading their favourite books in the original language in which they were written, but it does suggest that such a narrow interpretation of literature is not sufficient to capture everybody's preferences. A more representative view of literature broadens in scope to include modern novels, graphic novels, short stories, plays, poems, song lyrics, play scripts, screenplays, and even comics. When we consider using literature to teach L2 reading, we can extend this understanding of literature even further to include abridged and simplified versions of original texts, as is the case with many graded readers.

While we can identify particular text types that we associate with literature, it is far from easy to give a precise definition of what literature actually is. However, Thornbury (2005) provides the following useful list of characteristics of literary texts:

- Language is used expressively, i.e. to express feelings.
- Language is used playfully, e.g. forms are chosen and repeated purely for their effect.
- Language is used iconically, i.e. forms are chosen because their form is (part of) their meaning.
- Language is used imaginatively, to conjure up alternative worlds, or, put another way, texts represent reality, rather than simply referring to it.
- Language is used metaphorically, i.e. to say one thing in terms of another, and because of this texts can be meaningful on different levels.
- The point of view of the writer may be detached or involved, and this in turn effects the way the reader interprets the text, e.g. as irony, as matter-of-fact, etc.
- The text's meaning is partly intertextual, i.e. the text may only be fully understood by reference to other, related, texts.
- Texts conform to, and are constrained by, certain generic features; and very broadly they can be classed as poetry, prose or drama.
- Texts are often highly valued by the culture, at least in the case of 'literature with a capital L'.

We should remember, of course, that not all texts will have all of these characteristics because there will be variations according to genre.

Using literature in language teaching

Literary texts, particularly when the range of texts is interpreted broadly, open up interesting alternatives for classroom activities. Scripts, for example, are designed to be rehearsed and read aloud, with the possibility of adding a dramatic element to reading. Song lyrics are usually short, as are many poems, and this makes them easy to focus on in a single lesson, and both have a strong rhythm, which can be appealing to many learners. While some examples from these domains may be elusive and hard to understand, many more are written in a very accessible style, making them relatively easy to exploit in the classroom.

People are attracted to stories and they have been part of the human experience over very many centuries. Wright (2000) observes that 'Everybody wants to hear a story. That is why stories are so central to our society.' This means that using literature can potentially be highly motivating for learners. It is, by its very nature, intended to hook our attention and make us want to read. Importantly, literature is designed to engage our emotions and feelings, rather than simply provide information or examples of language patterns. This affective engagement with teaching material is important to learning (Tomlinson, 2010) but can often be missing from teaching material. If learners are emotionally engaged in a positive way in the lesson, they become more likely to want to participate and interact with their fellow learners.

Engagement can also be fostered through exploiting the narrative qualities present in much literature. Writers often build in 'cliffhangers', making us read on as we want to find out the next twist in the story. We can exploit these plot highlights by encouraging learners to predict and anticipate what will come next. We can develop this further by putting learners in the position of the author, encouraging creative responses to the texts they read, and providing tasks which demand an understanding of the choices the author has made.

The use of literature is also likely to develop both cultural awareness and critical thinking skills because literature often challenges us to examine the aspects of life we regard as 'normal' and those that are regarded as being in some way different, or 'other'. Furthermore, the use of literature in the classroom may act as a motivating force for learners to engage in further reading outside the classroom and the overall benefits of such extensive reading are well documented (see Chapter 10: *Encouraging extensive reading*).

However, there can also be downsides to using literature in the classroom. If learners are pressured to read texts that they instinctively dislike, they are unlikely to engage positively with lessons. This can particularly be the case if a narrow, 'classic text' view of literature is adopted. As with any reading lesson, selecting a text which is appropriate for the learners is essential to fostering motivation. A text which is seen as irrelevant, or is just too difficult for the group, is unlikely to lead to a successful lesson, however famous the author that produced it. Using a broader definition of literature, which allows for a much greater range of text types, is one solution to this potential problem. Learners can also be encouraged to select, or at least suggest, the texts that are read and studied in lessons.

Literary texts as part of a wider curriculum

In some teaching contexts, literary texts form part of a broader curriculum set out by a third party, such as an education ministry or examination board. For example, Cambridge English include a literature option in their B2 exam, First (FCE) for Schools, and also literature options in their

C2 exam, Proficiency (CPE). In principle, this may not be a bad thing because, as we have seen above, there are many advantages to using literary texts in classrooms. However, it may mean that the joy of reading is somewhat dissipated, particularly if the texts to be studied are prescribed and do not appeal to the learners. In many such teaching situations, assessment preparation comes to dominate reading lessons and this can lead to the benefits of using literary texts being further reduced. Wherever possible, teachers need to try to reclaim the benefits of using literary texts through using imaginative, motivating activities with their learners, although this must obviously be balanced with the needs of assessment preparation.

This chapter aims to give teachers a series of such activities to use with literary texts in the classroom. It is also worth keeping in mind that activities from other chapters can also be used when exploiting literary texts in many cases.

References

Thornbury, S. (2005) *Beyond the Sentence*, Oxford: Macmillan.

Tomlinson, B. (2010) 'Principles of effective materials development' in N. Harwood (ed.) *English Language Teaching Materials: Theory and Practice*, pp.81–108, New York: Cambridge University Press.

Wright, A. (2000). 'Stories and their importance in language teaching', *HLT Magazine* (5).

5.1 Questions, questions, questions

Outline	Learners answer a questionnaire about a book they have just finished reading.
Level	Intermediate and above (B1+)
Time	30 minutes
Focus	Reviewing a reading experience through answering questions
Preparation	Prepare a series of questions that could be answered about the book the learners have been reading, or use those provided here (see *Example*).

Procedure

1   Briefly ask learners about the book they have recently read.

2   Distribute (or display) the questions and check that the learners understand them.

3   Allow time for learners to think about their answers individually.

4   Divide the class into small groups and encourage the learners to share ideas on each question.

5   After an appropriate time, invite learners to report back their ideas.

Example

The questionnaire opposite may be copied or adapted for your learners.

Notes

If the questions are generic in nature, as in the example, they can be used for any text and this will save preparation time in future.

The example questions provided could be easily rewritten so that they apply to a book that has been started but not yet finished. For example: *Which parts of the book have been the most interesting, exciting, or in some way memorable so far?* In this way the questions can be used at various points as the learners make progress with the book.

Rationale

This activity encourages learners to share their reactions to the book. It allows for group discussion and the sharing of ideas that can both support understanding and also increase the motivation to read.

Where the activity is used while the book is being read (see *Notes*), it encourages ongoing summary building, a vital part of reading comprehension.

◤ *Questionnaire*

Questions, questions, questions

1 Summarize the key points of the story.

_____

_____

_____

2 Which parts of the book were the most interesting, exciting, or in some way memorable to you?

_____

_____

_____

3 Which character(s) in the book did you find the most interesting? Could you learn anything from these characters?

_____

_____

_____

4 Was the ending of the story what you expected? How did you feel while you were reading? How did you feel when you finished the book?

_____

_____

_____

5 Would the book make a good television series, or film?

_____

_____

_____

6 If there was a sequel to this book, would you want to read it? Can you think of any potential ideas for a sequel?

_____

_____

_____

From *Teaching and Developing Reading Skills* © Cambridge University Press 2017   PHOTOCOPIABLE

5.2 Literature circles

Outline	Learners each perform a specific role while reading a text.
Level	Intermediate and above (B1+)
Time	45 minutes
Focus	Reading collaboratively using a literature circle
Preparation	Select an appropriate text (or extract of a longer text). It could be from a book that the learners are studying in class.

Procedure

1 Explain to the learners that they are going to work together to read a text by each learner fulfilling a particular role. The first time the learners do the activity, the roles will need to be explained carefully.

2 Explain the roles:
   • chair: the person who manages the discussion, ensures everyone has the chance to speak and gives support to others, as necessary
   • summarizer: the person who summarizes the overall meaning and significance of the passage
   • word wizard: the person who makes sure they know most of the words in the text
   • connector: the person who says how the text connects to either other texts, real life, or anything else they can find a connection to.

3 Form groups and allocate roles so that there is at least one person with each role in each group.

4 Give learners time to read the text, and prepare their roles. If appropriate, all the students with the same role could prepare together (i.e. all the word wizards work together, for example) to share information.

5 Encourage learners to be supportive of each other as they work.

6 As groups finish, ask them to evaluate how they found the experience, making a bullet point list of two or three things they liked and one difficulty they had.

7 Ask learners to report back what they understood about the text and, if appropriate, how they found the process of doing the activity.

Notes

If necessary, some roles could be shared. For example, if there is a lot of new vocabulary in a particular text, each group could have two word wizards.

If necessary, the reading and preparation could be done as a homework task, with just the group discussion taking place in class time.

As learners get used to the activity through repeating it, they can take responsibility for selecting the text, with each group selecting a text for themselves. This often happens when literature circles are used in L1 reading programmes.

Rationale

Literature circles, such as the one described here, have been used in mainstream L1 reading programmes for many years and their proponents claim great successes for them. The allocation of roles allows an individual learner to focus on a key reading skill and the sharing of information 'scaffolds' the understanding of the entire group (i.e. the support gained from the intertaction allows the learners to operate at a higher level than they might if working individually). Clearly, as L2 is used in the discussion/information sharing stages, there is meaningful output generated, which is likely to support L2 acquisition more generally. The activity is clearly in a very learner-centred, collaborative tradition of language teaching.

5.3 Ask the author

Outline	Learners make up questions to ask the author of a book they have all been reading.
Level	Intermediate and above (B1+)
Time	30 minutes
Focus	Reflecting on a reading experience and the choices made by a writer
Preparation	None

Procedure

1   Focus the learners on the book that the class is currently reading or has just finished reading.

2   Elicit one or two questions that the class would like to ask the author (see *Example* for ideas).

3   Divide the class into small groups and ask them to think of some more questions.

4   Learners report back their questions.

5   As a group, speculate on what the most likely answers would be to some of the questions.

Example

Potential questions could include:

- *What inspired you to write the book?*
- *Are the characters based on people you know or have met?*
- *Did you always know how the story would end, or did you consider any alternatives?*
- *How much research did you have to do for the book?*
- *What is your favourite part of the book?*
- *Were any parts of the story particularly difficult to write?*
- *What message(s) would you like a reader to take away from the story?*
- *Do you think hard about the language choices (selection of vocabulary, for example) or do you simply know what sounds right?*
- *Would you like to see the story made into a film? If so, which actors would you like to play the main roles?*

Variation

Have the class interview a character from the book. They could ask the character about what they were thinking at a given point in the story, what happened to them after the story, and so on. Other members of the class could try to answer the questions in the role of the character.

Notes

It may be possible to find an interview with the author of the book through a simple online search. If this is available, it can be exploited as a follow-up activity.

Rationale

This activity allows the learners to reflect on what they have read and potentially ask questions about either their favourite sections of the book, or the process of writing. Through thinking of the questions and potential answers, they can start to understand the choices that the author made in creating the text.

5.4 Using a script

Outline	Learners read, rehearse and then perform a short extract from a script.
Level	Elementary and above (A2+)
Time	45 minutes
Focus	Reading aloud a prepared script
Preparation	Choose an appropriate scene from a film or play script. For lower level learners this could come from a story they are already familiar with in their L1. Make enough copies for each learner to have a copy of the script. Have a gist comprehension task ready for stage 2.

Procedure

1 Build interest in the text in the usual way.

2 Set a brief gist task to ensure reasonable comprehension.

3 Learners silently read the text. After an appropriate length of time, learners report back their responses to the gist task.

4 Ask learners to read again, deciding how each line should be said. Draw attention to some alternatives and support by asking questions such as *Should this line sound sad or excited?*

5 Encourage learners to annotate the text, identifying appropriate utterance stress, intonation patterns and pauses.

6 Put the learners into small groups to develop their ideas.

7 Allocate roles from the text to learners and ask them to perform what they have prepared within their small group.

8 After an appropriate amount of time, invite some groups to perform for the class.

Variation

Poems could be used as an alternative to scripts because they too often lend themselves to performance.

Notes

When the learners begin to perform their roles in small groups, it is a good idea to nominate at least one other learner to take the part of the 'director', who will give feedback, or encourage the 'actors' to experiment with alternative ways of delivering the lines.

Some learners may enjoy the drama element of this activity, while others may find it quite intimidating. Teachers need to make a judgement on the extent to which this reading practice should become a drama activity.

If a film script is used, one potential end to the lesson could be watching the way the scene was performed in the film.

Rationale

Reading aloud can be a very difficult skill to master. Most people will find that their intonation becomes very flat as they focus more on the form of words than the meaning of those words and this can affect comprehensibility. This is even more acute when reading in L2, where words are likely to be recognized less automatically. Moreover, some languages, such as English, do not have an entirely transparent relationship between the written form of words and their phonological forms and this can lead to further difficulties. Despite these challenges, reading aloud remains common practice in many classrooms.

This activity aims to make reading aloud into a positive and rewarding experience by building in a rehearsal stage, where meaning can be fully explored and discussed and by exploiting texts that were designed to be read aloud.

5.5 Listening to the text

Outline	Learners listen to a text being read aloud, while following on the page.
Level	Any
Time	20 minutes
Focus	Practising written and phonological correspondences
Preparation	Select an appropriate text for the learners. Make enough copies of the text for each learner to have a copy.

Procedure

1 Briefly introduce the text to the learners. For example, tell them the text type and why you chose it for them.

2 Explain that the learners should follow the text on the page as they listen to the text being read.

3 Read the text to the learners.

4 After reading, discuss the learners' reactions to the text.

Notes

The activity will work particularly well with texts that are written to be performed, at least to some extent, such as poems, fairy stories and other dramatic texts.

Rationale

Listening to other readers while following the text can help learners to establish written and phonological form correspondences. In addition, the activity can be used to develop reading fluency because the learners must follow at the rate at which the teacher chooses to read.

5.6 Read and talk, read and talk

Outline	Learners read short sections of text and then discuss their understandings before continuing to read.
Level	Elementary and above (A2+)
Time	30 minutes
Focus	Supporting reading through interaction
Preparation	None

Procedure

1   Lead in to the text in the usual way.

2   Ask learners to read a short amount of the text silently. This may be a few lines, a paragraph or several paragraphs, depending on the level of the learners.

3   After learners have read, put them into pairs to discuss what they have understood from the text. Encourage the learners to support each other in trying to resolve any difficulties of understanding.

4   Briefly, with the whole class, elicit summaries of the text and resolve any difficulties.

5   Repeat the above steps with the next section of text.

Notes

If appropriate, stronger readers could be paired with weaker readers. This will allow stronger readers to support the reading of the weaker reader through the interaction process.

Rationale

This activity encourages peer support in reading and also ensures that learners' misunderstandings will be resolved before continuing to read. This is essential because otherwise one misunderstanding is very likely to compromise the understanding of following sections.

5.7 Using graphic novels

Outline	The learners suggest the words to accompany a graphic novel.
Level	Intermediate and above (B1+)
Time	30 minutes
Focus	Supporting reading with images
Preparation	Select a graphic novel that the learners are likely to enjoy and make copies of the first page or so. Blank out the words in some of the later frames on the page.

Procedure

1   Lead into the text in the usual way.

2   Read the first few frames together and ensure that the learners understand the plot and who the main characters are.

3   Learners work in pairs to complete the frames where words have been blanked out, using the support provided by the visuals and any knowledge that they have of the genre. If you have an uneven number of learners, form a group of three.

4   After an appropriate time, pairs join together to form a group of four and compare their ideas.

5   Supply the original text and ask learners to compare the version they created with the original.

6   Lead a discussion on the differences.

7   Ask learners how they think the story will develop.

Variation 1

This could be set up as a jigsaw activity, with different learners working on different frames. For example, one group could work on even-numbered frames and another group on odd-numbered frames.

Variation 2

Another alternative is to supply all the text from the blanked-out frames in a jumbled order, with learners working together to decide which parts of text belong in each space.

Notes

Comics can be used in a similar way and can be appealing, particularly to younger learners.

Rationale

The visual element of this activity is likely to make it engaging for many learners. Graphic novels are also a well-established method of encouraging reluctant readers, not least because the pictures provide plenty of support for reading.

5.8 The best opening line, ever

Outline	Learners read the opening lines of several novels and choose which is the most appealing to them.
Level	Intermediate and above (B1+)
Time	25 minutes
Focus	Encouraging reading through using short extracts of texts
Preparation	Copy out the opening lines of some well-known books; 8–10 examples will work well in most cases. It is best to not to provide the names of authors or titles to begin with so that readers judge them 'cold', without the preconceptions that other information may evoke. Opening lines of novels can usually be found with a simple online search and it is important to include at least some that the learners are likely to find familiar and/or interesting.

Procedure

1 Ask learners about their favourite books.

2 Ask them how they choose what to read. Try to elicit that the learners may read the opening lines of a book before choosing.

3 Distribute the copies of the opening lines to the group.

4 Ask the learners to decide which lines they find most appealing and which ones are least interesting.

5 Allow time for learners to compare their ideas in small groups before reporting back. Encourage them to explain what makes the opening interesting or off-putting.

6 Ask the learners to suggest ways in which the stories might develop.

7 Encourage the learners to choose one of the books to read.

Variation 1

As an additional activity, the learners could try to match other information to the opening line, such as the author and/or the title.

Variation 2

The activity could also be done using the first line of poems, or indeed the first lines of any texts that are likely to engage the interest of the learners. As well as using opening lines, last lines could also be used. If song lyrics are used, invite learners to predict the genre of music, and be prepared to play a brief clip from each song.

Variation 3

The activity can also work well as a means of promoting reading material available to the learners. For example, the opening lines of various graded readers could be used.

Rationale

This activity introduces authentic texts in a non-threatening manner. The learners have plenty of opportunities for 'fresh starts' so if they do not understand one opening, they can quickly move on to another.

5.9 This doesn't belong here

Outline	Learners read three sections of text and decide which one is the odd one out.
Level	Any, depending on the texts used
Time	20 minutes
Focus	Reflecting on stylistic choices in texts
Preparation	Copy out two paragraphs from the text that the learners are currently reading. The paragraphs should come from different sections of the story. Copy out one paragraph from a completely different text. Remove any very obvious clues (such as the same name appearing in two of the texts). To save preparation time, a simple online search will provide appropriate sections of many texts.

Procedure

1 Give the three paragraphs to the learners and explain that their task is to decide which paragraph does not belong with the other two.

2 Give the learners some time to read, before inviting them to compare ideas in pairs or small groups. Encourage them to discuss the clues that they think may link the two paragraphs. These clues may relate to content, or be more stylistic in nature.

3 Learners report back their ideas.

4 Encourage learners to discuss what they know about the two paragraphs taken from the book they are reading, e.g. where they come in the text and why they are important.

Variation

For more advanced learners, two paragraphs from the same author (but from different publications) could be combined with one from a different author, with the learners asked to determine the odd one out on purely stylistic criteria.

Notes

The activity can be used before learners read a text, as a way of previewing it.

The activity is made harder by selecting a third paragraph that is similar in style to the other two, and perhaps taken from the same period.

Rationale

This activity allows learners to review (or preview) text and promotes a discussion of stylistic differences. The benefit to the learners is not necessarily in selecting the correct paragraph, but in discussing the similarities and differences in the texts.

5.10 Sentence detective

Outline	Learners decide which sentences are taken from the text that they are all reading.
Level	Any
Time	20 minutes
Focus	Reading for detailed understanding
Preparation	None

Procedure

1 Ask learners about the text that the group is reading. Ask what they like about it and what they think will happen next.

2 Explain that the learners should write six sentences. They select two sentences that they like from anywhere up to the point they have reached in the story. They then select two other sentences from the text and make small changes to them. Next, they make up two more sentences which sound like sentences from the text, but are not in the text. They should write these six sentences in a random order (see *Example*). Note that minor changes in form can make big changes to the meaning – see example 1 below.

3 Each learner swaps their sentences with another learner. They then decide which sentences are original to the story, which have minor changes, and which are made up.

4 Finish by having some learners read out a sentence and the rest of the class guessing its category.

Example
The following examples are taken from *Alice's Adventures in Wonderland* by Lewis Carroll.

1 'Speak English!' said the eaglet. I know the meaning of all those long words, and, what's more, I believe you do too!'

2 The table was a large one, but the three were all crowded together at one corner of it. 'No room! No room!' they cried out when they saw Alice coming.

3 'If you must whisper, whisper clearly and loudly: that is the only polite way to do it.'

4 'I think we might all have a better time,' Alice said, 'if we make up riddles that have no answers.'

5 'After three days any visitor is most unwelcome and should disappear without goodbyes of any sort: have you learned nothing in school?'

6 'They're dreadfully fond of beheading people here: the great wonder is that anyone is left alive.'

Key
1 Minor changes. The original is: 'Speak English!' said the eaglet. I don't know the meaning of half those long words, and, what's more, I don't believe you do either!'
2 Taken directly from the text.
3 Made-up sentence.
4 Minor changes. The original is: 'I think you might do something better with the time,' she said, 'than wasting it in asking riddles that have no answers.'

[5] Made-up sentence.
[6] Taken directly from the text.

Notes

This activity is particularly popular with young learners. The copying of the sentences and writing of new ones can be done as homework, if appropriate.

   If the learners find it hard to make up sentences, suggest that they read a sentence or two and then write the ideas in their own words.

Rationale

The activity demands quite careful close reading of a few sentences. It will also encourage the learners to skim though the text quickly to find examples to use. The activity also provides writing practice.

5.11 Watch and read

Outline	Learners study the changes made in adapting a book to become a film.
Level	Upper intermediate and above (B2+)
Time	45 minutes
Focus	Comparing written and film versions of a story
Preparation	Choose a book that has been made into a film and that you think the learners will be interested in. The *Harry Potter* and *The Hunger Games* series are obvious examples, although there are of course very many to choose from.
	Identify a short section of the book which will interest learners and its corresponding film scene. Make copies of the text from the book so that each learner has one. If possible, write out the transcript from the scene in the film. This may be available online with a simple search.

Procedure

1 Discuss in open class the sorts of changes that happen when books are adapted to become films. For example, typically they need to be made shorter, descriptive passages are omitted as these can be represented visually, and dialogues sometimes have to be made slightly more natural. Some characters may be left out of the film version.

2 Generate interest in the story and explain how the scene you have chosen fits into the narrative.

3 Show the scene from the film and check that learners have understood the key points. This could be supported with the transcript.

4 Ask learners to read the section from the book. As they do so, they should make notes about how it is different to the film. It can be a good idea to replay the film scene at intervals so that ideas can be checked and confirmed. This will support detailed responses.

5 Lead a discussion on the principal differences the learners have identified.

Notes

The learners could read the book version of the text before the lesson if time is short. In this case they can reread quickly during the lesson to remind themselves of key details.

Rationale

Many people find visual mediums, such as films, very attractive. This attraction can be used to foster an interest in reading the related text. This activity also has a strong affective appeal, as readers often form strong opinions about how the text has been interpreted.

5.12 Preparing a trailer

Outline	The learners design a film trailer for a book they have read.
Level	Intermediate and above (B1+)
Time	45 minutes
Focus	Identifying key parts of a text
Preparation	Choose two film trailers for films that you think the learners would like, or have already seen and enjoyed. Film trailers are available on IMDb and YouTube.

Procedure

1 Very briefly lead in to the trailers, asking learners if they have seen the films and so on.

2 Play both trailers, setting a gist type task, such as deciding which film they would be more likely to choose to watch. Learners report their answers.

3 As a group discuss the key features of trailers. For example:
   - They are very short.
   - They aim to excite/interest the audience through previewing key sequences.
   - They convey the genre of the film.
   - They introduce key characters.
   - They do not tell the whole story of the film.
   - There is usually a voice-over.

4 Explain that the book that the class has been reading is going to be made into a film and the learners must design a trailer for it.

5 Divide the class into small groups and give them time to design the trailer. If appropriate, the learners could be supported by answering questions, such as:
   - How will the trailer show the type of film this is? What sort of music will be used?
   - Which characters should be introduced? Which scenes will demonstrate their relationships?
   - Which key scenes will be used to give an idea of the story?
   - How much of the story will be revealed?
   - Will there be a voice-over? If so, what will be said?

6 After an appropriate amount of time, ask the groups to report back their ideas.

7 Encourage groups to comment on the similarities and differences of each group's suggestions for trailers.

Notes

If the book has already been made into a film, the learners can compare their ideas with the trailer that accompanied it.

Rationale

Film trailers can be thought of as adverts for a particular product. As such, they push the learners to make use of the positive parts of their reading experience, rather than any parts they may have found dull or boring. As trailers are very brief, learners need to summarize key messages from the book succinctly.

5.13 Summary charts

Outline	Learners complete a summary chart for each character in a particular scene from the book they are reading.
Level	Elementary and above (A2+)
Time	30 minutes
Focus	Analyzing characters in literature
Preparation	Choose an important scene in the book that the learners are studying. Produce a task sheet (see *Example*).

Procedure

1 Focus the learners on the scene you have chosen. If necessary, ask them to reread the relevant pages.

2 Distribute the task sheet and ensure that the learners understand what is required. See the example below.

3 Learners work individually to begin completing the task.

4 After an appropriate length of time, ask learners to compare their ideas in pairs. Give them a little more time to complete the chart together.

5 Learners report back their ideas.

6 Encourage learners to discuss the traits each character exhibits in the scene and the ways these are typical (or not) of them generally.

Example

In the task sheet opposite, the learners write the name of each character in the scene in the first column. More rows can be added if necessary. Learners should not write every word that is said in a dialogue, but sum up the key messages.

Through analyzing parts of the dialogue (second and third columns) and why some actions are important (fourth column), the learners are pushed to create links to other parts of the text. The final column, *Any other comments*, might include what the character is wearing (if it is significant), a particularly interesting/useful quotation, or what the character is thinking/plotting (if it is different to what they say).

Variation

Ask different groups of learners to focus on a different character in the scene. Regroup learners so that they can share information about all the characters.

Notes

Learners can be invited to select the scene to analyze.

Rationale

This activity can be a very useful revision for learners who need to prepare literary texts for assessment purposes. It helps them to focus on key moments in the text and understand a character's thoughts and motivations.

⬆ Task sheet

Character	What he/she does	What he/she says	Why it's important	Any other comments

5.14 Graphic organizer summary

Outline	Learners create a summary of a story using a graphic organizer.
Level	Elementary and above (A2+)
Time	30 minutes
Focus	Analyzing the structure of a text
Preparation	Select an appropriate fictional text for the learners. It could be a text that the learners have already read. Make copies of the organizer (see *Example*) and have a comprehension task ready, if required, for stage 2.

Procedure

1 Lead in to the text in the usual way.

2 If this is a text that the learners have not seen before, set a brief comprehension task. If it is a text that the learners have previously read, elicit the key points of the story.

3 Draw the organizer opposite on the board (or adapt it as appropriate) and ask learners to copy it.

4 Learners work in small groups to complete the organizer.

5 After an appropriate length of time, learners report back their ideas.

Example
The organizer opposite can be copied or adapted as required for the text you use.

Variation
This could be set up as a jigsaw activity, with different learners working on different parts of the summary before sharing information.

Notes
The activity works particularly well with short stories.

Rationale
Most fictional texts follow a pattern of establishing a situation, introducing a complication and then finding a resolution to that complication. A murder mystery is an obvious example of this pattern. This activity helps learners to see that pattern, which may in turn help with future reading and also writing.

⌖ Graphic organizer

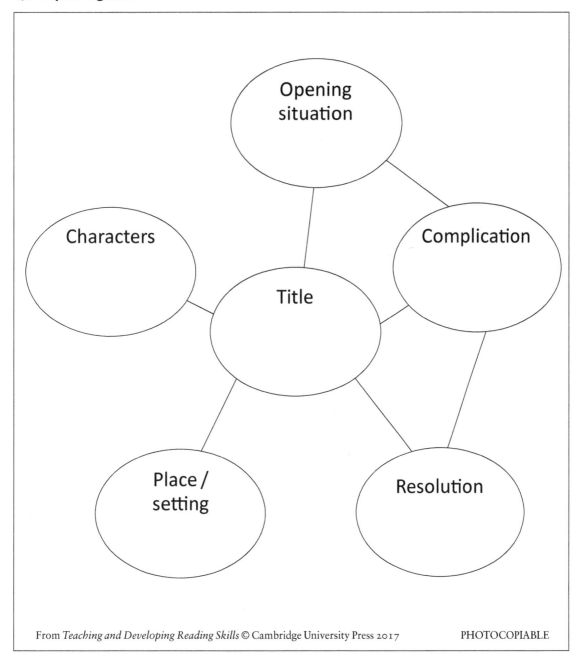

5.15 Which character would you most like to …

Outline	Learners discuss the traits of leading characters in a book.
Level	Elementary and above (A2+)
Time	10 minutes
Focus	Analyzing character traits
Preparation	Prepare a short series of questions (see *Example*).

Procedure

1   Focus learners on the book that the class has been reading.

2   Ask individual learners a question or two from the examples below and ask them to justify their decisions.

3   Write other example questions on the board, ensuring that the learners understand them.

4   Learners compare their ideas in small groups and justify their choices in each case.

5   Invite learners to report back their ideas.

6   Encourage learners to make up their own questions using the same formula (*Which character would you most like to …?*) for others to answer.

Example
- *Which character would you most like to go for a coffee with?*
- *Which character would you most like to sit next to on a long flight?*
- *Which character would you most like to see banished to a desert island?*
- *Which character would you most like to share a desert island with?*
- *Which character would you most like to have as a colleague?*
- *Which character would you most like to play a board game with?*
- *Which character would you most like to throw off a train?*

Variation
As an alternative, write all the questions on the board and then nominate a character from the book. The learners must guess which question you would apply to that character. Once this has been demonstrated, learners can take over nominating the character.

Rationale
The activity encourages learners to think about the traits of the characters in a light-hearted way. In justifying their choices they will also review and summarize key incidents from the book.

5.16 The story the author didn't write

Outline	Learners consider alternative story developments that the writer did not include.
Level	Intermediate and above (B1+)
Time	30 minutes
Focus	Analyzing critical incidents in a story
Preparation	Identify a few key points in the story, e.g.:

- where a character survives against the odds, or where a character dies
- where an important decision is made
- where characters' feelings towards each other change (they fall in love, argue and so on).

Procedure

1 Focus the learners on one of the incidents you have chosen. Ask them how the story might have developed differently if there had been a different outcome at this point. Elicit several ideas or possibilities.

2 Focus the learners on the other incidents selected. In small groups, learners discuss how the story could have been very different.

3 Learners report back their ideas.

4 Again in small groups, ask learners to identify other similar incidents in the book. They swap these with another group, which speculates about how the story could have been different.

Notes

The activity can be an interesting and communicative way of practising the so-called 'third' conditional. *If Katniss hadn't been kind to Rue, she might not have…*

Rationale

The activity helps the learners to place themselves in the position of the author and consider how each incident has impacted on the developing narrative. This helps the learners discover the structure of the writing and is also likely to help develop their own creative writing abilities.

5.17 The sequel

Outline	Learners consider how the story might develop if a sequel were written.
Level	Intermediate and above (B1+)
Time	20 minutes
Focus	Discussing possibilities for further stories, based on the reading of a text
Preparation	None

Procedure

1   After a class has finished reading a book, elicit from learners some of the key characters and incidents. Draw attention to any unresolved plot lines.

2   Tell the class that the book was such a success that the publisher is desperate to publish a sequel. In small groups learners discuss the best way to develop this, outlining the main plot lines, which characters will be the focus of the story, and any new key characters to be introduced.

3   Learners report back their ideas.

Variation

Instead of a sequel, learners could develop prequel ideas, where they explore the earlier life of the main character, for example, or a situation leading to the opening situation of the original story.

Notes

The activity will not work well with stories where there is already a well-known sequel. However, most other stories could have some kind of development. Even where a hero dies, we could pick up the story in the next generation. Alternatively, the focus could switch to a secondary character and how their life develops after the end of the book.

A homework task could be to write a pitch for the sequel idea to the publisher.

Rationale

Learners have the opportunity to discuss the book they have read and generate further ideas. This is a genuinely communicative task. In doing this task, the learners will also be pushed to review what they understood about plot and character from their reading.

Exploiting digital resources

Digital reading

Just as we read a huge variety of print sources, so we also engage with a range of digital text types. These may include as diverse formats as simple Word or PDF documents viewed on a screen, lengthy texts with numerous hyperlinks, and short instant messages to which we may, or may not, respond. Moreover, our reading experience is also impacted by the range of devices on which we view these text types: computers, tablets, smartphones, e-readers and so on. This diversity means that we should be careful about making broad generalizations about 'digital reading' as if it were a single, consistent entity.

One thing that does seem fairly certain is that the proportion of digital reading (as opposed to print) we engage in is likely to increase as we go through the 21st century. The growing ubiquity of digital media suggests that teachers and course designers have a responsibility to help learners develop the skills necessary for successful, efficient reading of a range of digital text types.

Print versus digital reading

Digital reading is a relatively new phenomenon and there is much that we still need to understand about it. However, some research has been done comparing levels of comprehension between print and digital reading. For example, Mangen, Walgermo and Brønnick (2013) studied 72 primary-age readers, who all read the same two texts. Half of the children read print versions of the texts and the other half read them as PDF files on a computer screen. The main finding of the study was that those who read the hard copies scored significantly better in tests of comprehension. This finding has been supported by other studies, suggesting that digital reading may generally lead to a reduction in comprehension. More research is required to confirm this, and we also need to understand how other variables, such as the use of different text types and the age of the learners, impact on digital reading comprehension. We should also remember that while comprehension studies are undoubtedly useful, they do not shed light on other areas that may also interest teachers, such as whether the learners find particular forms of digital reading more useful, motivating or pleasurable than traditional print reading.

If we tentatively accept that comprehension might be adversely affected by reading from a screen, an earlier study by Mangen (2008) gives some indication as to why this may be the case. In that study she found that digital reading was characterized by speed, using strategies such as skimming and scanning, and led to less focused attention on the text. Liu (2005) reached a similar conclusion and also found that readers tended to annotate and highlight digital texts to a lesser degree than print ones, perhaps another indication of reduced reader focus.

Online reading

Mangen et al's (2013) research referred to above was done using simple PDF files. Online reading is qualitatively different to reading linear texts from a screen, but again there is likely to be a push towards speed of processing. Wolf (2011) suggests that 'The characteristics of a medium like the internet invite the reader to move from one stimulus to the next in rapid fashion. The characteristics of a medium like the book invite more focused attention.' While books provide a finite amount of information to process, online reading can appear limitless and daunting, and this may add to a perception of a 'need for speed'. This is not to say that detailed, careful reading is impossible online, but that the medium itself militates against it, as Nicholas Carr observes:

> When we go online, we enter an environment that promotes cursory reading, hurried and distracted thinking, and superficial learning. It is possible to think deeply while surfing the Net, just as it's possible to think shallowly while reading a book, but that's not the type of thinking the technology encourages and rewards. (Carr, 2010, pp. 115–16)

Many online texts require the reader to navigate through them by clicking on links (for example, when we visit a website) and this demands quick decisions about which links to follow. Further research into how readers make such decisions is required but what is clear is that when we read texts with hyperlinks, the decision of whether or not to follow a link adds to the burden on cognitive processing resources and so reduces the attention we can give to the text itself. Further, if a link is followed, our reading of the original text is interrupted, perhaps impacting on our ability to build a coherent, developing picture from the text. As well as understanding more about how readers negotiate hyperlinks, we also need to know more about how readers use multimedia graphics, which may support understanding, and also how learners use other online tools, such as dictionaries, while they read. Answers to these questions will have implications not only for how we teach reading, but how we teach writing as well.

While hyperlinks, graphics and other multimedia input give potential support to reading, the online environment also poses less helpful challenges to our attention. If I read a print edition of a newspaper there may be advertisements on the page, but they are static and once reading of an article has started are unlikely to distract attention. However, when reading online those advertisements may include movement and sound effects, or even appear between paragraph breaks as I read. Each is calculated to maximally distract me from the newspaper article and draw me instead to the advertisement. Such competition for our attention is likely to impact on our ability to read in a focused manner.

Digital reading skills

It seems safe to say that all the skills that are required for successful print reading are also required when reading digital texts. However, it may be that additional skills are also needed, particularly when reading online. A simple internet search can produce thousands of results, requiring the reader to make quick decisions as to which seem the most relevant. Hyperlinks within texts may offer support and useful background information, or be a distraction, and so again require skilled decision making on the part of the reader. It is probably also the case that online reading requires ever greater criticality (see Chapter 8: *Developing critical reading skills*) so that readers can identify the true and the trustworthy from the untrue and the simply fabricated.

Online readers are also often working with new text types which blend features of written and spoken language to a very large degree. These texts, such as instant messages and posts to discussion forums, can make their own demands of a reader as they require an awareness as to whether contributions are intended to be serious, ironic, comical or even provocative. Face-to-face interaction usually provides sufficient context and supporting information (body language, tone of voice and so on) to allow us to make these judgements but the intentions of a writer are considerably harder to gauge.

With digital reading set to increase, it would seem appropriate that we include more digital reading in our classrooms where possible, and address the development of the skills and strategies it requires. The activities that follow in this chapter aim to support teachers in providing engaging and useful activities to their learners.

References

Carr, N. (2010) *The Shallows: How the internet is changing how we think, read and remember*, London: Atlantic Books.

Liu, Z. (2005) 'Reading behavior in the digital environment: Changes in reading behavior over the past ten years', *Journal of Documentation*, 61(6), pp. 700–712.

Mangen, A. (2008) 'Hypertext fiction reading: Haptics and immersion', *Journal of Research in Reading*, 31(4), pp. 404–419.

Mangen, A., Walgermo, B.R. and Brønnick, K. (2013) 'Reading linear texts on paper versus computer screen: effects on reading comprehension', *International Journal of Educational Research*, 58, pp. 61–68.

Wolf, M. (2011). 'Will the speed of online reading deplete our analytic thought?', *The Guardian* [online]. Available online at: https://www.theguardian.com/commentisfree/2011/aug/14/marshall-mcluhan-analytic-thought. [Last accessed 5 August 2017]

6.1 A quick experiment

Outline	Learners take part in a quick experiment investigating print and digital reading.
Level	Any
Time	30 minutes
Focus	Discussing the differences between print and digital reading
Preparation	Select a text that is appropriate for your learners. Ensure that there is both a print version and a digital version of the text. Write some comprehension questions to accompany the text.

Procedure

1   Explain to the class that they are going to take part in an experiment. Divide the class into two groups. One group will read the print version of the text and the other will read the text from screens.

2   Without much lead-in to the text, ask learners to read their allocated version of the text and answer the questions.

3   After an appropriate length of time, go through the answers to the questions. Ask learners to write on a small piece of paper the number of questions they got right. Learners fold the piece of paper, so that no one can see their individual score, and give it to the teacher.

4   Write each score on the board in two columns (one for print, one for digital). Ask learners to calculate the average score in each column.

5   Lead a discussion about the results, pointing out that some researchers would predict that print reading would result in higher scores (see the introduction to this chapter on page 135). Ask learners to consider why this might be.

Notes

It is a good idea to distribute slips of paper for the learners to write the number of correct responses. These can be colour-coded, e.g. blue paper for digital and yellow for print, making it easy for the teacher to manage the scoring.

The experiment, as set up here, is very unscientific and will not prove very much in itself. The learners may not be at the same level as each other, they may not report scores accurately and the group sizes are likely to be too small for reliable quantitative research to be undertaken. However, the experiment sets up the possibility of discussing print and digital reading.

Rationale

The activity is a fun way to discuss benefits and drawbacks of digital reading. If learners are aware of the potential challenges, particularly the possibility of distraction, they may be able to adopt and devise strategies to overcome them.

6.2 Same or different?

Outline	Learners compare print and digital reading.
Level	Intermediate and above (B1+)
Time	35 minutes
Focus	Discussing the differences between print and digital reading
Preparation	Select two short texts, one print and one digital, that are appropriate for the learners (see *Notes*).

Procedure

1 Lead in to the first text in the usual way.

2 If appropriate set a standard comprehension exercise, or select an appropriate activity from elsewhere in this book.

3 Repeat the process above with the second text.

4 Put the learners into small groups and give them the following sentence stems:
   - *I like reading hard copies because …*
   - *I like reading from a screen because …*
   - *The main differences between print and reading from a screen are …*

5 Learners complete the sentences in as many different ways as possible, drawing on their experience of reading the texts used in the lesson and also their wider experience.

6 Each group reports back its ideas.

7 Encourage discussion of the points raised and add to the ideas of the learners as appropriate.

Notes

For the purposes of the activity, it is useful to select texts that the learners can read comfortably. This allows for more reflection on the process of reading. The activity also works well if the digital text is an online one, allowing for hyperlinks, multimedia integration and so on. This gives the learners more to comment on.

If appropriate, add to the discussion by asking learners to consider different reading scenarios such as:
- reading for social purposes, such as staying in touch with friends
- reading for pleasure, such as a novel
- reading to learn, such as researching an essay
- reading for information, such as reading a newspaper.

Rationale

Learners will benefit from thinking about the pros and cons of online reading (links can give support and explanation, or be a distraction, for example). Learners may share strategies to overcome difficulties (such as sharing information about highlighting and annotating digital text).

6.3 How are they different?

Outline	Learners consider how print and digital coverage of a story in a newspaper differ.
Level	Intermediate and above (B1+)
Time	30 minutes
Focus	Comparing print and digital versions of the same story
Preparation	Select a print story from a newspaper that can also be accessed online.

Procedure

1 Start with the print version of the story. Lead in to the text in the usual way.

2 If appropriate set a standard comprehension exercise, or select an appropriate activity from elsewhere in this book.

3 Learners report back ideas/answers to the task.

4 Learners now read the online version of the story.

5 Set the following questions:
- *Was any information in one text but not the other?* (This is possible, as stories can be updated online.)
- *Were there any details in the two texts that were different?* (As above)
- *Were the images accompanying the two texts the same?*
- *Did the online text integrate any multimedia features, such as video and graphics? Were these useful and/or interesting?*
- *Did the online text use hyperlinks? If so did you follow them and were they useful?*
- *Did you search for any other information while reading online?*
- *Were there any other differences you noticed between the two versions of the text?*
- *Did it take more or less time to read the online text? Why?*
- *Did you understand more in the print text or the online text?*

6 Put learners into small groups to discuss their responses to the questions.

7 After an appropriate time, lead a discussion based on these questions.

Variation

This could be done as a jigsaw activity, with half the class reading the print version and half the digital version, and then discussing ideas.

Notes

The final two suggested questions above focus on the speed and depth of processing (see the introduction to this chapter, page 135). The responses here will obviously be affected by having read the printed version first (meaning that more might be understood from the digital version). However, the questions allow the teacher to discuss the issues of speed and depth of processing.

Rationale

The activity encourages learners to consider the differences between print and digital reading and to discuss the options that are available to an online reader. Also, the activity gives a reason to reread the text, which helps develop reading fluency.

6.4 Design it!

Outline	Learners design a piece of text.
Level	Any
Time	40 minutes
Focus	Responding creatively to a text
Preparation	Make a digital copy of a text that is appropriate for the learners. The text must be in a format that can be edited. Make the text as plain as possible. For example, use the same font and font size throughout and do not include any graphics. Prepare a brief comprehension task, if required for stage 2.

Procedure

1 Lead in to the text in the usual way.

2 If appropriate set a standard comprehension exercise, or select an appropriate activity from elsewhere in this book.

3 Learners read the text and briefly report back on the task set in stage 2.

4 Explain that the learners must now design the text, so that it could be published online. Brainstorm some of the features that the text could have (such as pictures, headings, links to video or other media).

5 The learners work in small groups to design the text, searching online for appropriate pictures and graphics. The design format may depend on the technology available but a simple Word document can be effective, or a Google Doc so that sharing is easy (see *Notes*).

6 After an appropriate period of time, encourage the learners to share what they have created with other groups.

7 Lead a discussion on the decisions that have been made and why the learners made the choices they did.

Notes

If appropriate, different groups of learners could work with different texts.

If appropriate, the learners could print their designs so that they can be displayed around the classroom. In this case, screenshots can be made of the links and the work can be turned into a poster.

Rationale

The learners will need to display an understanding of both the content and the genre of the text in order to create an appropriate design. The activity will also help to sensitize learners to the possibilities available to online writers.

6.5 Comment on the comments

Outline	Learners respond to the comments left by other readers.
Level	Intermediate and above (B1+)
Time	25 minutes
Focus	Understanding comments made about a text
Preparation	Select a digital text that is appropriate for the learners and has plenty of comments left by readers. Opinion pieces in newspapers are a good source. Before asking learners to read any comments, care should be taken to ensure that those comments are appropriate for the cultural context in which the teaching is taking place.

Procedure

1 Lead in to the text in the usual way.

2 Learners read the article (but not the comments). Set a brief gist task.

3 Learners report back on the task. Ensure that they have achieved a reasonable level of understanding before proceeding.

4 Now ask learners to read the comments, noting such things as:
   - those they agree with
   - those they disagree with
   - those that comment on another comment (rather than the text directly)
   - those that comment on the writer, rather than the text itself
   - any they think are meant ironically
   - any they think are inappropriate and should be deleted
   - those that they particularly like.

5 Put learners into small groups to share their reactions.

6 Lead a discussion based on what the groups have talked about.

Notes

The activity can be extended by broadening the discussion into how useful the learners feel such comment sections are and whether they usually read them, or contribute to them.

The tone (and indeed existence) of such comment sections may vary from culture to culture. If appropriate, explain to the learners where the text has been taken from and about the cultural expectations that accompany it. If preferred, contributions to a discussion forum can be used (rather than comments on a newspaper article).

Rationale

Comments are nearly always short and therefore give the learners an opportunity for 'fresh starts' as they read. Assuming the learners have understood the article, they should be able to follow at least some of the comments and the activity gives exposure to an informal style of writing that is becoming increasingly common.

6.6 Predicting from others' reactions

Outline	Learners predict the content of a text from the comments of others.
Level	Upper intermediate and above (B2+)
Time	15 minutes
Focus	Predicting content, becoming familiar with informal digital writing
Preparation	Select a text that has comments written about it. Opinion pieces in newspapers are a good source. Before asking learners to read any comments, care should be taken to ensure that those comments are appropriate for the cultural context in which the teaching is taking place.

Procedure

1   Show the learners the comments which have been made about the text. Put the learners in small groups and ask them to make predictions about the content of the article, based on the comments.

2   Learners read the text to see how accurate their predictions were.

3   In the light of their reading, learners say which comments they most agree with.

4   As a follow-up activity, ask learners to write a comment on the text, or to write a reply to an existing comment.

Notes

If the learners' predictions are very vague in the first instance it may be helpful to give additional information to help them, such as the title of the text or its source.

Rationale

As we saw in Chapter 1: *Preparing learners for reading*, pre-reading activities are very useful supports to both comprehension and motivation to read. If strong opinions are expressed (often in comment sections a range of strong opinions are voiced), learners are likely to be motivated to read to see how fair they think the comments are and which ones they agree with.

6.7 Background check

Outline	The learners search online to find background information and to check the accuracy of what is written.
Level	Elementary and above (A2+)
Time	20 minutes
Focus	Cross-checking information
Preparation	Choose an informational/opinion-based text that is appropriate for your class. For younger learners and low-level readers, texts can be simplified, with an emphasis on the checking of factual information. Design a brief, simple task sheet or copy the one opposite (see *Example*).

Procedure

1 Lead in to the activity by asking learners if they trust what they read online. Perhaps give some examples of sites and ask learners if they believe the information on them is unbiased and trustworthy.

2 Distribute the task sheet and ensure that learners understand it.

3 Learners read and complete the task sheet.

4 After an appropriate length of time, learners report back their ideas.

Example

The task sheet opposite can be copied or adapted if you prefer to create your own questions.

Notes

The activity works well with a variety of learners, and particularly those learning a language for academic purposes, who need to check that academic texts are reliable and to develop a sensitivity to the biases that may be inherent in them.

Rationale

One of the most important skills that online readers need to develop is being critical of what they read and this activity promotes cross-checking of information and basic research skills.

▧ *Task sheet*

1 Do an online search for the author of the text. What can you find out about the author? Have they written other texts? Do they appear to be an expert on this topic?

_____

_____

_____

2 Read the text. Use a coloured pen (or a highlight option, if reading from a screen) to underline the facts that are reported. Use a different coloured pen to underline the opinions of the writer.

3 Search alternative online sources to check whether the facts are correct. Make a note of any differences that you find.

_____

_____

_____

4 What opinions does the author put forward? Do you agree with these opinions?

_____

_____

_____

5 Who published this text? Do you think that influenced the writer?

_____

_____

_____

6 Quickly search online and choose two other texts that deal with the same topic. Read these texts very quickly. Do they put forward the same ideas as the original text? Is there any additional information which helps you understand the original text better?

_____

_____

_____

From *Teaching and Developing Reading Skills* © Cambridge University Press 2017   PHOTOCOPIABLE

6.8 Edit it

Outline	The learners edit a page of a shared document.
Level	Upper intermediate and above (B2+)
Time	Allow 15–20 minutes for stages 1–3. Allow 10 minutes per group to report (stage 5). Stage 4 is open-ended.
Focus	Developing critical reading skills
Preparation	Prepare a text that the learners can edit. The text should lack appropriate evidence to back up the assertions made (see stage 3 and *Notes*).

Procedure

1 Discuss with the class what they know and think about online information sources and what they perceive to be their strengths and weaknesses. They may mention that they are often free and open to everybody. However, some websites may make assertions that are not backed up with any evidence and are poorly referenced.

2 Explain to the learners that their task will be to edit such a source. This can be done in small groups.

3 Brainstorm the things an editor of a page would look out for (such as whether additional references are needed and can be added, whether the facts presented are actually true and can be cross referenced, and whether additional information could be usefully added).

4 Distribute the text to the learners electronically, or give a hard copy if preferred.

5 Before starting the editing, set the learners a time limit. This could be a homework project over a number of lessons, or even weeks. If this is the case, ask learners to report on their progress at regular intervals.

6 When the work is completed, ask learners to present their recommendations for changes to the class.

Variation 1

If desired, the document the learners edit could also include spelling, vocabulary and grammar errors. However, this may detract from the focus on reading critically and judging whether information is reliable.

Variation 2

If preferred, create a Google Doc so that the editing can take place online and be easily visible to other members of the class. If the technology is not available to allow the learners to work on computers, distribute a hard copy for the learners to annotate with the improvements they would make.

Notes

Teachers can prepare the texts relatively easily for classroom use. One way is to take a reasonably academic text and remove the citations from it (in other words, removing the evidence). The learners' task is to supply the missing evidence. In this case, the teacher can later show the original text as a model against which the learners can measure their own efforts. The teacher can explain where the text was taken from and also highlight the sources cited within it. The learners, of course, may well have found alternative evidence and they should record these sources on the document as they edit it.

The activity works particularly well with learners of EAP, who can be given a topic which is relevant to their academic specialism.

Rationale

Online reading demands a lot of criticality. Writers sometimes make claims that do not hold up when scrutinized. Checking that 'facts' are true seems a particularly important skill to develop. Also, some online information sources are criticized for lacking adequate referencing and this is a very important skill to develop, particularly if learners go on to higher education.

6.9 Rate the links

Outline	Learners judge the usefulness of the links in a text.
Level	Intermediate and above (B1+)
Time	30 minutes
Focus	Developing sensitivity to the usefulness of hyperlinks
Preparation	Select a text that is appropriate for the class and has several hyperlinks within it.

Procedure

1 Lead in to the text in the usual way.
2 If appropriate set a standard comprehension exercise, or select an appropriate activity from elsewhere in this book.
3 Learners read the text but should not at this point follow any of the links. Learners report back their answers/ideas on the task set in stage 2.
4 Tell the learners that they should read again and this time they should follow every link that is in the text. For each link, they should answer the questions given (see *Example*).
5 After an appropriate length of time, allow learners to compare their ideas.
6 Learners report back their ideas.

Example

Learners should complete the following for each link:

- *How useful was this link to understanding the text? (0 = not at all useful, 10 = very useful)*
- *What additional information did the link give you?*

Variation

This activity could be done as a jigsaw activity, with different learners being given different links to follow.

Rationale

Hyperlinks have the potential to support reading but can also reduce the cognitive processing resources available to focus on the text. It is useful for learners to develop an understanding of the ways in which links can help them and this sort of analysis can also help them make quick decisions as to whether links are worth following in the future.

6.10 Search results

Outline	Learners practise skim and scan reading skills as they decide on the most useful search results.
Level	Intermediate and above (B1+)
Time	15 minutes
Focus	Identifying the most useful results of an online search
Preparation	None

Procedure

1 Divide the class into small groups. Give each group a topic that will allow for some research. See the examples below.

2 The learners search online to find relevant information for this topic. As a group, they decide on the three most useful sources that they find. If necessary, help learners to refine their search terms to get useful results.

3 Learners report back on the sources that they found.

4 Encourage learners to reflect on what made some sources better than others and the process they went through in making their selections.

Example

The following topics are likely to work well, but there are many others and the teacher is best positioned to decide what will most interest a particular group of learners.
- the extent to which other animals use language
- the causes of climate change
- the effects of climate change
- what value there is in space exploration
- a period in the history of a particular country
- the ways in which shopping may change in the future
- the origins of a given festival

Notes

It is a good idea to set a time limit so that learners are pushed to read quickly. In this case, ensure that they understand that the task is not to understand each source in detail but just to identify sources that they could return to and read in more detail later.

A follow-up activity could be to write about the topic using the sources, or to give a presentation.

Different groups of learners can research different topics, or indeed, they can choose their own topic.

It may be useful to remind learners that it is a good idea to use several sources when writing essays or giving presentations, so that the views of one writer are balanced against those of other writers.

Rationale

Being able to refine searches and make quick assessments of results is likely to be an increasingly important reading skill in the 21st century and this activity encourages learners to discuss and share the strategies through which they do this.

6.11 Find it

Outline	Learners work in small groups to answer questions taken from websites.
Level	Intermediate and above (B1+)
Time	40 minutes
Focus	Finding information from non-linearly organized sources, such as websites
Preparation	Prepare a task sheet (see *Example*).

Procedure

1   Put the learners into pairs or small groups.

2   Distribute the task sheet and ensure that the learners understand it.

3   Give learners time to complete the task.

4   Learners report back their ideas.

Example

The task sheet opposite can be copied or adapted if you prefer to create your own questions.

Variation

If the class responds well to competition, this activity can be set up as a racc between the different groups, with the first to answer all the questions appropriately being the winner. This is likely to push learners to use more skimming and scanning strategies, as they attempt to work quickly.

Notes

If the task sheet is designed with relatively generic questions (as in the example) it will be quick to prepare.

Rationale

Navigating websites, where information is organized in a non-linear way, can be very challenging for learners and this activity gives direct practice in this skill.

▶ Task sheet

Find it

Imagine you want to study Business Communication (or a related course) at university, either in the UK, or elsewhere using English as the medium of instruction.

Find a potential course and write the name of the institution and the precise name of the course.

_____

_____

What are the entry criteria?

_____

_____

What modules or content is offered?

_____

_____

What fees would you pay?

_____

_____

What accommodation is offered?

_____

_____

What is the application procedure?

_____

_____

Would you like to study at this university? Why/Why not?

_____

_____

From *Teaching and Developing Reading Skills* © Cambridge University Press 2017   PHOTOCOPIABLE

6.12 Learner research

Outline	Learners read to find out information they need or want to know.
Level	Intermediate and above (B1+)
Time	15 minutes for stages 1 and 2. The rest is open-ended.
Focus	Using information needs to stimulate reading
Preparation	Activity 6.10: *Search results* can be used as a precursor to this activity. Think of some possible research topics in case learners need support with stage 1 (below). See Activity 6.10 for some example topics.

Procedure

1 Put the learners into groups of three or four and ask them to select a topic that they would like to research and find out more about.

2 Ask each group (either in class or as a homework activity) to identify four or five websites that are relevant and appropriate to their research. The majority of the sites, if not all, should be in the target language.

3 The learners must use the information they find to prepare a presentation to give to the class. This could be in the form of a formal presentation but could equally be through a poster, a discussion, or question and answer formats.

4 Give each group a completion date.

5 The learners research the topic through reading the websites and following appropriate links. Emphasize that the learners are expected to present information that they have discovered, rather than simply stating their existing opinions.

6 On the completion date, the learners present what they have learned to the class.

Notes

If teachers feel that their learners are not ready to take responsibility for selecting topics and websites, they can assign these. In this case, teachers may want to limit the number of topics and have some groups do the same topic, in order to make their own workload more manageable. If available, the research could be done in a computer lab.

It is sensible to group learners according to their interests for this activity sequence.

The level of the task can be adjusted through the scale of the task (essentially, how much learners are expected to find out and report) and the support they are given in finding appropriate texts.

Rationale

Much reading in language learning classes tends to focus on prescribed texts from which information is extracted. The pattern is 'Here is a text, what information can we extract from it?'. However, in many instances outside the classroom, we start with information we need to find an answer to and then search for relevant texts. This activity aims to create a pattern of a desire for knowledge leading to text/source identification, and then to reading. This is both realistic and potentially motivating. The learners also practise identifying appropriate texts (a relevant reading skill in the 21st century) and then synthesizing information from multiple sources, which can be very challenging.

6.13 Predicting the conversation

Outline	Learners predict the development of an instant messaging conversation based on the opening exchanges.
Level	Elementary and above (A2+)
Time	20 minutes
Focus	Discussing the content and style of instant message conversations
Preparation	Select a conversation from an instant messaging app. *Football conversation* on page 278 is an example.

Procedure

1 Lead in to the text by asking the learners how much they use instant messaging apps in the target language.

2 Give the learners the opening contribution or two from the conversation.

3 Ask them what the topic of the conversation is (if it has been established in the opening lines) and what they think the relationship is between the people.

4 Ask the learners to predict how the conversation will develop, writing what they think the next contribution will be, taking into account the style in which they think it will be expressed.

5 Show learners the next contribution and elicit feedback on how accurate their predictions were. Focus on both accuracy of content and the tone/style adopted.

6 Continue building and analyzing the conversation in the same way. If appropriate, learners could predict two or three turns ahead.

Notes

An alternative to this is to give the learners one participant's turns in the conversation and ask them to use the information from those to predict what the other participant wrote in the gaps.

If it is more appropriate, an invented conversation could be used for this activity but in this case care should be taken that it retains features of a genuine conversation.

Rationale

Learners are likely to find the text type motivating as many of them will probably use it in their everyday lives. Here they can compare their own attempts at extending the conversation with the authentic (or semi-authentic) version, helping them to notice the discourse patterns and style adopted in such texts.

6.14 Following the conversation

Outline	Learners study an instant messenger app conversation.
Level	Elementary and above (A2+)
Time	20 minutes
Focus	Developing awareness of discourse and pragmatic features of an instant messaging conversation
Preparation	Take a conversation from an instant messaging app. Edit and simplify as necessary so that the conversation can be followed. Devise some questions to accompany the text. At least some of the questions should focus on the discourse and pragmatic elements of the text (see *Example*).

Procedure

1 Lead in to the text by asking the learners how much they use instant messaging apps in the target language.

2 Contextualize the chosen conversation, explaining the topic that is being talked about and the relationship of the people involved.

3 Ask the learners to read the conversation quickly.

4 Put the learners into pairs or small groups to answer the questions devised.

5 After an appropriate period of time, learners report back their ideas.

Example
The following example is based on the text *Football conversation* on page 278.

1 *Which team scored? How do you know?* (Portugal – Monika is disappointed and clearly supports Poland)

2 *What is there 'still time' for?* (Poland to score/win the game)

4 *What is the effect of Monika using 'we'?* (She identifies with the team and sees the team as representing her)

5 *What might the tattoo depict?* (Something that indicates love for Poland, such as the national symbol – a white eagle)

6 *What does 'this' refer to?* (Watching the game)

9 *What does 'Yeeessssssssssssssssssss!' indicate?* (Excitement and pleasure at Poland scoring a goal)

11 *Why does Monika not want the match to be decided by penalties?* (Probably because she considers it too stressful, given her next contribution)

14 *What does 'It' refer to?* (The next goal)

Notes
If a text is used where real people can be identified, their permission should be sought, or their identities concealed through changes to the text (such as changing names and places).

Rationale

Instant messaging is increasingly common and results in a relatively new type of text, which draws quite substantially on the patterns and conventions of oral conversation. Context is therefore very important, with a lot of shared knowledge between the participants. The questions are used to draw attention to the discourse and pragmatic elements of the conversation, which learners can find difficult to understand in an L2.

6.15 Phone detective

Outline	Learners work out as much as they can about a person from reading mobile phone messages.
Level	Intermediate and above (B1+)
Time	20 minutes
Focus	Understanding implicit messages
Preparation	Select a text message exchange for learners to read. If anyone can be identified from the exchange, details (such as names) could be altered. Make copies so that learners can have one each.

Procedure

1 Explain that the learners have found a mobile phone and can access some of the messages.

2 The learners read one of the messages and work out as much as they can about the owner of the phone (see key opposite).

3 Ensure the learners are clear as to which person in the conversation they are investigating. (This could be achieved by shading one part.)

4 Learners read the text and then work in small groups to discuss ideas.

5 Learners report back their ideas.

Example

Key
Love Actually and *The Hunger Games* are both films. *The Hunger Games* is also a best-selling series of books.
Learners may be able to work out that the person whose contributions are in the darker shade of grey:
- is Polish (or at least living in Poland)
- is health conscious (references to running)
- socializes with friends
- likes and is knowledgeable about films and popular culture (*Hunger Games* book and film mentioned, and *Love Actually*).

Notes
After the text has been read, a further exchange could be used so that learners can work out more information about the person.

The learners may speculate about the age, sex, personality and interests of the person. Ask learners to make their contributions based on the evidence produced by their reading. Try to avoid learners making judgements based on stereotypes, e.g. *The person is male because he likes football.*

Rationale
Learners need to read in detail in order to gain as much information as possible about the person. The text is also likely to be motivating for the learners to read because it is a type that they will deal with in their everyday lives.

7 Exploiting texts as objects of study

Teaching grammar and vocabulary

While it may be that traditional syllabuses have over-emphasized the teaching of grammar, there are few who would now argue that the teaching of grammar is not important. Norris and Ortega (2000) analyzed nearly fifty research studies and found clear evidence for the usefulness of language instruction.

However, traditional teaching has often relied on teaching language at sentence level and this sentence level approach has often resulted in learners being unable to use their language knowledge for communicative purposes (Celce-Murcia, 2016). This may be because the vast majority of grammar and vocabulary choices are context-dependent. In other words, we only truly know the meaning of a word, phrase or sentence when we know who said it to whom and in what circumstances (the context of situation) and also the words that preceded it (the co-text).

Here is an example from an instant message conversation:

M: How's your day been?

P: Yeah, OK. How about you?

M: Yeah, good. Just off to the gym with Joanna. What are you doing?

Here the sentence *What are you doing*? seems to mean something like *How are you occupying your time at this moment*?. However, if we change the preceding words, we change the meaning:

M: Yeah, good. I'm going to the gym with Joanna tomorrow. What are you doing?

In this case, it would more likely become an enquiry about future plans, and possibly be the opening to an invitation (*Would you like to come with us?*).

These are not the only possible meanings, of course. In the following example a teacher is discussing the first lesson with a new class:

It was a nightmare! I turned my back to write on the board – then there was all this commotion and I spun round. One kid had picked up their chair and was about to throw it and I just screamed 'What are you doing?'.

In this case, *What are you doing*? seems to actually mean *Stop! Put the chair down and behave*. So an apparently simple sentence has a variety of meanings, depending on the context in which it is used. Individual words also often rely on context and co-text for meaning, as is demonstrated by the use of the word *way* in these examples:

Can you tell me the way to the station?

You paid way too much.

By the way, have you heard about next week?

Be the best. Play the Lionel Messi way.

Moreover, there is a lot more to learning words than their semantic value (Nation, 1990). Learners also need to know the connotations words bring with them, how they collocate with other words, whether they are used in formal or informal contexts, and the grammar patterns associated with them, e.g. whether a verb requires an object. There is a strong argument that this 'incidental' information is best presented to learners through repeatedly seeing words in context.

So, providing context is essential in language teaching as it impacts so significantly on how words and sentences are used. If we do not provide sufficient context, we may actually make it harder for learners to infer meanings. Using texts to teach new language is an ideal way to provide that necessary context.

Teaching discourse patterns

In addition to the teaching of vocabulary and grammar, texts are an obvious way of teaching learners about how texts are organized at discourse level. Research evidence is consistent in showing that learners' reading comprehension improves when they have an understanding of the text structures they are reading (Geva and Ramírez, 2015). This is not surprising as the way particular types of text (such as an academic argument) are structured can vary from culture to culture and so an explicit awareness of those differences is helpful to L2 readers. Typical patterns that learners may benefit from having highlighted include such things as main point and supporting evidence, comparison and contrast, cause and effect, and problem-solution patterns.

One common way of teaching these patterns is to use graphic organizers. A graphic organizer is a diagram representing the concepts and arguments in a text. It shows how those ideas are interconnected, and, as the name suggests, how they are organized.

Using texts

Using texts to teach vocabulary, grammar and discourse is a very useful tool for teachers but that is not to say that there is no place for any sentence level instruction, which may well fit the learners' expectations and also serve to give additional highlighting to a new item of language.

Where texts are used to teach new language, care should be taken that learners have a good understanding of the meaning of the text before they study any elements of it. Particularly at lower proficiency levels, materials writers (or teachers) may choose to write a text specifically for learners in order to promote easy understanding or to allow for a particular language item to be presented. Where this is the case, it is important that the text produced is realistic in terms of being a recognizable text type that learners may one day read outside the classroom, following its basic conventions. This realism is likely to add to greater motivation to read, as well as help learners to become familiar with the structure of real texts.

This chapter aims to provide teachers with a range of activities that can be used to focus learners' attention on vocabulary and grammar in context, as well as on the structure of texts.

References

Celce-Murcia, M. (2016) 'The importance of the discourse level in understanding and teaching English grammar', in E. Hinkel (ed.), *Teaching English Grammar to Speakers of Other Languages*, pp. 3–18, Abingdon: Taylor & Francis.

Geva, E. and Ramírez, G. (2015) *Focus on Reading*, Oxford: Oxford University Press.

Nation, I.S.P. (1990) *Teaching and Learning Vocabulary*, Boston: Heinle, Cengage Learning.

Norris, J. M. and Ortega, L. (2000) 'Effectiveness of L2 Instruction: A Research Synthesis and Quantitative Meta-analysis', *Language Learning* 50(3), pp. 417–528.

7.1 Vocabulary swap

Outline	Learners work in groups to study vocabulary in a text and then share it with other learners.
Level	Intermediate and above (B1+)
Time	20 minutes
Focus	Studying vocabulary from a text
Preparation	Select appropriate vocabulary sets for stage 1.

Procedure

1 After the learners have read a text and their understanding of it has been checked, split them into four groups, A, B, C and D. Assign each group a vocabulary set to work on and develop. These sets might include categories such as 'Words to do with …' or might focus on a particular word class (see *Example*).

2 The learners work in groups to identify the appropriate words and their meanings, along with any other relevant information, such as collocation pattern or connotation. As well as pooling existing knowledge, they can use dictionaries or translating devices to help them.

3 Circulate, encourage and support the learners.

4 When the groups have finished the teacher pairs members of group A with group B, and members of group C with group D.

5 The learners share their findings with their new partners, explaining the words they have chosen. Learners write down the new words (i.e. those they learn from their partner from the other group).

6 When the learners have finished, again form new groups, with those from AB being paired with those from CD. The learners again explain all the new words they have learned to that point. This means that each learner should have a record of all the words from all the groups.

7 To round off the lesson, the teacher can dictate sentences from the text with a missing word or phrase. Ask learners not to look at the text and then dictate a sentence, clapping where the missing word or expression goes. For example, *There is one day that has* [clap] *for all the wrong reasons.* The learners complete the sentence. Once demonstrated, the teacher can nominate a learner to choose and dictate a sentence in the same manner. This can be done in groups if preferred. The gaps should focus on the new words learned in the lesson.

Example

The following groups and words arose from *A true story* on page 273:

- places: *lodge, game reserve, the grounds, Masai Mara*
- verbs: *leap, plead, brush (it) away, overreact, crawl*
- common expressions: *stuck in my mind, sure enough, in a flash, pleased with myself, I told you so.*
- animals/related to animals: *snake, lizard, slither, coiled up, crawl*

Notes

The studying of vocabulary in this way will not necessarily ensure learning. The vocabulary needs to be recycled in lessons, or the learners could be encouraged to review it regularly for themselves.

Having read a text, the learners themselves could be asked to decide the categories for the vocabulary sets.

Rationale

Texts are an excellent potential source of vocabulary learning and knowing vocabulary is essential to successful reading. The learners work in groups and share what they have learned in order to ensure that the new vocabulary is activated soon after initial contact with the word. In order to identify vocabulary, learners will need to reread the text, which will also support the development of reading fluency.

7.2 Translating phrases

Outline	Learners focus on formulaic chunks of language through comparing L1 and L2 versions.
Level	Any, dependent on the text
Time	10–15 minutes, depending on the number of phrases given
Focus	Studying chunks of language through translation
Preparation	Select an appropriate text. Choose six to eight phrases from it that you would like learners to focus on and translate them into the learners' L1.

Procedure

1 First, ensure that learners have a fairly good understanding of the text either by setting standard comprehension questions, or using an appropriate alternative activity from this book.

2 Dictate the L1 translations to the learners and ask them to locate the corresponding English phrases in the text.

3 Discuss the translations and any alternatives that might have also been possible.

4 If necessary, recap strategies for learning vocabulary, such as reviewing new items regularly.

Example

The following phrases could be used from the text *A true story* on page 273. They have been translated into Spanish as an example of learners' L1.

- for all the wrong reasons: *y no por buenas razones*
- just in time: *justo a tiempo*
- I was overreacting: *estaba exagerando*
- an overactive imagination: *una imaginación desbordante*
- she looked bored: *parecía aburrida*
- I told you so: *te lo dije!*

Notes

When the learners have experienced the activity once, they could be invited to select and translate phrases for themselves, and then dictate them to other learners.

Rationale

The teacher draws attention to set phrases and chunks of language through the translation and therefore aids the noticing process associated with learning. At higher levels, the activity can also be used to highlight the difficulty of translating idiomatic phrases.

7.3 Rebuilding a text from fragments

Outline	Learners read a text and then reconstruct it from fragments.
Level	Elementary and above (A2+)
Time	45 minutes, depending on the length of the text used
Focus	Studying the linking within a text
Preparation	Choose an appropriate text. The longer the text, the more challenging the activity will be. Reproduce the text in short sections and phrases (see *Example*).

Procedure

1 Introduce the text in the usual way. For example, pre-teach any necessary vocabulary and build interest in what the learners will read.

2 Display the text and ask learners to read it briefly and check that they have understood the key points.

3 Divide the class into small groups and give each learner a copy of the chunked text (see *Example*). The learners work together to recreate the text by putting the fragments in order.

4 If the learners find it very difficult or become stuck, briefly display the complete text again and ask them to read quickly, before removing it.

5 When the learners have finished, ask them to compare their versions with the original.

Example
The example on page 167 uses the text *An unusual meeting* on page 269. It is at B1–B2 level.

Variation 1
Read the complete text to the learners (rather than re-show it) if they need additional support.

Variation 2
Prepare different versions of the text, one with longer (and therefore fewer) chunks. This will make the task easier and so is a way of differentiating the material if there are readers of markedly mixed proficiency in the class.

Variation 3
Cut the text into individual chunks and distribute them so that learners assemble the pieces as a jigsaw task, thus forming a complete text in the correct order. This will make it easier to connect the chunks of text.

Notes
Although this example is at B1–B2, the essential activity of rebuilding texts in this way can work successfully as soon as learners move beyond sentence level reading. However, very long texts may seem daunting, even for quite advanced learners.

The example here retains the original punctuation, with capital letters and full stops. This makes the task marginally easier, but they could be removed, if desired.

Some learners may choose to draw lines between each section to show connections. Others may choose to number the sections and some may want to write out the text. You may wish to clarify which approach you would like the learners to take.

Rationale

The activity pushes the learners to read and reread in great detail. They must also pay attention to how the text is constructed, and particularly the linking devices in order to recreate it.

⬐ *An unusual meeting*

A woman was sitting alone at a table.		Paris, 1936, and bright lights flickered in the night
	embroidered with roses.	
from the Café des Deux Magots,		and repeatedly stabbed it into the table between her fingers.
	before driving the penknife one more time	
Eventually, he spoke to her, using French.		a popular meeting place for intellectuals and artists.
	She was wearing black gloves,	
She spread her left hand on the table.		between her spread fingers.
	A man watched her, transfixed.	
Sometimes she missed and traces of blood		In her right hand she held a small penknife
	Her name was Dora Maar	
as a reminder of the occasion		could be seen soaking through the gloves and onto the tablecloth.
	and soon began a stormy, passionate relationship.	
She was a brilliant woman		for the rest of his life.
	and his was Picasso.	
and replied in perfect Spanish		and successful photographer
	He was unable to take his eyes off the woman.	
and he was one of the greatest artists in history.		
	She looked at him, paused,	
He kept the bloodstained gloves		They immediately fell in love

7.4 Narrow reading and vocabulary

Outline	Learners study vocabulary and read a number of texts on the same topic.
Level	Intermediate and above (B1+)
Time	45 minutes
Focus	Recycling vocabulary through reading texts on the same topic
Preparation	Choose a text that is appropriate but challenging for your learners. Ensure that similar texts on the same topic are available (see *Notes*).

Procedure

1 Ask learners to read the text for a gist-level understanding.

2 Tell learners that they can underline up to 15 words that they do not understand.

3 Learners use dictionaries and electronic translators to find out about these words. They should make detailed notes on each item they look up. This could include a translation, synonyms, collocations, example sentences and so on.

4 Learners can discuss the words they chose to study either in open class or groups.

5 Learners read the text again and use a simple self-assessment instrument (such as a numerical scale) to grade their comprehension.

6 After a few days, repeat the task with a different text on the same topic. This step can be repeated as many times as the learners maintain interest.

Notes

The activity relies on there being several texts on the same topic being available. These could be a number of reviews of the same film, play, or concert. Alternatively, reports of a sports event could be used. The texts could also be a 'big' news story which will be covered in newspapers for several days. Learners can read and see how the story develops. If the story is particularly significant, L2 reading will be supported by what learners have read and heard in L1.

The activity will work best if three or four texts are used on the same topic. However, this does mean that the majority of learners must find the subject intrinsically interesting. If this is not the case, the teacher can use just two texts.

The learners may benefit from being reminded about good vocabulary-learning strategies and habits. For example, they should review their notes regularly.

Rationale

Most coursebooks base each unit around a different topic. In contrast, advocates of 'narrow reading' suggest that as learning either structural or vocabulary items is likely to be facilitated by multiple exposures to those items, it makes more sense to strictly limit the range of text types and topics so that the learner is more likely to see the same items repeatedly. This activity works well because the vocabulary is met in context and so is likely to be recycled in subsequent lessons, increasing the likelihood of retention. The reading done in one lesson is effectively preparation for the reading done in the next, meaning that learners can often cope with texts that would usually be beyond their linguistic level.

7.5 One sentence to many sentences

Outline	Learners read and study a complex sentence and break it into as many smaller ones as they can.
Level	Elementary and above (A2+)
Time	15 minutes
Focus	Understanding complex sentences
Preparation	Write a complex sentence (see *Example*). For lower-level learners the sentence could make more use of simple conjunctions and use less subordination.

Procedure

1   Ask learners to read the sentence. Ask them to identify what they consider to be the most important piece of information. Various arguments could be made for this. In the example below, it may be that nobody was hurt in the accident, or that Alex has learned a valuable lesson.

2   Ask learners to work individually to write as many true sentences as they can based on the sentence they have read.

3   After an appropriate length of time, ask learners to compare what they have written and then report back to the class.

Example

> If Alex had been more careful when overtaking on the motorway, it is possible that the accident could have been avoided and the events, which caused so much inconvenience for so many people, would never have happened but at least nobody was seriously hurt and Alex is certainly a better driver as a result.

Key

- Alex was driving on a motorway.
- There was an accident.
- Alex was responsible (at least in part) for the accident.
- The accident may have occurred even if Alex had been more careful.
- Nobody was seriously hurt in the accident.
- Alex is now a better driver.
- A lot of people were inconvenienced by the accident.

Variation

The activity can be used in reverse to practise writing, with learners being given some short sentences, which they combine into one.

Notes

This activity can be used to change the pace of a lesson. As it is largely done individually, it can calm a boisterous class.

   The sentence given to learners can recycle vocabulary and/or grammar recently studied.

Rationale

Learners can find it difficult to follow complex sentences, sometimes missing important information. This activity helps learners to follow the links in a sentence and understand how sentences are put together and therefore supports reading.

7.6 Grammar race

Outline	Learners race against each other to locate grammar features in sentences taken from a text they have read.
Level	Any
Time	15 minutes
Focus	Identifying key grammatical elements in a sentence
Preparation	Prepare a comprehension task, if required for stage 1.

Procedure

1 First, ensure that learners have a fairly good understanding of the chosen text, either by setting standard comprehension questions, or using an appropriate alternative activity from this book.

2 Divide the class into two or more groups.

3 Write a complex sentence from the text on the board.

4 In their groups, the learners must identify the main verb in the sentence as quickly as possible.

5 The first team to send a representative to the board who correctly underlines the main verb wins a point.

Notes

The activity requires the learners to have some knowledge of metalanguage (i.e. language that describes language, such as 'verb').

For lower levels, a simple sentence could be used, with learners asked to identify the verb. Alternatively, two or three short sentences could be written on the board, with learners asked to identify items of vocabulary from synonyms, antonyms, or L1 translations.

Rationale

Reading is a complex skill, with different knowledge bases used in parallel as text is processed. One of the things we do as we read is to break the words into meaningful units (parsing the sentences). Identifying the main verb is an important step in this process.

7.7 Chasing the meaning

Outline	Learners practise identifying the referents of pronouns.
Level	Elementary and above (A2+)
Time	15 minutes
Focus	Studying backward and forward referencing devices
Preparation	Choose a text that the learners have read or are about to read. Identify appropriate words (usually pronouns) to focus on (see *Example*).

Procedure

1 Ensure that the learners have at least a gist-level understanding of the text.

2 Ask the learners to highlight the words you have chosen. This can be done either by dictating the words (line numbers on the text will help) or displaying them.

3 Learners work individually to identify what the words refer to. An example may help in the first instance.

4 After an appropriate time the learners compare their answers before reporting back.

Example

The following example is based on the last two paragraphs of *A true story* on page 273 and is appropriate for B1–B2 learners.

She looked bored but finally she picked up a stick and with a sigh went over to the towel to check what was there[1]. Gently, she hooked the stick under the towel and lifted it[2] out of the way. And sure enough, there on the grass, under the towel, was a green snake coiled up. We got a clear view for just a few seconds and then in a flash it[3] shot off into longer grass.

I was quite pleased with myself at this point, satisfied that I had been right and that I had indeed seen a snake. I turned around to my friend to say 'I told you so!' but was surprised by her expression. The calm face from earlier was replaced by a quite different one[4]. 'What is it[5]?' I asked. She was silent and shaking, and then she told me in a quiet voice that the snake that had been under my towel was one of the most poisonous snakes in Africa. One bite and you[6] start to bleed out of your eyes, your mouth, your ears … If you[7] don't get to hospital within a couple of hours, you bleed to death. We[8] were in the middle of the game reserve. There was no hospital or even airstrip anywhere near us. In short, if it[9] had bitten me[10], I would have died there in the lodge.

Key

[1] there: under the towel
[2] it: the towel
[3] it: the snake
[4] one: literally 'face', or expression
[5] it: the problem (unstated but implied in the text)
[6] you: people in general
[7] you: people in general
[8] we: the narrator and her friend
[9] it: the snake
[10] me: the narrator

Notes

The activity is appropriate for all learners who are able to read beyond clause level although obviously the choice of text will need to be appropriate.

The activity is probably best used in short, frequent bursts (e.g. 10 minutes) with other activities, rather than as an extended activity on its own.

Rationale

Research suggests that one of the main reasons for comprehension to break down, even at quite high levels, is that learners find it difficult to trace these kinds of backward and (less commonly used) forward referencing devices across clause boundaries. This activity explicitly addresses this difficulty.

7.8 Arrows

Outline	Learners identify what pronouns refer to.
Level	Any
Time	15 minutes
Focus	Studying backward and forward referencing devices
Preparation	None

Procedure

1 Ensure learners have a reasonably good understanding of the text.

2 Choose a section of the text and ask learners to identify the pronouns within that section.

3 Check that the learners have correctly identified the pronouns.

4 Write a simple example on the board. Highlight a pronoun and draw an arrow, pointing to what it refers to.

5 Ask learners to work on the text, drawing arrows from the pronouns identified to their referents.

6 After an appropriate length of time learners compare ideas before the teacher confirms answers.

Notes

The activity is probably best used regularly for short periods of time.

Rationale

One of the key causes of communication breaking down in reading is that readers have difficulty in tracing the links between pronouns and their referents. This activity gives specific practice in this.

7.9 Focus on linkers

Outline	Learners study the use of linkers as a preview to a reading activity.
Level	Elementary and above (A2+)
Time	15 minutes
Focus	Studying discourse marking devices
Preparation	Choose an appropriate text for the class.

Procedure

1 Outline to the class very briefly what the text is about, e.g. say *This is an email of complaint to an online company that sells film posters.*

2 Pick some linkers (such as *and*, *but* and *or* for lower levels, and *such as* and *on the other hand* at higher levels) from the text.

3 If necessary, explicitly teach the function of these linking devices.

4 Dictate the first sentence in which a linking device occurs up to and including the linker.

5 Ask learners to complete the sentence.

6 Elicit some suggestions from the learners as to how the sentence may be completed, before showing them the version from the text. Highlight the relationship between the information before and after the linking device (i.e. the function of the device).

7 Continue with the next sentence.

8 When all the sentences have been completed in this way ask the learners if they can predict any other details about the text.

9 When the learners have done this, proceed with a reading task focusing on overall meaning.

Example
The following example is based on *An email of complaint* on page 276.

The teacher dictates:

I am writing with regard to …

First of all, I had to wait over two months for the delivery, although …

I did not get any explanation for the delay despite …

This was very inconvenient as the poster had been purchased as a birthday gift. Moreover, …

Your website claims that you provide 'an expert and professional service for dedicated collectors of movie memorabilia'. However, …

Notes
If there is unknown vocabulary in the dictated parts of the sentence, this can be pre-taught.

It is important that learners complete the sentence in a coherent way, rather than guess the exact information.

Rationale

Understanding how discourse markers point the reader in the direction that the text will turn is essential to efficient reading. In addition, this activity allows the learners to preview the text and gives a reason to scan for the sentence stems and read the original version.

7.10 Study the genre

Outline	Learners study the structure of a specified text type.
Level	Intermediate and above (B1+)
Time	15 minutes
Focus	Studying the structural conventions of texts
Preparation	Select two texts of the same genre. As two texts are used, they should be relatively short. Identify the principal structural features.

Procedure

1　Ask learners to read the first text quickly for a gist understanding.

2　Draw attention to different sections of the text with the whole class, eliciting and/or briefly explaining the purpose of each feature.

3　Distribute the second text and ask learners to read.

4　Check that the learners have understood the text.

5　In small groups, learners compare the two texts, looking for similarities in how they are organized.

6　Learners report back their ideas.

7　Confirm the main structural features of the texts.

Notes

A follow-up activity to this reading would be to ask the class as a group, or in pairs, or individually to write a text of the type studied, following the structure as closely as reasonable.

While not all texts are absolutely predictable in terms of structure, many are sufficiently predictable to be useful to learners. Academic texts, while varying with discipline, tend to have reasonably predictable structures and so learners of English for academic purposes can benefit greatly from activities such as the one here.

Rationale

Research evidence is clear that the more familiar learners are with the structural conventions of a genre, the easier they will find reading texts of that genre.

7.11 Making changes

Outline	Learners study how changes to vocabulary and grammar choices would affect meaning.
Level	Intermediate and above (B1+)
Time	15 minutes
Focus	Studying the impact of grammar and vocabulary choices in texts
Preparation	Select an appropriate text for the learners. This could be one that they have read before. Copy the text, making changes to such things as modal verbs, verb forms, the distribution of active and passive voice, determiners and so on. If appropriate, some items of vocabulary can also be changed for synonyms (see *Example*).

Procedure

1 Ensure learners have a good understanding of the text.

2 Show the learners the rewritten section of text and talk through an example with the group, showing how the vocabulary and grammar choices have impacted on meaning. Ensure that the learners understand that the rewritten text is still grammatically accurate – they are not correcting mistakes.

3 Allow learners to read the two texts and make notes about the ways in which the changes affect meaning.

4 Learners compare their ideas in pairs or small groups.

5 Learners report back their discussions in open class.

Example

This short example is taken from the text *It's time to accept that elephants, like us, are empathetic beings* on page 270. It is appropriate for a B1–B2 group.

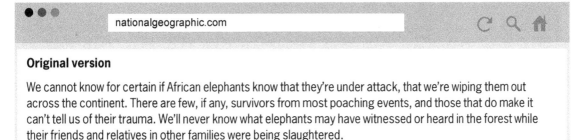

nationalgeographic.com

Original version

We cannot know for certain if African elephants know that they're under attack, that we're wiping them out across the continent. There are few, if any, survivors from most poaching events, and those that do make it can't tell us of their trauma. We'll never know what elephants may have witnessed or heard in the forest while their friends and relatives in other families were being slaughtered.

Rewritten version

We do not know for certain if African elephants know that we are attacking them, that we will wipe them out across the continent. There are few, if any, survivors from most poaching events, and those that do make it don't tell us of their trauma. We'll never know what elephants may have witnessed or heard in the forest while their friends and relatives in other families were being murdered.

- *Do not* suggests we do not know yet but may in the future, whereas the original *cannot* suggests it is impossible to know.
- *We are attacking them* plainly identifies who is attacking (humans) whereas *they're under attack* does not identify the attackers.
- *We will wipe them out* suggests that the eventual outcome is certain. *We are wiping them out* suggests that it is happening at the moment but that we could change the course we are on.
- *Don't tell us* suggests (improbably) that they could choose to tell us, whereas *can't tell us* makes it clear that this is impossible.
- *Murdered* is usually used about humans and so this equates an elephant life with a human life. Also, *murder* is used to describe a crime, whereas *slaughter* does not necessarily imply this.

Notes

The potentially open-ended nature of the activity can lead to lessons becoming rather dry discussions of grammar points. It is therefore best to use a short section of text and limit the changes to no more than four or five, keeping explanations brief. Additionally, teachers can choose to focus on a single grammar point (such as the use of modal verbs, or active and passive voice) rather than a mixture of points as are used in the example above.

Learners can also be encouraged to make changes to texts they have read and these can be used as short tests for other learners or the whole class.

Rationale

Writers (and speakers) make choices depending on the precise meaning they wish to convey. This activity allows vocabulary and grammar choices to be studies in context, seeing how the choices impact on meaning.

7.12 Mixed lines

Outline	Learners sort lines of short texts into the correct order.
Level	Intermediate and above (B1+)
Time	20 minutes
Focus	Reading and rereading lines of text for detailed understanding
Preparation	Choose two short texts, or extracts of texts. These might be short poems, or a verse of a song, for example. Copy out the texts and cut them up line by line. Each group will need one complete set of lines.

Procedure

1 Introduce the activity and divide the class into small groups. Give each group a set of lines.

3 Learners work in small groups to sort the lines, first separating the lines from the two texts and then sequencing the lines from each text.

4 After an appropriate length of time the learners report back their ideas.

Notes

If a group is finding the task difficult, allow one member to get up and look at the work of another group. This member can then report back to their original partners.

The more similar the texts, the more difficult the task becomes. The texts may be similar in terms of topic or structure, e.g. the number of syllables per line.

If the technology is available, this activity can also be done on screen, with learners dragging and dropping the lines into the appropriate place.

Rationale

The activity requires learners to read and reread text closely in order to separate the lines and to sequence them successfully.

7.13 Who, what and how

Outline	Learners study texts, focusing on the contexts in which they were produced, particularly the relationship of the participants, the topic of the communication and the 'mode' of communication, e.g. email or instant messaging.
Level	Upper intermediate and above (B2+)
Time	10 minutes
Focus	Studying the context in which a text was produced
Preparation	None

Procedure

1 This activity can be used either before or after a standard comprehension type activity. Set questions which focus on contextual factors (see *Example*).

2 Divide the class into small groups. The learners work together to answer the questions.

3 After an appropriate period of time, the learners report back their ideas.

Example
Who
- *Who wrote this text?*
- *Who were they writing for?*
- *Did they know the reader(s) personally?*
- *What is the relationship between the writer and the reader(s)? Is it friendly? Are they equals, or does the writer have expertise that the reader doesn't?*
- *For each of the above questions, how do you know?*

What
- *What is the main topic of the communication?*
- *What is the text about?*
- *Does it cover more than one topic? If so, how does it move between topics?*
- *Are there parts of the text which are concerned with building the relationship between the writer and the reader, rather than giving new information, developing an argument. etc.?*
- *Which parts of the text allow you to make these decisions?*

How
- *What is the 'channel of communication' used? Is it an email, a text message, an essay, a newspaper article, etc.?*
- *Which parts of the text allow you to make these decisions?*
- *How would the communication be different if it took place in a spoken form? For example, a face-to-face conversation or a telephone call?*

Notes
If time is short, each group could be allocated a different set of questions.

Rationale

Texts will have particular features depending on the contexts in which they are produced. This activity focuses on three contextual variables in order to increase the learners' awareness of how texts are created.

7.14 Using graphic organizers

Outline	Learners break texts into component parts, using diagrams to help them.
Level	Intermediate and above (B1+)
Time	20 minutes
Focus	Studying the structure of a text
Preparation	Choose a text that is appropriate for the learners and draw a diagram of its structure. Do not at this stage include sentences from the text (see *Example*).

Procedure

1 Show the 'empty' diagram of the text to the learners (see example opposite).

2 Ask learners to read the text and identify the component parts. They should record which parts of the text fit each section of the diagram.

3 Learners should work individually in the first instance and then collaboratively in small groups.

4 After an appropriate length of time, groups report back their ideas.

Example

The short example opposite is taken from the text *It's time to accept that elephants, like us, are empathetic beings* on page 270. It is appropriate for a B1–B2 group. Answers are given below.

Key

1 The elephant population is falling rapidly.
2 Humans are killing elephants because their ivory is valuable.
3 There are fewer, perhaps far fewer, than 500,000 wild African elephants.
4 They recognize and empathize with each other's pain. They want to help other elephants that are suffering.
5 Humans are killing elephants and reducing their numbers. This killing increases the pain and fear of the elephants that survive.
6 climb up muddy banks.
7 find a safe path.
8 help them break through electric fences.
9 Elephants help other injured elephants
10 Elephants help and comfort dying friends.

Notes

If the learners are not used to this kind of activity, they could be initially supported by supplying diagrams with parts of the relevant information already completed.

Rationale

When the learners have completed activities such as this one, they can be encouraged to draw their own diagrams of other texts after reading. This stage leads to learners being able to apply what has been learned from the lessons to the reading of new material outside the class.

◤ Graphic organizer

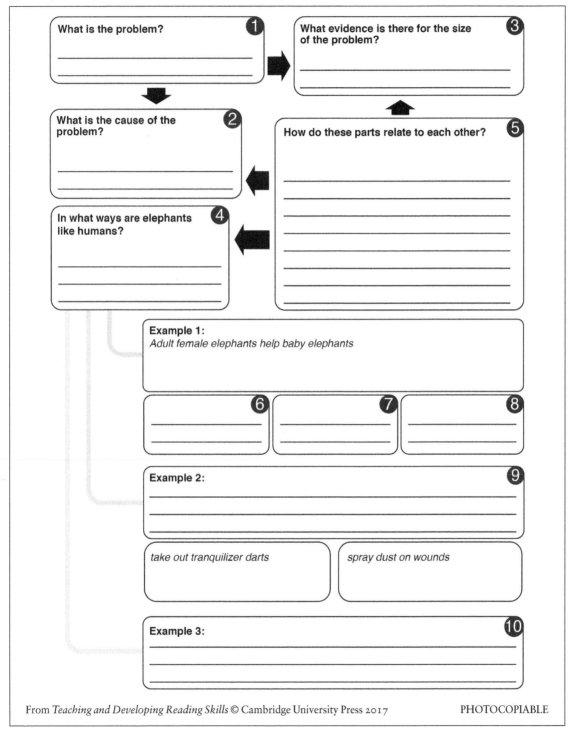

What is the problem? **1**
_____
_____

What evidence is there for the size of the problem? **3**
_____
_____

What is the cause of the problem? **2**
_____
_____

How do these parts relate to each other? **5**
_____
_____
_____
_____
_____
_____
_____

In what ways are elephants like humans? **4**
_____
_____
_____

Example 1:
Adult female elephants help baby elephants

6
_____
_____

7
_____
_____

8
_____
_____

Example 2: **9**
_____
_____
_____

take out tranquilizer darts

spray dust on wounds

Example 3: **10**
_____
_____
_____

8 Developing critical reading skills

What is critical reading?

'Critical' can be used to mean many things in educational contexts (Goatly and Hiradhar, 2016) and in some uses it is concerned with no more than evaluating the evidence and arguments put forward for any given point of view. This is the sense that is often associated with 'critical thinking'. However, 'critical' is also used to describe the process of uncovering the ideological beliefs that underpin social practices, and in particular the ways in which relations of power are enacted. For example, in the context of journalism, we may critique the portrayals of minority groups in the media.

Critical reading starts with the assumption that many texts – and all texts that try to persuade us in some way – are not neutral but instead are influenced by the writer's beliefs and attitudes. The writer attempts to 'position' their readers – to make them see the world from a particular point of view. It is important, therefore that readers are aware of how they are being positioned and that they are able to 'read' the subtext – to see any hidden agenda – as well as more explicitly stated messages. Is the reader pushed towards accepting a particular view of the world, for example? Does the writer make assumptions about norms and behaviours that, given time to reflect, we would want to question?

A writer may use their position in quite subtle ways to promote their own judgements. For example, if we read *Jay gushed about being in love* we are positioned by the verb *gush* to see this emotion as something trivial, even infantile. But the verb was chosen by the writer. In the sentence *Jay talked about being in love* there is no negative assessment. Therefore, critical reading requires constant questioning, not just of comprehension (*Do I understand the text?*) but of the judgements and views that underpin the text. This can be a difficult task because often those views are only implied, rather than being explicitly stated.

When we start to think carefully about text types, it is clear that very many are persuasive in some form or other. Obviously, advertisements try to persuade us that a particular product or service is worth paying for. But there are many less obvious examples too. Media texts (from news organizations and the like) will aim to persuade us that a story is both true and has importance. Literary texts persuade us that fictional characters and places are believable and reflect, or shed light on, our own world experiences. Even academic texts are persuasive in nature in that they aim to persuade us that the arguments put forward have relevance and explanatory power.

Critical readers are sensitive to the implicit as well as explicit messages of a text, and test the text against alternative explanations and views. As such, critical readers are constantly making judgements as to how plausible and trustworthy a text is.

Why is critical reading important?

Texts depict the world we live in and so contribute to us constructing views of what we find normal and acceptable as a society (Stubbs, 1996). This is equally true in specific domains and so the texts we read about language teaching, for example, help to shape what we consider to be 'standard practice' and normal learner and teacher behaviour. As the texts we read have such power, it would seem self-evidently important that we can differentiate reliable from unreliable information.

There is also a strong case to suggest that in the 21st century critical reading is more important than ever. Katharine Viner, the editor-in-chief of *The Guardian* and *The Observer* newspapers, points out that the need for news organizations to attract advertisers to their websites can lead them to pursue clicks at the expense of all else:

> The most extreme manifestation of this phenomenon [the pursuit of clicks] has been the creation of fake news farms, which attract traffic with false reports that are designed to look like real news, and are therefore widely shared on social networks. But the same principle applies to news that is misleading or sensationally dishonest, even if it wasn't created to deceive: the new measure of value for too many news organizations is virality rather than truth or quality (Viner, 2016).

Holmes (2014) quotes Neetzan Zimmerman, a specialist in high-traffic, or 'viral' internet stories, as saying: 'Nowadays it's not important if a story's real. The only thing that really matters is whether people click on it.'

In a world where 'fake news' is just another product that competes with other news, it is essential that readers are critical when they read. Moreover, traditional filters of information are disappearing. People are now able to publish very quickly and cheaply online, without even submitting copy to an editor. This lack of pre-publication screening increases the need for readers to question what they read. This is not only true of news stories but academic publishing too. While many academic and quasi-academic blog posts may be inspiring, readers still need to critically assess which are evidence based (not to mention the quality of that evidence) and which rely solely on a writer's personal theory and opinion. Of course, that personal theory may still be appealing but a reader needs to scrutinize and question it before accepting the argument – and that requires an ability to read critically.

What are the most common techniques used to persuade us?

There are many techniques that creators of text can use to persuade readers, including the use of carefully selected images that accompany the text. One of the principal linguistic devices is in word choice, exploiting the connotations the words bring with them. There may also be a conflation of one thing with another, making one seem better (or worse) by association. For example, a fizzy drink manufacturer may have a big advertising campaign around a holiday festival, suggesting that their product is part of the happy feelings we associate with the festival. Another key persuasive device is to omit parts of the story, or parts of the information, to make a case seem stronger. For example, in order to portray someone as an essentially bad person, the acts of kindness they are responsible for may be missed out from the story. In academic contexts, poor academic writing may simply omit reference to contradictory studies, thus portraying the claims made as being stronger. Above all, it is important that the reader remembers that texts will have both explicitly stated messages and those that are implied and they may covertly persuade us towards the values and viewpoints of the writer.

In this chapter we will introduce activities that are designed to promote critical reading in an L2.

References

Goatly, A. and Hiradhar, P. (2016) *Critical Reading in a Digital Age* (2nd ed.), Abingdon: Taylor & Francis.

Holmes, D. (2014). 'It's not important if a story is real …' Available online at: https://pando.com/2014/07/31/whisper-eic-its-not-important-if-a-storys-real-the-only-thing-that-really-matters-is-whether-people-click-on-it. [Last accessed 5 August 2017]

Stubbs, M. (1996) *Text and Corpus Analysis: Computer-assisted Studies of Language and Culture*, Oxford: Blackwell.

Viner, K. (2016) 'How technology disrupted the truth'. Available online at: https://www.theguardian.com/media/2016/jul/12/how-technology-disrupted-the-truth. [Last accessed 5 August 2017]

8.1 Investigate

Outline	Learners analyze a text to find the persuasive devices used.
Level	Intermediate and above (B1+)
Time	30 minutes
Focus	Studying persuasive devices in texts
Preparation	Have a comprehension task ready for stage 1.

Procedure

1 Lead in to a persuasive reading text in the usual way and set a standard comprehension task.

2 After checking the comprehension task, set learners a series of questions (see *Example*) to encourage them to investigate the views, values and stance inherent in the text.

3 Give learners time to compare their responses in small groups before reporting back.

Example

1 *Who wrote this text?*

2 *Why did they write it? What do they want me to think / believe / buy / do?*

3 *Are there hidden values/messages implicit in the text?*

4 *Is any contradictory evidence available from an internet search? Is there anything that is not said in the text that could have been said?*

5 *What techniques are used to attract my attention?*

6 *Could other people understand this text differently to me? In what ways?*

Notes

The activity will work with any news media or persuasive text. Question 4 in the example above focuses on the information that is missing from the text. For example, manufacturers of big cars will promote the luxury of the brand but rarely comment on the environmental impact of their products.

Rationale

The activity prompts learners to actively engage with the text and to find the means by which the writer positions them to accept certain arguments.

8.2 Investigate (EAP)

Outline	Learners analyze a research report to determine the strength of the evidence and argument put forward.
Level	Upper intermediate and above (B2+)
Time	30 minutes
Focus	Analyzing the strength of an argument
Preparation	Select a research report, or a summary of a report, and have a comprehension task ready for stage 1.

Procedure

1 Lead in to the reading text in the usual way and set a standard comprehension task.

2 Set learners a series of questions, such as those below, to encourage them to analyze the strength of the arguments put forward.

3 Give learners time to compare their responses in small groups before reporting back.

4 Encourage learners to get into the habit of asking themselves these questions every time they read an academic text.

Example

1 *Is the methodology used in the research described clearly? Does the author acknowledge any weaknesses in the methodology? Can you see any weaknesses?*

2 *How strong is the evidence? Is there any obvious influence or bias?*

3 *Are the interpretations made reasonable? Do they clearly link to the evidence presented?*

4 *How does the study fit in with other research on the subject? Does this study support other research or does it contradict it?*

5 *Am I prepared to support the author's claims?*

Notes

The questions above will work with any academic text that presents primary research findings.

Rationale

Learners are sometimes so busy decoding the argument of a text that they fail to scrutinize the strength of that argument and are therefore likely to take what they read at face value. The aim of this activity is to push learners to explicitly question the strength of the argument.

8.3 Cross examination

Outline	Learners prepare detailed questions that challenge the views put forward in a text.
Level	Intermediate and above (B1+)
Time	30 minutes
Focus	Analyzing the strength of an argument
Preparation	Have a comprehension task ready for stage 1.

Procedure

1   Lead in to the reading text in the usual way and set a standard comprehension task.

2   Explain what *cross examination* means, perhaps using a video to make the point (see *Notes*).

3   Explain to the class that they need to prepare detailed questions on specific short sections of text. Use one short section as an example, creating questions as a whole class (see *Example*).

4   Divide the class into groups, giving each group a short section of the text to work on.

5   After an appropriate time, invite learners to report back their questions.

Example

The following questions were written after reading this short extract from the web page *SueZe Lashes* on page 277.

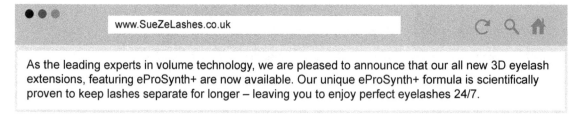

As the leading experts in volume technology, we are pleased to announce that our all new 3D eyelash extensions, featuring eProSynth+ are now available. Our unique eProSynth+ formula is scientifically proven to keep lashes separate for longer – leaving you to enjoy perfect eyelashes 24/7.

1   *What makes you 'experts'? What qualifications do you have?*

2   *Who are the other experts in the field? What evidence is there that you are better than them and are indeed 'leading experts'?*

3   *In what way are these 3D eyelash extensions different to former versions?*

4   *What exactly is unique about the formula? Can we be sure that no one else uses it?*

5   *What exactly is the evidence that these extensions last longer? How was it gathered? Can it be trusted?*

6   *How much longer do these extensions last?*

Notes

The questions asked will not have obvious answers in most cases and indeed, the questions will probably be unanswerable because the writers of the text will not be present to provide the necessary information. Instead, the questions act as a mechanism through which the learners can articulate their scepticism over particular claims in the text.

As an optional lead-in, find a short film clip that will set up the idea of courtroom drama and cross examination, e.g. *Witness for the Prosecution* (directed by Billy Wilder), *Anatomy of a Murder* (Otto Preminger) or *The Verdict* (Sidney Lumet).

Rationale

By asking learners to prepare 'cross examination' type questions, they are pushed to look for what information is either contradictory in the text or is missing altogether.

8.4 Facts / opinions / reactions

Outline	Learners divide a text into facts, the writer's opinions, and their own reactions and judgments of the text.
Level	Upper intermediate and above (B2+)
Time	30 minutes
Focus	Separating facts and opinions
Preparation	Select an appropriate text. This could be one that the learners have previously read.

Procedure

1 Focus on the text and check general comprehension.

2 Ask the learners to copy the table below into their notebooks.

Facts	The writer's opinions	My reactions

3 Explain to the class that they should divide the text into the facts and the writer's opinions. They should also record their own reaction to the text.

4 Remind them that opinions may not be explicitly stated but may be implied.

5 Learners work in small groups to complete the table.

6 After an appropriate time, the learners report back their findings.

Example
The following is based on the web page *SueZe Lashes* on page 277.

Facts	The writer's opinions	My reactions
There is a new product.	The writer thinks this is good news.	It isn't important news.
Eyelashes are made longer.	This makes people feel more confident.	Women should not be made to feel that they have a problem that needs solving, however they look.
	Women should spend money and effort on making themselves more attractive to others.	This is rubbish. And it is a dangerous message, particularly for young girls.
Appointments can be booked through the website.		

Notes
In some cases, facts may be included that are not linked to any particular opinion, or opinions may be given that are not based on facts. In these cases, there will be boxes left blank in the table.

If the text is long, each group could be given a separate section of text.

It may be a good idea to go through an example section of the text with the class first.

Rationale
This activity focuses on being able to separate facts from the opinions of the writer, which is a key aspect of critical reading.

8.5 Replacing words

Outline	Learners consider the significance of word choices in creating an argument.
Level	Intermediate and above (B1+)
Time	20 minutes
Focus	Studying how vocabulary choices can position the reader
Preparation	Choose an appropriate text. Select some words from the text that have strong connotations or position the reader in some other way. Write alternatives that could replace the words selected (see *Example*). Have a comprehension task ready for stage 1.

Procedure

1 Lead in to the reading text in the usual way and set a standard comprehension task.

2 When they have read the text, ask learners to focus on both the original words and the alternatives.

3 Divide the class into small groups to consider the effects of the choices the writer made, by considering how each alternative would affect meaning.

Example

The following is taken from the web page *SueZe Lashes* on page 277. An example answer is given for *gift* as one of the possible alternatives for *treat*.

---

*The perfect **treat***

gift: *A treat is something that is out of the ordinary and gives pleasure. It suggests indulgence. Gifts are often linked to particular events, such as birthdays. Gifts are generally bought for other people, whereas treats can be bought for oneself.*

surprise: _____

extravagance: _____

*… we are pleased to **announce** …*

say: _____

report: _____

disclose: _____

*Our **unique** eProSynth+ formula*

luxury: _____

special: _____

expensive: _____

Notes

Learners could also research and provide alternatives for other lexical choices as a homework task.

Rationale

Readers are often positioned to form particular judgements based on the lexical choices a writer makes. This activity aims to push learners to question those choices and their effects.

8.6 Two views

Outline	Learners consider a news story from two perspectives.
Level	Intermediate and above (B1+)
Time	30 minutes
Focus	Analyzing texts for bias
Preparation	Choose two texts that report the same event from two different perspectives. Have a comprehension task ready, if required, for stage 2.

Procedure

1 Lead in to the texts by discussing the topic briefly. Ask learners whether they think that different groups of people may have different views on the topic.

2 Give the learners the first text. If necessary, set a short comprehension task in order to ensure that they have a reasonable understanding of the story.

3 Give the learners the second text. Tell the learners the origins of the two texts and ask them to decide which source is which and how they know (see *Notes*). This is likely to require rereading the texts. Learners can compare ideas before reporting back.

4 Ask the class to identify specific differences between the two stories. These may include 'facts' included in one but not the other, or different evaluations of the same events. Again, learners can compare before reporting back.

Notes

The texts could come from a variety of sources. One option would be to use coverage of a political event from two different perspectives. Alternatively, a big sports event could be used, such as an important football match, with a comparison of how the local media of each side report the occasion. Football clubs generally put their own reports of matches on their websites and so these are both easy to access and not unbiased!

Rationale

A key critical reading skill is the ability to identify bias in a text and this activity gives specific practice in that skill.

8.7 The tourist trap

Outline	Learners compare a tourist brochure for a particular town or region, with an encyclopaedia entry.
Level	Upper intermediate and above (B2+)
Time	30 minutes
Focus	Studying features of persuasive writing
Preparation	Select a text, or section of text, from a tourist brochure for a specific tourist destination. Look up the same place in an encyclopaedia and print out the result.

Procedure

1 Lead in to the texts by presenting some factual information about the place chosen (but withhold the name) and asking learners if they would like to visit it (see *Example*).

2 Ask learners how this information could be made more persuasive.

3 Tell the learners the name of the place and distribute the encylopaedia text and ask learners to briefly identify any additional information not already given.

4 Distribute the tourist brochure text.

5 Learners work in small groups to identify the differences between the content and style of the two texts and particularly the evaluative language in the tourist brochure.

6 As a follow-up activity, learners could write a text trying to persuade people not to visit the chosen place, or they could write a persuasive text for a different destination.

Example

This example describes Barcelona.

Fact sheet

Would you like to visit a place …

- with a population of 1.6 million (although 3 million live in the surrounding area)?

- an area of approximately 101 km^2?

- which has around 16,000 inhabitants per km^2?

- which has around 8 million visitors a year?

- which has approximately 35,000 stores?

- which has approximately 4 km of beach?

Notes

If time is short, just a fact sheet (such as in the example) and the tourist brochure could be used.

The activity is likely to work best if the learners can identify with the place chosen, and where possible, have visited it.

Rationale

Tourist brochures are a source of particularly clear examples of persuasive language and are generally easy to find. By comparing the factual and the persuasive texts, learners will become familiar with some of the features of persuasive writing.

8.8 What's changed?

Outline	Learners analyze a short section of text and consider the impact of particular linguistic choices.
Level	Intermediate and above (B1+)
Time	30 minutes
Focus	Analyzing the impact of grammatical and lexical choices
Preparation	Prepare two texts that are similar in content but differ on a particular linguistic point. Fruitful areas for analysis include the use of active and passive voice, modality, and transitivity. Try to ensure that there are at least two or three examples of the key point for learners to comment on. Occasional lexical choices could also be altered (see *Example*). Have a gist comprehension task ready, if required, for stage 2.

Procedure

1 Lead in to the text in the usual way.

2 Distribute the first text. If necessary set a short gist task and ensure that the learners have a reasonable understanding of the text.

3 Distribute the second text. Explain that the content is largely the same. Ask learners to identify the differences in language choices. If necessary, work as a whole group to identify the first change as an example, before asking the learners to look for others.

4 Confirm that the learners have identified the changes appropriately.

5 Put learners into pairs or small groups and ask them to discuss the effect of the changes.

6 Learners report back their ideas to the group.

Example

The texts opposite are appropriate for a B1 or B2 class. The first uses examples of the passive voice to avoid direct blame for the events (*has been destroyed, has been cleared, can only be farmed, has to be cleared*) and also uses the verb *die out*, which suggests a natural process and avoids apportioning blame, in the last line. Of course, farming is a uniquely human activity and so the agent can be recovered but it is not made explicit.

On the other hand, the second text identifies the agent of the verbs explicitly, and makes clear that human beings are the cause of the problem. Also *kill* (a transitive verb here) is used in the last line, suggesting a deliberate act.

Notes

The activity works best with relatively short texts so that the learners can analyze the differences and the effects of the changes thoroughly.

A similar activity can be used to analyze reporting verbs, particularly those associated with academic research, e.g. *state*, *claim*, *hypothesize*, *suggest*. Again, learners can be asked to discuss the effect of different linguistic choices.

Rationale

This activity allows learners to focus on key linguistic areas that are used to subtly position readers. The language items are seen in context and so learners can see the effects of the changes more easily.

▶ *What's changed?*

The Amazon rainforest produces about 20% of the earth's oxygen but more than 10% of the rainforest has been destroyed since the 1960s, with 1.5 acres being lost every second. Much of it has been cleared to make way for farmland, although the land is actually often of poor quality and can only be farmed for a year or two before another patch has to be cleared. Rainforests cover around 6% of the Earth's surface but are home to over 50% of the world's species. However, some estimates suggest that as many as 137 species are dying out every day.

The Amazon rainforest produces about 20% of the earth's oxygen but human activity has destroyed more than 10% of the rainforest since the 1960s, with 1.5 acres being lost every second. Often people clear areas for farmland although the land is frequently of poor quality and farmers move on after a year or two and clear another patch. Rainforests cover around 6% of the Earth's surface but are home to over 50% of the world's species. However, some estimates suggest that we humans are killing as many as 137 species every day through our activities.

From *Teaching and Developing Reading Skills* © Cambridge University Press 2017   PHOTOCOPIABLE

8.9 Analyze that!

Outline	Learners analyze a section of their coursebook for underlying assumptions and bias.
Level	Intermediate and above (B1+)
Time	25 minutes
Focus	Analyzing some of the values implicit in the learners' coursebook
Preparation	Select a text from the coursebook that the class is using. It could be a text that has already been read. Have a gist comprehension task ready, if required, for stage 1.

Procedure

1 Lead in to the text in the usual way. If the learners have not read it before set a short gist task to ensure they have a reasonable understanding of the text.

2 Divide the class into small groups. Set a task that guides the learners to analyze the text (see *Example*).

3 Ensure the learners understand the questions.

4 Allow learners time to analyze the text before reporting back their ideas.

Example

Learners could analyze the text using the questions below. However, it is likely that some adaptation will be required to suit specific texts.

1 *Can you find any examples of stereotyping (either positively or negatively)?*

2 *How are males and females represented in the text? Do they represent stereotypical roles?*

3 *Do the text, or the images that accompany it, represent people from a range of ethnic origins?*

4 *Are people with disabilities represented in this text, or the images that accompany it?*

5 *Do the activities and life style choices represented in the text require a lot of money?*

6 *What other values are promoted?*

7 *Do the pictures support these messages?*

Notes

Learners could be encouraged to analyze more of the book, perhaps a unit, or even the whole book.
Different groups of learners could analyze different texts so that a more complete picture emerges.

Rationale

Coursebooks have educational goals and like all educational texts have some underlying assumptions within them. Most obviously these assumptions are about what to teach and how to teach it. However, English teaching textbooks also tend to represent an 'aspirational culture'. This may be a result of assuming that learners will identify with such a culture because learning languages (and particularly English) is associated with improved career prospects. As educational material is so influential, it is appropriate for learners to question the material they use.

9 Using learner-generated texts

Learner-generated texts

Most reading in the classroom involves using texts selected by a course designer, whether that be a remote professional materials writer, or the teacher of a particular class who takes on the role. There are good reasons why this should happen because these individuals have professional expertise and we assume that their decisions are based on an understanding of the learners' needs, levels and interests. They may deliberately sequence texts using carefully considered criteria, such as the level of difficulty. Alternatively, material may be chosen that introduces a particular text type or contextualizes particular items of language. In addition, texts may be selected to ensure that language items are recycled from earlier input and in these regards professionals can be expected to make well-informed decisions.

However, there is often space in a reading curriculum to include texts that are either written or selected by the learners themselves and this too can have advantages.

Advantages of using learner-generated texts

Learner-created texts

Both research and more practice-based literature (e.g. Anderson, 2012; Watkins, 2014) often makes a case for the teaching of the four skills (reading, writing, speaking and listening) to be integrated. In the case of reading, this is frequently achieved by using a text as a prompt for speaking and/or writing work. However, the benefits of integrating skills can equally be achieved by reversing the sequence, with learners reading what other learners have written.

One of the key advantages of using such learner-generated texts for reading practice is that it tends to be motivating. Where learners write texts for others in the class to read, there is a natural interest generated which comes from wanting to read the thoughts and ideas of people we actually know. Moreover, from the writer's point of view, the knowledge that what we write will be read by others creates a sense of readership and is likely to make the task more genuinely communicative. In addition, if learners read what more skilled peer writers produce, it may have a positive impact on their own writing.

Further, much reading in the 21st century involves the co-construction of text, with two or more participants taking turns to read what another has written and then contributing the next part of the developing text. This is the case with text message exchanges, for example, or where a shared text is revised and edited online (such as when using wikis or Google Docs). Learners simply have to be involved in generating texts to gain practice in these types of genre.

Learner-selected texts

Where learners select texts for the group to read, those texts are more likely to have an immediacy and relevance to the particular group of learners than texts selected by someone remote from the situation, as is the case with much coursebook material, for example. Learners are likely to have an instinctive understanding of what others may want to read.

Another advantage is that the process of selecting texts, along with making suggestions for how those texts might be exploited, will provide much reading practice in itself. There is also a clear purpose to the reading (to find a suitable text) and a potential outcome attached to the reading (it is used in class). Again, these factors are likely to be a source of motivation.

Drawbacks of using learner-generated texts

As well as advantages, there are some drawbacks to using learner-generated texts to practise and develop reading skills.

Learner-created texts

It may be that the texts written by learners lack the degree of sophistication in terms of linking and organization that learners need to be exposed to. While there are benefits to the comfortable intelligibility of texts and the promotion of fluent reading, a fully rounded course also needs challenge. The texts produced by learners are also likely to be relatively short and so not provide for more extensive reading.

Learner-selected texts

Where learners select texts for classroom use, teachers may be concerned about their appropriacy, both in terms of content and linguistic level. This may lead to the need for the teacher to vet texts before they are made available to other learners. If the selected texts are particularly challenging, learners could be encouraged to supply a glossary, which is likely to benefit their own vocabulary growth as well as support the reading of others.

On balance, while learner-generated texts may not be able to provide a complete reading syllabus that meets all the needs of a group of learners, they can add variety to reading and be a useful part of a course.

The activities focused on in this chapter are designed to give teachers some practical ideas about how to create and exploit learner-generated texts in the classroom.

References

Anderson, N. (2012) 'Reading instruction' in A. Burns and J.C. Richards (eds.), *The Cambridge Guide to Pedagogy and Practice in Second Language Teaching*, pp. 218–215, New York: Cambridge University Press.

Watkins, P. (2014) *Learning to Teach English* (2nd ed.), Peaslake: Delta Publishing.

9.1 Beginner reading

Outline	Learners read a text that they have previously created orally.
Level	Beginner and above (A1+)
Time	25 minutes
Focus	Reading at text level for beginner readers
Preparation	None

Procedure

1 Select an appropriate topic and elicit information from the learners using language that is known to them. Use visual support where necessary (see *Example*).

2 When sufficient information has been elicited, incorporate it into a short text and write it on the board.

3 Read the text to the learners. The learners follow and/or join in the reading (see *Notes*).

Example

The following is a brief example of just the beginning of an elicitation phase and how it is written up. The elicitation would go on longer in order to produce more details and therefore a longer written text.

Teacher:	Look at this picture *(holds up picture of a woman)* What's her name? What shall we call her?
Student 1:	Alessandra.
Teacher:	OK, good, so this is Alessandra. And where does Alessandra live?
Student 2:	England.
Teacher:	OK, and where in England?
Student 2:	London.
Teacher:	Good. OK, and Alessandra has a job. She works at … *(holds up picture of a hospital)*. Where is this?
Student 3:	ospedale.
Teacher:	That's right. And in English?
Student 4:	hospital.
Teacher:	Excellent. Yes, she works at the hospital. So what job does she do?
Student 1:	doctor

The teacher incorporates this information into a short text, such as:
Alessandra lives in the UK and works at a hospital in London. She is a doctor and works …

Variation

Instead of using a picture as a prompt for the elicitation phase, narratives that the learners themselves volunteer can be exploited, or shared group experiences. This would make the activity more personalized and potentially more powerful as a result.

Notes

The activity works well with beginner learners and also young learners.

The activity can be adjusted for the level of the class by eliciting more (or less) text before the teacher writes a version for the learners to read.

The task set to accompany the reading text can also be made more demanding. For example, the teacher could change some details in the text and ask the learners to identify those changes.

Rationale

Learners who are beginning to read need to work with words that they are familiar with orally. This activity helps learners progress from reading individual words to texts by ensuring that they are well prepared for the challenge through having co-created the text that they eventually read.

9.2 Who is who?

Outline	Learners create and then read a series of short paragraphs about each other.
Level	Intermediate and above (B1+)
Time	45 minutes
Focus	Combining writing and reading skills
Preparation	Copy the questionnaire (see *Example* – one for each learner) or adapt it as necessary.

Procedure

1   Distribute the questionnaire and ensure that learners understand it.

2   Learners complete the questionnaire for themselves.

3   Put learners into pairs and ask them to swap questionnaires.

4   The learners use the information to write a short paragraph about their partner. They should not use their partner's name but refer to them as *she* or *he*.

5   Display the paragraphs around the room in a random order.

6   If possible, learners circulate and read all the descriptions. If class size, space or some other constraint, makes this impossible, learners can pass their text to a learner near to them (but not their original partner). After a set amount of time that learner passes it on to another person, and so on.

7   Having read the description, the learners write on it who they think is being described. Ensure there is space for this, or provide an additional sheet of paper next to each description.

8   After the reading of texts is completed, the learners report back their ideas.

9   Feedback on the learners' writing can also be offered.

Notes

The example questionnaire given is appropriate for B1 (intermediate) learners. The activity can be adapted by adjusting the written statements. These particular statements are designed to help the teacher understand the learning preferences of their class. However, the questionnaire could be designed around any appropriate topic.

The activity can also be used to teach the use of *they*, *their*, etc. to stand in place of singular nouns (often used to disguise gender). If this is desired, instruct learners to refer to their partner as *they* etc.

The writing task could be done for homework, if preferred, with the reading in the following lesson.

Rationale

This activity combines reading and writing and exploits the fact that learners are often motivated to read what their colleagues have written. The reading of other learners' writing is likely to be at an appropriate level for comfortable intelligibility and so will promote fluent reading.

The reading of several short texts allows learners to have 'fresh starts'. This can be reassuring, particularly at lower proficiency levels.

The moving around the room provides energy to the lesson and contrasts with much reading work, in which learners are sat silently.

▶ *Questionnaire*

Who is who?

Read the following statements. Underline the options that are true for you. Add any comments you wish.

1   Education is about learning *facts / about yourself*.

   _____

   _____

   _____

2   It's *important / not important* to study rules when you start learning a language.

   _____

   _____

   _____

3   I like studying *in groups / on my own*.

   _____

   _____

   _____

4   I like *studying grammar / communicating with language*.

   _____

   _____

   _____

5   I *like / worry about* performing in front of the class.

   _____

   _____

   _____

6   Making mistakes is *a good way to learn / embarrassing*.

   _____

   _____

   _____

From *Teaching and Developing Reading Skills* © Cambridge University Press 2017   PHOTOCOPIABLE

9.3 Read and comment

Outline	Learners read texts produced by others and comment on them.
Level	Intermediate and above (B1+)
Time	45 minutes
Focus	Combining writing and reading skills
Preparation	None

Procedure

1 Lead in to a writing activity, through such things as establishing the task, brainstorming ideas and discussing options for organizing the text.

2 Put the learners into pairs. Each pair writes their response to the task on a large sheet of paper.

3 Give learners time to write their texts, circulating and helping as necessary.

4 When the learners have written their texts, display them around the room.

5 The learners comment on the texts written by others. Before this, give guidance as to the sorts of things that learners may want to comment on. For example, they may write that they agree or disagree with an idea, or they could indicate if they find part of a text difficult to follow. They could also correct any spelling or grammar mistakes they find.

6 If possible, learners circulate, reading and commenting on the texts. If class size, space or some other constraint makes this impossible, learners can pass their text to the pair to their left. After a set amount of time to read and comment, that pair passes it on to the next on their left and so on.

7 After an appropriate amount of time, learners sit down (or stop passing the texts on).

8 Lead a brief discussion on which texts the learners found particularly effective, or interesting.

9 Return the texts to the original writers so that they can look at the comments and ask any questions they want to. They can now redraft the text, using the comments.

10 Lead a brief discussion highlighting the features that were generally done well in the writing phase.

Notes

It is a good idea to ensure that learners understand that their work will be displayed before they start writing.

The learners' comments can be either written directly onto the texts or they can be given sticky notes to use.

Rationale

The activity creates a readership for the writing and this is likely to increase motivation for the task. Learners are also likely to be motivated by seeing how others have approached the same task and there may well be opportunities for them to learn from what others have done. The movement around the room helps create energy and purposeful discussion of each text.

9.4 Questions to story

Outline	Learners are guided to create versions of a text before they read the original.
Level	Intermediate and above (B1+)
Time	45 minutes
Focus	Preparing learners for reading by having them write a similar text beforehand
Preparation	Select an appropriate narrative text.

Procedure

1 Before the learners see the text, give a series of prompts which relate to it. These prompts could be in the form of questions (see *Example*).

2 Ask learners to write a paragraph (or whatever length of text is appropriate) containing their responses to the prompts. This can be written in pairs or small groups, if appropriate.

3 When the learners have finished writing, nominate some learners to read out their versions of the story.

4 Distribute the original text to the learners. The learners read the text and compare their versions with the original.

5 In small groups, learners discuss the differences in both content and writing style between their own text and the original.

6 After an appropriate length of time, learners report back their ideas.

Example

The following questions would be appropriate for the text *An unusual meeting* on page 269.

A woman is sitting alone – describe her and say where she is.
She is playing a game – what game?
Someone approaches her and speaks – does she know this person? Describe the exchange.
What happens after this meeting?

Notes

To some extent the teacher can manipulate the degree of similarity between the learners' versions and the original text through giving more (or less) information. For example, the first prompt (above) could be written as *A woman is sitting alone in a café in Paris – describe her and where she is.* The inclusion of *in a café* guides the learners' thought and is likely to lead to versions closer to the original text.

Rationale

The writing stage of the activity introduces learners to some of the main points in the text and increases the motivation to read the original version as there is a natural curiosity in finding out the accuracy of our own predictions. The creation of the learners' version of the text also encourages discussion of stylistic differences.

9.5 Paper text messages

Outline	Learners have a conversation with a partner through reading and writing.
Level	Any
Time	20 minutes
Focus	Reading and responding in order to co-construct a text with a partner
Preparation	None

Procedure

1   Put the learners into pairs.

2   Tell the learners that they are about to have a text message conversation in the target language. Explain that there is one difference: they will write the conversation on paper. Learners can draw the equivalent of emojis if they wish.

3   From this point on, there should be no talking until the conversations have been completed. One learner should start. The second learner reads what has been written and responds (on the same piece of paper). The first learner reads and makes their next contribution. The conversations proceed in this manner.

4   Allow time for the learners to begin their conversations and then circulate, offering support and guidance as appropriate.

5   When the learners have finished their conversations, lead a discussion on the activity. Focus on any elements of the conversation that were difficult to understand or where the tone was unclear, e.g. whether a comment was intended seriously or ironically.

6   Lead a brief discussion on how the conversations on paper were different to those that take place outside the classroom. This could be in the sense of being different to face-to-face conversations, or in the sense of being different to standard text conversations.

Notes

Some teachers like to guide learners on the topic(s) they should talk about when doing this activity, while others prefer the conversation to develop naturally and without guidance or a lot of planning.

The activity requires only very simple instructions. One way to make the lesson stand out and be different is to start the lesson without saying anything at all, but getting attention and then writing on the board *Nobody will speak in this lesson. If you have any questions, please come and write them on the board for me*. The few instructions that are needed can then be displayed on the board. The silence should continue until the written conversations have been finished.

If appropriate, learners could do this activity by messaging each other using their phones. However, this requires sharing of numbers and so should be done cautiously. Also, it is important that the learners receive feedback on their work and having the learners write on paper makes it easier for teachers to monitor and offer support.

Rationale

Co-constructed texts where participants are both readers and writers are becoming increasingly common and have distinctive features, such as a high degree of assumed knowledge and short turns. This activity gives specific practice in dealing with this type of text.

9.6 Using voice recognition software

Outline	Learners read back what they have dictated to voice recognition software and correct any errors.
Level	Any
Time	10 minutes
Focus	Decoding the forms of words
Preparation	Ensure that learners have access to voice recognition software. Most smartphones will have some form of this if no other software is available.

Procedure

1 Explain that learners will use voice recognition software. Briefly elicit any experiences of using such software that the learners may have had.

2 Allow learners a short time to prepare what they want to say.

3 Learners work individually, dictating sections of text to the voice recognition software.

4 Learners compare the version printed out for them with what they intended to say.

5 Ensure learners check the accuracy of the written version very carefully.

6 Where necessary, learners can dictate their messages again.

7 After an appropriate length of time (see *Notes*), lead a brief discussion on the sources of any difficulty. Difficulties most usually arise from shortcomings in the software, or from unclear pronunciation.

8 Encourage learners to repeat the activity on a regular basis outside lessons.

Notes

If smartphones are used, the learners may have to select the target language from the settings menu.
   This activity tends to work best when done frequently for short bursts of time.

Rationale

The activity combines reading and speaking, and particularly pronunciation work. The learners will be pushed to read in detail (and are therefore likely to use a lot of bottom-up processing) because any words that are misrepresented will most probably have similarities in form to the dictated/intended word.

9.7 Read my text

Outline	Learners supply a text and questions for other learners.
Level	Elementary and above (A2+)
Time	25 minutes
Focus	Deciding where difficulties may arise for a reader in a particular text
Preparation	Ask learners to select and prepare a text that can be used in class. This should include the text, a gloss (or translation) of words they feel may be difficult, and some comprehension questions.

Procedure

Learners exchange texts and answer the questions.

Notes

Teachers should be prepared for some learners not bringing texts at the designated time. If this happens, some learners could work in pairs, reading one text between two people. Alternatively, the teacher could collect the texts from those who have prepared them and then select a sample to use with the class in a subsequent lesson.

Teachers may also wish to guide learners in the selection of their texts by providing links to particular websites.

Rationale

Learners are likely to be motivated to read the texts supplied by other members of the group. Also, the preparation of the glossary and questions will provide much useful detailed reading practice.

9.8 Whose is it?

Outline	Each learner supplies a short text and others must guess who supplied which text.
Level	Intermediate and above (B1+)
Time	25 minutes
Focus	Providing motivation for reading
Preparation	Ask the learners to select and bring in to class a short text that they find interesting or is in some way important to them.

Procedure

1 Choose three to five of the texts supplied. How many texts exactly are used will probably depend on their length. Display the selected texts around the room.

2 Tell the class the names of the learners whose texts are displayed.

3 Learners circulate and read the texts. Learners should:
   • match the texts to the person who brought them in
   • decide which text they find most interesting.

4 After reading, learners report back their ideas.

5 Finish by having the learners whose texts were used explain why they chose those particular texts.

Notes

The activity can be repeated with other texts that have been supplied on other days.

If appropriate, learners could be asked to supply a short glossary with their text to support fluent reading. There are likely to be benefits to the learner preparing this in terms of vocabulary growth.

If appropriate, learners could also supply a few comprehension questions with their text for the class to answer.

Rationale

Learners are likely to have an instinctive understanding of the level of difficulty appropriate for their group and also the topics that are likely to interest and motivate fellow learners. Therefore this should provide a motivating and engaging reading experience.

9.9 Next year's class

Outline	The class designs a reading course for another group of learners.
Level	Upper intermediate and above (B2+)
Time	30 minutes for the first five stages and open-ended for the following stages
Focus	Combining skim reading and detailed reading
Preparation	None

Procedure

1 Lead a brief discussion of why reading is important in language learning. Point out though that some learners may not read much, or may not look forward to reading lessons.

2 Tell the class that their task is to help design a reading course for another group of learners. For example, it may be the class that will be doing the same course the following year, or another group of a similar level in the school.

3 Give clear parameters for what is expected such as:
   • the number of texts required
   • the ideal length of the texts
   • the genre(s) required, e.g. factual versus expressive texts (if expressive discuss what can be included – poetry, extracts of novels, etc.).

4 If necessary, brainstorm appropriate sources of texts.

5 Discuss with learners the types of activity that could accompany the texts. This could be done by reflecting on tasks that the learners have used during their own course.

6 Give the learners time to locate the texts, write accompanying tasks and sequence the texts. This could be done as a homework project, and could extend over several weeks, depending on the scale of the course to be designed. Learners could work in groups and be assigned particular topics to work on.

7 Large classes may produce more texts than can be realistically used. In this case, put time aside in lessons for 'editorial meetings', where texts are discussed and selected for final inclusion or rejected.

8 When the sequence of reading lessons has been designed, be sure to save them in a safe place so that the lessons can be used. If possible, arrange how feedback will be given to the current class (the designers) on how well their lessons work.

Notes

The parameters for the design can change to suit the teaching context. For example, it may be that learners design a short reading programme to be done outside of class time (rather than during class time). The programme that the learners design may consist of just a few texts, or many.

An engaging follow-up to this project work, is to ask the learners to record a short video that can be played to the next class. This should introduce the aims of the project (to provide a motivating reading course) and the process they went through to create it.

Rationale

The learners will engage in plenty of reading, including quick gist reading to get the main ideas within texts and more detailed reading as they set tasks. The learners are likely to be motivated by knowing that others will use their work in the future and particularly by the responsibility that is given to them and the trust that it implies. The future learners who use the materials are also likely to be motivated to see what their predecessors included.

9.10 Photo captions

Outline	Learners read the captions to a series of photographs.
Level	Elementary and above (A2+)
Time	25 minutes, depending on the number of photographs
Focus	Motivating learners to read through focusing on a shared positive experience
Preparation	Choose a school occasion, such as an excursion, a party/celebration, or school play/performance. Take photographs regularly throughout the event. (As the photographs will not be published this should not present a problem, but you may wish to check what your institution's policy is on the taking and use of photographs and also that nobody objects to being in a photograph.)
	Choose a selection of photographs and print them. Write captions for each photograph (see *Example*). Print each caption on a slip of paper. Display the photographs on the classroom wall but retain the captions.

Procedure

1 Ask learners what they remember of the event and what they enjoyed.

2 Distribute the captions to the learners (or pairs of learners if there are more learners than photos).

3 Ask learners to match their caption to the appropriate picture, sticking it next to the picture they choose.

4 Monitor the activity, supporting where necessary.

Example

The following example is taken from a Macau primary school trip to a panda reserve. In all, the teacher used twenty photographs, for a class of forty children. Here are four examples from her twenty.

Photo	Caption
bus arriving at the school to pick up the children	We are ready to leave. We have a long journey!
panda eating bamboo	This panda is eating her breakfast. She looks hungry!
the children on benches, eating lunch	We are eating our lunch. It tastes good!
teacher on the bus, counting children	Is everyone here? I must not forget anybody!

Variation 1

Instead of captions, write speech bubbles that are 'attached' to people in the photographs.

Variation 2

Display additional photographs taken from the set and ask learners to write captions for them.

Notes

Captions can be made shorter or longer, according to the needs of the class. So, higher-level learners would be expected to read longer, more sophisticated captions.

The photographs and captions should ideally stay on the wall for a period of time, helping to create a rich reading environment.

Rationale

Matching activities are quite frequently used in reading lessons. However, the focus on an event which was real and memorable for the learners is likely to increase engagement with the task.

The photographs provide some context for reading very short (sometimes sentence-level) texts, making the activity appropriate for low-level learners.

10   Encouraging extensive reading

What is extensive reading?

There are several characteristics that distinguish extensive reading from the more intensive reading that we usually associate with the classroom. One defining feature is that extensive reading should be relatively easy. Rather than working with texts that are at the limit of the learners' ability, as is frequently the case with intensive reading in the classroom, learners work with texts that they can understand without undue effort and which contain few unknown words. The ease with which learners can process the text leads to a second characteristic of extensive reading and that is that learners read much longer texts than those that they generally experience inside the classroom. Extensive reading also promotes reading fluency and speed, rather than close attention to detail, with learners often encouraged to either guess or ignore unknown words. Another feature of extensive reading is that it is self-directed, with learners choosing what they read and there being a clear emphasis on reading for pleasure. This in turn leads to very little use of comprehension questions or testing of any sort. If there is a follow-up activity, care should be taken that it encourages learners to read more, rather than risking discouraging learners from reading (Bamford and Day, 2004).

The teacher's role in extensive reading

The teacher has two principal roles in extensive reading programmes. One is to ensure that learners have a wide variety of texts that they can access. Related to this, teachers also need to help learners find materials that are both at an appropriate level of comfortable intelligibility and are also of interest. This is vital if learners are to participate in extensive reading. The second main role of the teacher is to act as a motivator, encouraging learners to engage with extensive reading programmes as much as possible. This may come about partly through modelling reading behaviour and prompting discussions about what learners are reading outside class. For example, teachers may take a few moments at the start of some lessons to talk about what they themselves are reading, why they like it, and then move on to invite learners to comment on what they are reading.

The benefits of extensive reading

The research literature suggests that learners can get great benefits from extensive reading. Not only do general reading skills improve, but learners also report a greater degree of motivation, which may be partly explained by the development of learner autonomy (frequently associated with increased motivation), which is implicit in extensive reading. As well as these benefits, many studies over a long period of time have shown that extensive reading also contributes to vocabulary growth (e.g. Nagy, Herman and Anderson, 1985; Horst, 2009) and this supports the development and performance of all language skills.

There is also evidence that extensive reading impacts positively on grammar learning. This may be because reading is a key provider of the input that cognitive views of learning identify as being necessary to fuel language acquisition. Extensive reading is also compatible with more associative models of learning (such as connectionism), as the more times associations between words are made, the stronger those links become.

On top of these linguistic benefits, extensive reading can also promote an increased knowledge of the world and other cultures. In sum, many researchers believe that extensive reading programmes do not just support reading skills development, but also gains in overall linguistic proficiency (Ellis and Shintani, 2014).

Challenges in implementing extensive reading programmes

Given the general agreement on the advantages that extensive reading can bring, it is perhaps surprising that the practice is not promoted more widely. One reason for this may be that in many contexts the learning and teaching process is still seen as being centred around traditional teaching, with any more learner-centred initiatives being viewed with some scepticism. Certainly, one argument often put against extensive reading is that teachers cannot be sure that learners have actually done the reading that they claim. However, where this is a concern, it is fairly easy to check what learners have read. For example, a discussion of only a few seconds usually reveals whether the learner has read the text in question.

It may also be that teacher education programmes could do more to foreground the benefits of extensive reading, while also making the argument that classroom reading alone may not produce effective readers. Teachers would then be in a position to extend these discussions to learners as a form of learner training (see Activity 10.1: *The benefits of reading* as an example).

Another reason that extensive reading programmes do not form part of more courses is that they can be seen as quite resource-intensive, with their success being linked to the provision of a wide variety of materials at a range of levels. While the internet provides an almost limitless range of potential authentic material, which is useful for high-level learners, there is much less freely available that is graded to lower proficiency levels. As a result, most programmes, particularly at lower levels, are built around 'graded readers' (books that are graded for difficulty, particularly with regard to word frequencies) but these materials obviously have to be paid for.

However, perhaps the biggest challenge in encouraging learners to read extensively is the learners themselves. Some learners simply may not see reading as a pleasurable activity (in any language) but advocates of extensive reading assume that learners will find pleasure and enjoyment through reading. One way in which to counter the 'but reading isn't fun' argument is to foreground the linguistic benefits of the reading (as outlined above) so that otherwise reluctant readers see the possibility of tangible benefits as a result of their labour. Also, classroom conversations about reading and what people read may help to motivate learners. In order to counteract any negative perceptions of reading for some learners, the material available needs, wherever possible, to move beyond the provision of traditional books to include such things as comic books, graphic novels, interactive quizzes, popular magazines and so on.

The aim of this chapter is to give a few activities that could be used to encourage extensive reading and help teachers who wish to set up, or develop, extensive reading programmes. In the end, we learn to read through reading and we learn a lot more besides. The benefits to learners of engaging with extensive reading are very clear.

References

Bamford, J. and Day, R. (2004) *Extensive Reading Activities for Teaching Language*, New York: Cambridge University Press.

Ellis, R. and Shintani, N. (2014) *Exploring Language Pedagogy through Second Language Acquisition Research*, Abingdon: Taylor & Francis.

Horst, M. (2009) 'Developing definitional vocabulary knowledge and lexical access speed through extensive reading' in Z. Han and N. Anderson (Eds.), *Second Language Reading: Research and Instruction*, Ann Arbor, MI: University of Michigan Press.

Nagy, W., Herman, P. and Anderson, R.C. (1985) 'Learning words from context', *Reading Research Quarterly*, 20, pp. 233–253.

10.1 The benefits of reading

Outline	Learners take part in a discussion of the benefits of extensive reading.
Level	Elementary and above (A2+)
Time	30 minutes
Focus	Discussing the benefits of extensive reading
Preparation	Prepare and copy a short questionnaire (see *Example*).

Procedure

1 Explain any statements on the questionnaire that are not clear and ensure that learners understand that the statements refer to L2 reading.

2 Ask learners to respond individually to each statement before comparing their responses in small groups. Encourage learners to give reasons for what they think.

3 In open class, learners report back what they discussed.

Example

The questionnaire opposite may be copied for your learners.

Notes

Statement 1 will elicit personal responses. Statement 2 is probably not true because some reading texts should encourage fluent reading and be quite easy to understand. There is research evidence to support all the other statements (see the introduction to this chapter for a brief summary).

If necessary, the statements and discussion could be in L1 for low-level learners.

Rationale

The research evidence is very clear that extensive reading benefits language learners – and not just in the development of reading. However, many learners do not use extensive reading material even when institutions make it available. It is possible that if learners come to understand the benefits of reading, they will become more likely to read.

⬉ Questionnaire

Reading

Circle the most appropriate response for each statement.

1   Reading can be enjoyable.

   I'm sure this is true.   *This might be true.*   *I don't think this is true.*

2   I learn best if reading texts are always quite difficult for me.

   I'm sure this is true.   *This might be true.*   *I don't think this is true.*

3   Learners who read outside class become quicker at reading.

   I'm sure this is true.   *This might be true.*   *I don't think this is true.*

4   Learners who read outside class understand more when they read.

   I'm sure this is true.   *This might be true.*   *I don't think this is true.*

5   Learners who read outside class get better at writing.

   I'm sure this is true.   *This might be true.*   *I don't think this is true.*

6   Learners who read outside class report that they enjoy learning the language more.

   I'm sure this is true.   *This might be true.*   *I don't think this is true.*

7   Learners who read outside class learn more vocabulary.

   I'm sure this is true.   *This might be true.*   *I don't think this is true.*

8   Learners who read outside class learn more grammar.

   I'm sure this is true.   *This might be true.*   *I don't think this is true.*

9   Learners who read outside class learn more about the world.

   I'm sure this is true.   *This might be true.*   *I don't think this is true.*

10.2 Taking reading to the learners

Outline	The teacher takes a selection of reading material to the class so that learners can select what they would like to read.
Level	Any
Time	15 minutes
Focus	Encouraging learners to engage with extensive reading programmes
Preparation	Select a wide range of texts that you think will interest your learners and be at an appropriate level for them. These may be a selection of graded readers. However, you could collect texts from elsewhere too. Some could be taken from newspapers, magazines or printed from online sources. The important thing is that the texts will both interest and be appropriate for your learners. The texts need not all be the same length.
	Ensure there are more texts than learners so that there is always a choice. Prepare a simple record sheet so that you know who has borrowed which text. Put the texts into a box and take it to a lesson.

Procedure

1 Tell the learners that the aim of this section of the lesson is that they should all choose one text to read outside class.

2 Place the texts around the room so that learners can move and browse among them.

3 When the learners have chosen a text, they can record their choices.

4 Set a time (for example the following week) when the learners will be expected to report on their progress.

Notes

This can become a regular activity if the learners respond well. Learners can use a self-assessment activity (see Chapter 11: *Assessing reading*) if appropriate.

When selecting the texts, think carefully about what you think may interest your learners. For example, if there is interest in particular brands of clothing, electronic gadgets, or drinks, an online search for the history of those brands will probably produce many results of varying lengths and complexities.

Once the box has been created, it will be a resource you can use on an ongoing basis. You could invite learners to contribute texts and/or suggestions for future inclusion.

Rationale

Many institutions have reading resources for learners to access. However, a fairly common complaint is that learners do not use them! This activity brings the texts to the learners.

It can be useful to have texts of varying levels, as longer texts may be off-putting for some learners at first.

10.3 The first page

Outline	Learners listen to the beginnings of three books and decide which one they would most like to read.
Level	Intermediate and above (B1+)
Time	20 minutes
Focus	Encouraging learners to engage with extensive reading
Preparation	Choose three texts in L2 that you think the learners may want to read. These may be graded readers at the appropriate level, but need not necessarily be. Plan to read for no more than a couple of minutes from each text.

Procedure

1   Explain that the class is going to hear the beginnings of three stories (or other text type that you have chosen).

2   Give the learners the three titles. Show the learners the cover of each book before you read.

3   The learners should listen and rank the books in the order in which they would like to read them.

4   When they have finished, they should discuss their choices in small groups, explaining what they liked (or not) about each one.

5   Encourage learners to borrow the books that they most liked.

Variation

Copy the openings of the three titles and ask learners to read silently and then make their choices.

Rationale

Learners will be more likely to engage with extensive reading if the opportunities and possibilities are presented in class. The task is reasonably realistic, in that we often make choices about which books to read by sampling the opening page or two.

10.4 The readability test

Outline	Learners use a simple self-assessment technique to check if a book is at an appropriate level.
Level	Any
Time	15 minutes
Focus	Ensuring texts chosen for extensive reading are at an appropriate level
Preparation	None

Procedure

1 Learners choose a book or graded reader that they may be interested in reading.

2 Learners open the book randomly somewhere near the middle and choose a stretch of text. They count 100 words of running text, making a note of any words they do not know (excluding proper nouns).

3 Learners calculate the percentage of unknown words in the chosen stretch of text.

4 In open class, discuss the implications of the results with the learners (see *Notes*).

5 In the light of the evidence, learners can change their choice of text and, if they wish, repeat the stages above.

Notes

If learners understand less than 95% of the text, it is likely to be beyond what they can understand comfortably and may not therefore be ideal for extensive reading. This can be discussed with the learners (stage 4, above). However, extensive reading programmes seek to build learners' autonomy, so the final choice of text is probably best left to the learners themselves in most situations.

Rationale

Extensive reading programmes promote the fluent reading of large amounts of text and as such typically make use of texts that are reasonably easy for learners to read. This activity empowers learners to make informed choices about what they read, in terms of selecting texts which are at an appropriate level of difficulty.

10.5 Let's fly to Mars

Outline	Young learners earn points for extensive reading and go on a trip.
Level	Elementary and above (A2+)
Time	5–10 minutes on a regular basis
Focus	Using rewards to promote extensive reading
Preparation	Select and print a picture of Mars and a picture of Earth. Draw (or print out) a picture of a space rocket. Stick the picture of Earth low down on one classroom wall. Stick the picture of Mars high on another. The space rocket starts on Earth.
	Label your extensive reading materials with how many kilometres each is worth. For example, long reading texts could be worth 15 million kilometres, but shorter ones could be worth 10 or 5 million. On average, Mars is approximately 225 million kilometres from Earth, so award more (or fewer) kilometres per read depending on how many days or weeks you want the activity to last.

Procedure

1 Tell the learners that their task is to fly to Mars, as a group. Explain that each time they read a book (or other text) the class will fly more kilometres.

2 Each week (or other convenient period) ask the learners to report what they have read and the kilometres they have earned. Add these together and move the rocket an appropriate (approximate) distance.

3 Involve the learners by asking them when they think the class will arrive at their destination.

4 Have a small celebration in class (such as cakes) when you arrive. And plan your next voyage!

Notes

One variation is that as learners report what they read to you, you encourage them to move the space rocket.

This activity gives points for reading. Any destination can be chosen and you could include other sites to see as you travel. For example, rather than a space trip, you could plan a tour of Europe with different cities to see on the way.

Rationale

The idea of awarding points for reading can be controversial because it implies that reading is not a reward in itself. However, some learners find such external motivation helpful.

Where learning the L2 is part of a broader curriculum, this activity could be integrated with other subjects. As described here it could complement maths and also science as there is potential to discuss the solar system and other planets. If the scenario of a trip around the world (rather than to Mars), for example, were used, the activity could support geography.

10.6 Reading log

Outline	Learners record and comment on their reading in a shared online space.
Level	Intermediate and above (B1+)
Time	30 minutes in the first class and then open-ended
Focus	Encouraging extensive reading through seeing what peers read
Preparation	Set up a shared online space. This could be in the form of a blog or something as simple as a Google Doc. Allow space for brief summaries and comments.

Procedure

1   Show the learners the document. Explain that they can record their L2 reading on it. They start by writing the title of what they read, saying what type of text it is, e.g. a ghost story, and finally they provide a brief evaluation.

2   Explain that if other learners read the same text, they should add their own comments/evaluation.

3   If possible, ask all learners to make one entry during the first class.

4   Encourage learners to read the document regularly as they may find useful recommendations of what to read.

5   Monitor the document entries as appropriate.

Notes

You may like to start by providing a model entry based on something you have read so that the learners have a model to follow.

Learners can also upload short videos of themselves reviewing their chosen books.

Rationale

The activity creates an opportunity for learners to record their reading. It also allows learners to see what their peers are doing and this may foster motivation to read. The activity also provides communicative writing practice.

10.7 But would it be a good film?

Outline	Learners discuss whether the books they are reading would make good films.
Level	Intermediate and above (B1+)
Time	30 minutes
Focus	Promoting extensive reading through the discussion of books
Preparation	None

Procedure

1 Lead in to the lesson by asking learners to describe some of their favourite films, actors, and the last film they saw.

2 Tell the learners that they should imagine that they are part of a focus group to decide if they think that the book they are reading in L2 should be made into a film. Put the learners into small groups. Within the group, each learner should describe the book they are reading and whether they think it would make a good film.

3 Monitor carefully. When the learners have finished, invite three or four people to describe their book and give their opinions to the class.

4 The class can vote on which film they would most like to see.

Notes

If there are learners in the group who are not reading a book (or have not read one recently) they could be given a role solely as part of a panel which has to decide which book would make the best film, as there is only enough budget to make one.

See also Activities 5.1: *Questions, questions, questions* and 5.3: *Ask the author*.

Rationale

The task is essentially one of describing the plot to others and giving opinions. The vote provides an outcome and to some extent an element of competition.

10.8 Casting the film version

Outline	Learners discuss which actors would be appropriate to play characters in the books that they are reading.
Level	Upper intermediate and above (B2+)
Time	15 minutes
Focus	Promoting extensive reading through the discussion of books
Preparation	Have ready a selection of pictures of well-known actors to prompt learners if necessary.

Procedure

1 Ask learners who their favourite actors are. If necessary, be prepared to prompt using pictures of well-known actors.

2 Give learners time to prepare a brief summary of the plot of a story that they have read in the target language. When this has been done, ask them to prepare more detailed summaries of the main characters.

3 Learners share what they have done in small groups.

4 Tell the learners to imagine that film versions of the book are going to be made. Learners work together in their groups to make casting suggestions for the different stories that they have summarized.

5 After an appropriate length of time, learners report back what they have discussed.

Notes

You may like to give an example before the learners start by summarizing a book, focusing on the characters and explaining who you think would be good actors to play the various parts in the films. In this case it would be a good idea to have pictures of the actors that you suggest, in case the learners do not know them.

   See also Activity 5.11: *Watch and read*.

Rationale

This activity gives a meaningful purpose for the learners to summarize and comment on books they have read.

10.9 Writing the script

Outline	The learners write dialogue for a scene from a book.
Level	Intermediate and above (B1+)
Time	45 minutes
Focus	Promoting extensive reading through the discussion of a key scene
Preparation	Select a film that you like and have access to. Select a key scene that you like. Be prepared to say why you like it and why it is important to the story.

Procedure

1 Show the scene you selected. Explain why you like it.

2 Ask learners to think about the book they are reading in L2 and to identify a key scene within it. When they have had time to prepare, divide the class into small groups.

3 Each learner should describe the scene they chose and why it is important in the story.

4 Monitor carefully. When the learners have finished, invite three or four people to describe and explain their book and key scene to the class.

5 Select one scene (or let the learners vote for one) and invite more questions about the characters and the situation so that learners have plenty of information.

6 Put the learners into pairs to write the dialogue for the scene described. While they do this, they can ask the 'expert' (the learner who is reading the book) further questions if they need to. Rather than taking part in the writing, this learner could monitor groups, along with the teacher.

7 When they have finished, invite some learners to read their dialogues.

Variation

As an alternative ending to the lesson, you could display the dialogues and discuss the similarities and differences between them.

Rationale

The task involves describing a key scene to others. The interest taken in what learners are reading is likely to promote further reading.

10.10 Don't judge a book by its cover

Outline	Learners design a book cover.
Level	Any
Time	45 minutes
Focus	Promoting extensive reading through the discussion of books
Preparation	Select a few books that have striking covers that can be discussed with the class.

Procedure

1   Show the learners one of the selected covers. Elicit suggestions about the genre, characters, setting, or anything else that is suggested by the design. In pairs, learners make similar predictions for another cover. If appropriate, these predictions can be checked by reading the blurb on the back of the book.

2   Put the learners into pairs. Ask them to describe the book they are reading in L2 (or one they have recently read) in as much detail as possible. The description should include a brief outline of the plot, the main characters and the genre. They should also include the title and the name of the author.

3   Explain the phrase 'don't judge a book by its cover' and how in English it is used metaphorically to mean 'don't judge the value of something by its appearance'. However, book covers are actually a key way of attracting a potential reader's interest. Explain that they do so through using carefully selected images (photos or illustrations) to create a particular mood and expectation. The positioning of the author's name is also important, and if they are well known it is likely to be very prominent.

4   Each learner should now design a cover for their partner's book, based on the description they were given.

5   Once you have outlined the task, you may want to allow a few more moments of interaction for the 'designers' to clarify any more information that they need.

6   Allow time for the learners to design the covers.

7   When they have finished, they could compare their efforts with the original design.

8   Encourage learners to discuss what they were trying to capture in their designs.

Notes

If time is short, the actual designing of the cover could be set for homework.

   The activity works well if learners have access to computers so that they can experiment with fonts and import images.

   At very low levels the discussion could take place in L1. The aim of this particular activity is to encourage learners to be enthusiastic about reading.

Rationale

The task promotes extensive reading through valuing that reading and asking learners to summarize, comment and so on.

10.11 Retell it

Outline	Learners give, listen to, and retell summaries of books.
Level	Intermediate and above (B1+)
Time	30 minutes
Focus	Promoting extensive reading through the summarizing of stories
Preparation	Choose a book that you like and prepare answers to the questions set out below.

Procedure

1 Ask the learners to answer the following questions individually about a book that they have recently read in L2:
   - *What is the title?*
   - *Where is it set?*
   - *When is it set?*
   - *Who are the main characters?*
   - *What happens in the story?*
   - *Would you recommend this book to other people?*

2 When the learners have finished, give your own summary and evaluation of a book you have read (see *Preparation*). Do not read out the answer to each question, but use the information from the questions to frame a reasonably natural piece of discourse. Encourage learners to ask questions both to ask for clarification and to elicit more detail.

3 When the learners are ready, put them into pairs and ask them to talk about their respective books in a similar way. Again, encourage questions.

4 When they have finished, ask them to stand up and find a new partner. They should now give the account of the book that they have heard (not the one they produced themselves).

5 When the learners have finished, ask them to sit down and invite individuals to talk about the last book they heard about.

6 Invite the original reader of the book to comment on the accuracy of the summary and anything important that was omitted (or, indeed, added).

Notes

If time is short, you could ask learners to prepare their summaries before the lesson for homework.

If you think that the activity would be useful and enjoyable for most of the class but are put off because one or two people may not engage with reading in L2, those learners could be allowed to discuss an L1 book. If this is still problematic, they could talk about a film.

Rationale

The teacher can be an important role model in demonstrating good reading habits and this gives an opportunity for the teacher to convey this to the learners.

The preparation time (when thinking about the questions) gives learners the opportunity to think about what they say, which will result in more accurate, fluent and complex language production, according to research (e.g. Skehan, 1998).

Reference

Skehan, P. (1998) *A Cognitive Approach to Language Learning*, Oxford: Oxford University Press.

10.12 The shortlist

Outline	Learners try to persuade others that a book that they like is worth reading.
Level	Intermediate and above (B1+)
Time	30 minutes
Focus	Encouraging extensive reading through listening to peers talk about their own reading
Preparation	Ask the learners to prepare a short promotional pitch for a book (or other text) that they have enjoyed reading in L2. Explain that they should try to convince everybody else that it would be a good idea to read the book/text.

Procedure

1 Explain that the class are all members of a reading club. They must select a book or text to read for the next meeting of the club. The suggestions they will hear are the shortlist from which to choose.

2 Select three or four learners to give their pitches.

3 After each pitch allow the class to ask further questions.

4 Ask the class to vote for a winner. If you feel that this might embarrass a learner who got very few votes, have a secret ballot and simply announce a winner.

5 Encourage the learners to read the text that was voted for.

Variation

Ask learners to describe the worst book they have read and explain why they did not enjoy it. Other learners could then vote for the presentation they found most convincing.

Rationale

Learners can motivate each other to read by being enthusiastic about what they have read. The task allows learners the opportunity to show their peers that they have enjoyed reading.

10.13 Pictures of my reading

Outline	Learners keep a photo diary of what they have read.
Level	Any
Time	15 minutes for stages 1 and 2 and then 5–10 minutes per person for stage 3
Focus	Noticing the variety of texts that can be engaged with
Preparation	Over the space of a day or two, the teacher takes photographs of what they read in the target language. This may include the cover of a book, but also billboards, shop signs, magazine covers, digital texts, graffiti, and much more besides.

Procedure

1 Show the class the pictures that you have taken and comment on each. Say where you were when you saw it, whether you liked it, whether it made you laugh and so on.

2 Explain to the learners that you want them to keep a similar photo diary of what they read in the target language.

3 At regular intervals (for example, each lesson, or each couple of lessons), invite one or two learners to present their photos to the class, commenting as they go. This will work best if you give the learners a little notice of when they will present so that they can prepare.

Notes

The activity relies on learners having a mobile phone with a camera and also a classroom in which they can project the images.

The activity may promote questions from learners about the meaning of the language they have photographed and so the teacher needs to be ready to answer such questions.

At very low levels learners may prefer to present their diaries in L1, or in a combination of L1 and L2.

Rationale

The activity encourages learners to notice the target language they see around them and to engage with it. This helps learners to make the most of the opportunities that exposure to text outside the classroom gives them in developing reading skills. The activity is a productive way of filling a few spare minutes in a lesson, or can be used to change the mood of a lesson.

11 Assessing reading

Assessment and testing

Assessment and testing are far from synonymous. Assessment is the gathering of data on the progress and performance of a learner (or group of learners) and this data could come from a variety of sources, including informal activities such as noticing how learners work during classroom tasks. Teachers inevitably assess their learners' abilities and progress on an ongoing basis as they teach, making judgements about which learners are progressing, which are finding things difficult and so on. On the other hand, testing has connotations of objectivity and correct or incorrect responses and tends to be quantitative in nature, with learners' performances given a score. In reality, testing is just one means, a more formal means, of assessing learners.

Although reading often forms part of high-stakes language tests, in the classroom the main aim of assessing reading should be to improve the learners' reading through identifying what they do well and what they find difficult.

Traditional tests of reading

There are many question types that are commonly used in the testing of reading. These include:
- multiple choice questions
- *True/False* questions – a modification of multiple choice questions, but with a single distractor (wrong answer)
- questions requiring a short written answer
- cloze tests, where a word is deleted at regular intervals, such as every seventh word, for learners to supply the missing item
- gap fills, where a word is deleted at irregular intervals, allowing the test writer to decide on where to place gaps
- using information from a text to complete a table, chart, or diagram
- putting sentences or paragraphs into a correct sequence
- inserting sentences or paragraphs into a text
- correcting errors in a text.

Some of these techniques test reading in isolation (such as multiple choice questions) and some require other skills and knowledge to be used alongside reading skills (such as when learners write a short answer). Each test type has its own advantages and disadvantages and a discussion of these can be found in Alderson (2000). Research (e.g. Francis et al, 2006, cited in Geva and Ramírez, 2015) has shown that different test types can give different indications about an individual learner's reading ability. This is perhaps not surprising given that different test formats test slightly different aspects of reading. Therefore in high-stakes tests it is important to use a range of reading tasks so that a rounded picture of ability emerges.

The test types listed above are probably very familiar to most readers and we will move on to consider alternative forms of assessment.

Assessment

Even where teachers choose, or are obliged, to use formal tests at points in a course, they can still adopt alternative assessment practices to run alongside those tests. The different forms of assessment can then be used in whatever combinations best suit the needs of the particular learners being taught.

As assessment can take the form of careful observation of how a learner engages with a task, most of the activities in this book could, in theory, be used for assessment purposes. In this sense, assessment can be very unobtrusive in the classroom, with learners unaware of it happening. However, the activities we will outline in this chapter have a particular and explicit focus on assessment.

As a general principle, when we are assessing learners' reading abilities we should endeavour to use texts that are, wherever possible, aligned to the types of text that learners will deal with outside the classroom. This allows us to draw more accurate conclusions about how successfully a learner will deal with reading texts in 'real life' situations. In reality, of course, this can be problematic. For example, primary level learners may not come into contact with texts outside the classroom, or if they do, the texts may be more complex than a primary level learner can realistically engage with.

As well as using realistic texts where possible, we should also try to set realistic tasks, so that learners read and use the text in ways that mirror life outside the classroom. Clearly, some of the test types listed above are very far removed from any kind of real world task.

Another consideration in assessment is to ask *Who does the assessing?*. In traditional high-stakes tests, this is done by an external body, such as an exam board. In less formal situations, the responsibility for assessment usually falls to the teacher but there are alternatives to this. After all, if we believe in learner-centred learning and teaching then it makes sense to consider the extent to which learners can be involved in their own assessment. This may take the form of self-assessment and/or peer assessment. One of the great advantages of using learners in making assessment judgements is that it almost inevitably increases their awareness of the aims of the course because they engage with learning outcomes and assessment criteria (Douglas, 2010). This may help them appreciate their own strengths and weaknesses, which may in turn help them to set realistic goals for themselves (Chapelle and Brindley, 2010). In addition, as with any form of autonomy, there may be enhancements in motivation as learners take more responsibility for their own learning (Ryan and Deci, 2000). This chapter aims to give teachers a series of practical activities to assess learners' reading abilities.

References

Alderson, J.C. (2000) *Assessing Reading*, Cambridge: Cambridge University Press.

Chapelle, C. and Brindley, G. (2010) 'Assessment' in N. Schmitt (ed.) *An Introduction to Applied Linguistics* (2nd ed.), pp. 247–267, Abingdon: Taylor & Francis.

Douglas, D. (2010) *Understanding Language Testing*, Abingdon: Taylor & Francis.

Francis, D., Rivera, M., Lesaux, N., Kieffer, M. and Rivera, H. (2006) *Practical guidelines for the education of English language learners: Research-based recommendations for instruction and academic interventions*, Portsmouth, NH: U.S. Department of Education. Available online at: http://www.centeroninstruction.org/files/ELL1-Interventions.pdf. [Last accessed 5 August 2017]

Geva, E. and Ramírez, G. (2015) *Focus on Reading*, Oxford: Oxford University Press.

Ryan, S. and Deci, E. (2000) 'Self-determination theory and the facilitation of intrinsic motivation, social development, and well-being', *American Psychologist*, 55(1), pp. 68–78.

11.1 Ten texts

Outline	Learners read a range of texts in preparation for a test.
Level	Any
Time	5–50 minutes for the test, depending on the test used, and open-ended for the preparation
Focus	Encouraging learners to read widely
Preparation	Choose ten texts that are of similar difficulty and are appropriate for your learners. Write an appropriate task (or tasks) for one of the texts and put the text and task(s) into the test.

Procedure

1   Explain to the learners that one of the texts will be used in an upcoming test (such as an end of term/year test). So, one of the ten texts will be in the test but the learners do not know which one.

2   Make all the texts available to the learners well in advance of the test. They should read them at regular intervals so that they are prepared for the upcoming test.

3   Learners complete the test.

Notes

The number of texts used can be adjusted to suit the teaching context.

As with all assessment, the learners should be familiar with the types of question/task that accompany the text.

Rationale

One argument for regular assessment is that it can have a motivating effect on learners. This activity harnesses the natural desire to do well in the assessment to encourage learners to engage with reading.

I learned this technique from Will Forsyth.

11.2 Reading to write

Outline	Learners select relevant information from texts to complete a written task.
Level	Intermediate and above (B1+)
Time	10 minutes for stages 1–3 and then dependent on the texts and task set
Focus	Combining reading with writing
Preparation	The learners will select information from texts to complete a written task. For example, learners studying language for business purposes could be asked to write about the benefits and risks attached to the potential merger of two companies, and be given a profile of each company with which to work. Set a clear written task that can be achieved through using the chosen texts.

Procedure

1 Explain the task carefully to the learners.

2 Explain how they will be assessed (see *Notes*).

3 Give each learner a copy of the texts they will use.

4 Allow sufficient time for the task to be completed successfully.

Notes

The reading of multiple texts, combined with writing, makes this a demanding task. Therefore it is most likely to be effective with higher-level learners.

Texts can quite easily be found from different sources reporting on the same event or phenomenon.

This task also works well with EAP classes, where texts can be sourced quite easily based on subject discipline. In EAP contexts learners particularly need to select, prioritize and synthesize information.

If learners are to receive a score for their work, careful thought needs to be given as to how marks should be distributed between the reading phase (being able to select appropriate information and seeing which points are most important) and the written aspect of the work.

Rationale

We often read for a particular purpose and this task replicates that. Learners may be motivated by the 'real world' nature of the task (unlike traditional reading tests).

11.3 Free recall

Outline	Learners recall what they remember from a text.
Level	Any
Time	5–20 minutes, depending on the text used
Focus	Recalling information from a text
Preparation	Choose a text that is appropriate for your learners and if necessary, make copies for the learners, although a coursebook text could be used.

Procedure

1 Ask the learners to read the selected text within a given time limit.

2 At the end of the time limit, take the text away from the learners.

3 Ask the learners to write what they remember from the text. This could be done in L1, particularly at low levels.

4 In assessing the learners' achievement, credit should be given both for the quantity of what is remembered and also the prioritizing of essential information.

Variation

If time allows, an alternative to this procedure is to interview learners about the text. This would allow the teacher/assessor to prompt and support where necessary. Again, this could be done in L1.

Notes

The sooner the recall takes place after the reading, the less burden it places on memory. You could allow learners a short time to make notes before removing the text.

Rationale

Some research suggests that free recall assessments can shed light on the causes of misinterpretation of texts. By removing the text, learners are forced to use what they have understood (and can remember), rather than being able to disguise a lack of understanding by copying sections of text that have only been partially understood. In addition, in recall situations proficient readers tend to prioritize the most important information over any that is less relevant.

11.4 Portfolios

Outline	Learners create a portfolio, detailing their reading.
Level	Any
Time	10 minutes for stages 1–3 and then open-ended
Focus	Encouraging extensive reading
Preparation	Ensure that your learners have a plentiful supply of texts. The texts could be online, in the form of graded readers, or from some other source. They need not be all of the same type. Devise a simple grading system to indicate the relative difficulty of the texts if they are not already labelled in some way. This could be a simple numerical system based on your quick impressions.
	Decide how many texts you expect learners to read in a given time period. If the texts are of very different lengths you may prefer to express this in terms of how much time you expect learners to devote to reading.
	Make enough copies of the reading portfolio sheet for every learner (see opposite).

Procedure

1 Tell the learners the number of texts they are expected to read in a given period (or the amount of time they should spend). You may wish to dedicate some class time to reading at first but most of the reading can be done outside class time.

2 Each time a learner completes a text they should fill out a reading portfolio sheet and file it as part of their reading portfolio. The one opposite can be used or adapted for your learners.

3 Explain to learners that if they choose a text that is too difficult for them, they can change it for one graded at a lower level.

4 Check each learner's portfolio at regular intervals. Where possible, use it as a basis to discuss each person's development as a reader.

Notes

If you determine text difficulty yourself, be prepared to re-grade texts based on learner feedback of difficulty. For example, if learners routinely regard a particular text as 'difficult' for the level, you may wish to alter its grading.

If the completion of the portfolio sheet is likely to be off-putting to learners, it could be translated into L1.

Rationale

There is a lot of research evidence that shows the benefits of extensive reading and this assessment type is designed to encourage that. Learners are not tested on the texts they read but are assessed on their engagement with the programme.

▶ *Reading portfolio sheet*

My reading portfolio

Title of text: _____

Grade of difficulty: _____

How easy or difficult did you personally find this to read?

very easy _____ *very difficult*

Date completed:

What I liked about the text:

_____

_____

_____

What I didn't like about the text:

_____

_____

_____

I would like to read other similar texts: *Yes/No*

Circle the words that you would use to describe this text. Circle as many as you wish.

This text was *funny / boring / interesting / useful / informative.*

This text made me feel *angry / excited / enthusiastic / sad / hopeful.*

Are there any other words you would use to describe this text or your feelings towards it?

_____

_____

_____

From *Teaching and Developing Reading Skills* © Cambridge University Press 2017   PHOTOCOPIABLE

11.5 That text was …

Outline	Learners assess their own reading of a text.
Level	Any
Time	10 minutes post-reading
Focus	Developing learner autonomy through self-assessment
Preparation	Choose a text and task that is appropriate for the learners. This activity can be used immediately after a standard reading lesson. Make copies of the assessment form for each learner (see *Example*).

Procedure

1 After reading, ask learners to complete the form opposite, or one similar. Take time to explain the form, as necessary.

2 If appropriate, learners could share their assessments. However, it may be that some learners would rather not discuss how they did, particularly if they find it difficult.

3 Collect the self-assessment sheets so that you can see how each learner views their own progress.

4 After the lesson, comment on the self-assessment sheets as necessary. Return them to the learners.

Example
The self-assessment sheet opposite may be copied or adapted for your learners. It may be translated into L1 if necessary.

Notes
Learners could complete a form such as this after each reading they do.

Rationale
The activity is designed to promote self-assessment. Self-assessment is part of developing learner autonomy, which in turn can lead to increased motivation. The teacher can use the information to guide future teaching and support for individuals.

▶ *Self-assessment sheet*

That text was …

Title _____

I enjoyed reading the text.	agree _____	disagree
I understood the text.	agree _____	disagree
I could read the text quickly.	agree _____	disagree
The text was interesting.	agree _____	disagree
I knew most of the words in the text.	agree _____	disagree
I'd like to read similar texts.	agree _____	disagree

I learned the following words: and phrases

Teacher's comments:

From *Teaching and Developing Reading Skills* © Cambridge University Press 2017   PHOTOCOPIABLE

11.6 Reading ladder

Outline	Learners assess their own reading ability by considering 'can do' statements.
Level	Any
Time	10 minutes
Focus	Promoting learner autonomy through self-assessment
Preparation	Copy the reading ladder opposite, or develop one that is more appropriate for your learners.

Procedure

1   Explain the 'can do' descriptors on the ladder.

2   Ask learners to tick the things they think they can do.

3   If possible, try to spend time with each learner to discuss their decisions and how they can move up the ladder.

Notes

It is a good idea to return to the activity regularly during the course so that you and the learners can monitor progress.

You may wish to add detail for the level of learners you are teaching. For example, the highest parts of the ladder given below will be irrelevant to very low level learners, and it may be better to include more specific descriptors for that level, such as *I can recognize letters and letter combinations when they are written down.*

Clearly, at least at low levels, the descriptors on the ladder will need to be translated for learners.

Rationale

The activity promotes self-assessment and focuses on what learners can already do, rather than on what they cannot do. Self-assessment is part of developing learner autonomy, which in turn can lead to increased motivation.

▶ *Reading ladder*

The reading ladder

Start at the bottom of the ladder. Tick the things that you can do.

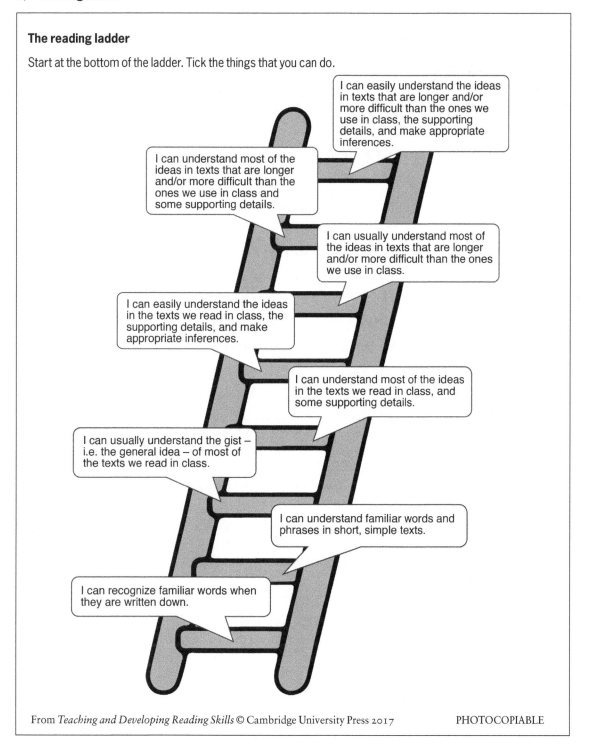

I can easily understand the ideas in texts that are longer and/or more difficult than the ones we use in class, the supporting details, and make appropriate inferences.

I can understand most of the ideas in texts that are longer and/or more difficult than the ones we use in class and some supporting details.

I can usually understand most of the ideas in texts that are longer and/or more difficult than the ones we use in class.

I can easily understand the ideas in the texts we read in class, the supporting details, and make appropriate inferences.

I can understand most of the ideas in the texts we read in class, and some supporting details.

I can usually understand the gist – i.e. the general idea – of most of the texts we read in class.

I can understand familiar words and phrases in short, simple texts.

I can recognize familiar words when they are written down.

From *Teaching and Developing Reading Skills* © Cambridge University Press 2017   PHOTOCOPIABLE

11.7 Learners as testers

Outline	Learners write questions for each other.
Level	Intermediate and above (B1+)
Time	45 minutes
Focus	Promoting learner-centred assessment
Preparation	Choose at least two texts that you think are suitable for your class and make enough copies for each learner to have one text.

Procedure

1   Divide the class into two groups (or as many groups as you have texts).

2   Give one text to each group.

3   Learners should take some time to read the text and then work together in their group to write questions about the text.

4   When they have finished, pair learners so that they are working with someone from a different group.

5   Learners swap texts and questions.

6   Give learners time to read the text they are given and answer the questions.

7   When the learners are ready, they should compare the answers they have written with the answers the test writer was expecting.

Variation

Learners interview each other in pairs about topics they are each interested in. They then find a text that they think will appeal to their partner and write questions based on that text.

Notes

You can support the process of writing the questions by reminding learners of examples of question types.

Rationale

Peer assessment, on which this draws, can promote a learner-centred environment and foster group cohesion when done sensitively.

11.8 Product and process assessment

Outline	Learners are assessed on both the product and the process of their reading.
Level	Any
Time	Around 30 minutes, depending on the text used
Focus	Assessing the process of reading
Preparation	Choose a text that is appropriate for your learners. Set some standard comprehension questions to go with the text (see the introduction to this chapter for ideas). Ensure the text has plenty of space around it so that learners can annotate it. If this is not possible (for example, if the text is part of a coursebook), supply additional paper.

Procedure

1   Explain to the learners that they going to do a reading assessment. 50% of the marks will come from the answers to the comprehension questions. The other 50% of the marks will come from the annotations that they put on the text. For low-level learners these could be written in L1.

2   Ensure the class are familiar with the sorts of annotations they could add (see *Example*).

3   The learners complete the assessment.

4   After the assessment, mark the work, taking note of the strategies that learners have used. Give feedback to the entire class, sharing good practice.

Example

This is not an exhaustive list, but learners could:

*   comment on pictures accompanying the text (*This looks as if the story is set in the past.*)
*   comment on headlines / titles / subheadings (*It seems this story will be about …*)
*   list their predictions about the text, or subsections of the text
*   comment on the accuracy of those predictions
*   write summaries of sections to build comprehension as they go
*   indicate key words that they have looked up in a dictionary or translating device
*   indicate sections they translated into L1
*   indicate words they have guessed the meaning of (perhaps with an indication of how they arrived at their guess)
*   indicate sections that were difficult and what they did as a result (e.g. reread, or used a dictionary)
*   indicate sections that they cannot fit into their developing understanding of the text – the parts they therefore don't understand
*   indicate sections that fit in with their background knowledge (i.e. confirm that knowledge) and parts that they find surprising or that contradict existing knowledge.

Notes

A text that the learners find quite challenging is likely to allow more opportunities for learners to consciously consider how they can deal with difficulties.

The product part of the assessment will be easy to mark as there will be 'correct' answers. The process part will be far more challenging for the assessor as it will be subjective to some extent. It is useful to work out some criteria in advance (perhaps based on the number of strategies/processes used, along with their appropriacy). This is not intended as a high-stakes assessment (i.e. one that has a great influence on a learner's future) so an impressionistic mark is perfectly justifiable. However, it is useful to discuss the criteria with the learners beforehand. You could, for example, show annotated texts from another class, explaining why some got higher scores than others.

Rationale

Reading assessment is almost always based on the product of reading (correct answers to comprehension questions) rather than the process of reading (focusing on how learners can improve). This activity gives equal weighting to the process of reading and therefore provides positive washback in the assessment process (i.e. the assessment process has a positive impact on teaching procedures).

11.9 One-to-one reading assessment

Outline	Learners read aloud to their teacher, discussing their reading strategies as they do so.
Level	Any
Time	10–15 minutes, depending on the texts used
Focus	Reading in a one-to-one situation
Preparation	Select a text (or range of texts) appropriate for the learners.

Procedure

1   Give each learner the chance to read the selected text silently by themselves.

2   Have each learner read to you on a one-to-one basis. As well as listening to the learner, try to create a conversation about the reading.

3   If a reader is having difficulty, help them by using questions (see *Example*).

4   At the end of the session, praise and encourage, while also outlining ways in which the reader could continue to improve.

Example

It is important to focus on the process of reading as much as possible. This can be done though using prompts such as:

- *What does this picture suggest about the text?*
- *What sort of text do you think this might be?*
- *What does the headline/title suggest?*
- *Can you summarize that section (you have just read)?*
- *Are there parts that were difficult to understand? Would you like to reread any of the text?*
- *Before we go on, what do you think will happen next? What makes you think that?*
- *Do you understand this word? If you look at these other words, can you work out what it might mean?*

Notes

When learners read to teachers, it can often be little more than a test of pronunciation. Reassure learners that this is not the case in this instance. Tell them you want to understand more about how they read the text.

Clearly, one-to-one teaching is very demanding in terms of time. Other learners will need to be doing something productive during this time and it may only be possible to schedule the individual meetings outside class time or with the help of a teaching assistant.

Rationale

This activity draws on the sort of processes proposed by advocates of reading recovery programmes. The teacher intervenes and supports the reading process, potentially guiding learners to using appropriate strategies. For example, if a summary is inaccurate, the teacher could prompt the learner to reread a section, or find a word in a dictionary. This support by a more skilled other person clearly draws on sociocultural learning theory. The activity does not test the learner as much as it provides the chance for the learner to achieve more in their reading than they would be able to on their own. The teacher meanwhile gathers a lot of data on the reading ability of each learner.

12 Developing expertise in the teaching of reading

Expertise in language teaching

There is no clear definition of what being 'expert' in language teaching might involve. Indeed, given the varied nature of language teaching contexts, it is unlikely that any single definition is possible (Tsui, 2009). However, there is general agreement that one characteristic of expert teachers is that they are more likely to be flexible when teaching and be more prepared to divert from their original plans. This is probably the result of having more options at their fingertips that they feel comfortable switching to. In the case of teaching reading, this might take the form of having more ideas of how to exploit a text, or more options for providing learners with support if the text proves difficult, for example.

Becoming expert

We should not assume that all experienced teachers become expert. Tsui suggests that in order for teachers to convert experience into expertise, they need to continually relate their practical classroom experience to the supporting theory, generated by research. So, in the case of teaching reading, teachers would need to reflect on what happens during reading lessons and relate that to the literature on reading and how people learn to read. See the introductory chapter for a brief overview of this and works such as Grabe (2009), and Grabe and Stoller (2011) for much fuller accounts.

It also seems that expert teachers are more prepared to experiment in their practice, rather than rely on previously learned routines. Experts continually question their own practice and positively look for ways to do things better. Moreover, they are more likely to be able to make appropriate selections from their repertoire of options for the context in which they are operating. This is in line with seeing teacher learning as a process of construction, with a teacher as an independent decision maker, rather than an operator of a system dictated by others, as is the case if a teacher is given strict guidance on both what and how to teach.

We could perhaps also add that those teachers who are recognized as 'expert' are not just prepared to invest in their own learning but are also prepared to share their understandings and practice with others.

Sources of knowledge

There are two principal sources of knowledge, which can each be further subdivided. The first is accessing the knowledge that has been generated by others. This would include such things as reading about the subject in question (in this case, the teaching of reading), attending conferences, or following webinars. Through engaging with these activities we learn from the insights of other practitioners and researchers.

The second source of knowledge is generated personally by the teacher, and as such is likely to be a knowledge based on practice, situated in the context in which it occurs. One common model of learning often recommended to teachers is that of reflective practice (e.g. Farrell, 2007), which is also incorporated into other forms of teacher learning, such as action research. In the case of action research, a teacher (or often a group of teachers) will develop a plan (based on reading or some other form of evidence) to improve the practice currently in place. The plan is implemented and evidence is gathered about its impacts. This leads to further reflection and potentially another cycle of planning and action. It is easy to see how this model fits Tsui's (above) view that practical knowledge should be integrated with current theory. The 'action' of changing some aspect of teaching is informed by 'research', in the form of relevant reading.

Teacher development need not be a solitary process. There is good reason to believe it can be most effective when undertaken collaboratively with supportive colleagues (Osterman and Kottkamp, 1993). Not only can fellow teachers prove a useful source of information, they can contribute to the co-construction of ideas. Another source of information that teachers can exploit is the learners they work with. Understanding more about their motivations and strategies can lead to more appropriate teaching practices. Finally, we should remember that teaching is often mediated by materials of some sort (which will of course always be the case with reading) and so holding those materials up to critical analysis and investigating the extent to which they meet the needs of particular learners is also a hugely valuable exercise in developing our practice.

The activities that follow in this chapter aim to support the learning of teachers and the development of expertise in the teaching of reading. They draw on the sources of learning, outlined above.

References

Farrell, T. S. C. (2007) *Reflective Language Teaching: From Research to Practice*, London: Continuum.

Grabe, W. (2009) *Reading in a Second Language: Moving from Theory to Practice*, New York: Cambridge University Press.

Grabe, W. and Stoller, F. (2011) *Teaching and Researching Reading* (2nd ed.), Abingdon: Taylor & Francis.

Osterman, K. and Kottkamp, R. (1993) *Reflective Practice for Educators: Improving Schooling Through Professional Development*, Thousand Oaks, California: Corwin Press.

Tsui, A. B. M. (2009) 'Teaching expertise: Approaches, perspectives and characterizations' in A. Burns and J. C. Richards (eds.) *The Cambridge Guide to Second Language Teacher Education*, pp. 190–197, New York: Cambridge University Press.

12.1 Group interviews

Outline	The teacher interviews small groups of learners about their reading abilities and habits.
Level	Any (see *Notes*)
Time	20 minutes per interview approximately
Focus	Understanding what and how learners read
Preparation	Tell the learners that you will interview them about their reading habits in small groups. Plan the questions that you want to ask (see *Example*).

Procedure

The interview

1 Try to ensure that the interviews take place in a relaxed environment. Make clear to the learners that there are no 'right' or 'wrong' answers and that you just want to understand more about their reading habits.

2 The interviews could take place in either L1 or L2.

3 With the permission of the learners, record the interviews so that you can listen again later.

After the interview

4 If the interview was recorded, listen again to the interview and pick out the key things that you learned. These may relate to what learners read, what they want to read in the future, the time they devote to reading in L2, or the strategies they use when reading.

5 From the information you have gathered, think through any changes you could make to your teaching, and the teaching of reading in particular.

Example

The following are examples of interview questions that could be used or adapted for your learners:

* *How much do you read in L1? Do you enjoy reading? What sort of texts do you read?*
* *How much of your reading is done online?*
* *What about L2 reading? How much do you read?*
* *Outside the classroom, do you think it is better to read texts that are quite easy to understand, or quite difficult?*
* *What sort of texts do you read now in L2? And what sort of texts will you need (or want) to read in the future? What sort of texts do you enjoy reading?*
* *Do you enjoy reading in the classroom? Do you find it useful? Do you think it is necessary?*
* *What do you do when you have difficulty understanding a text? Do you always use the same strategies or do you have different strategies depending on the situation?*
* *When you read a text outside the classroom, do you try to guess what it will be about before you start? Do you go back and reread difficult sections? Do you study the text and try to learn grammar and vocabulary from it?*

Notes

The activity could be adapted to interview individual learners. The advantage of using small groups is that it is more time-efficient and also a member of the group may challenge the views put forward by another participant. This can be difficult in a one-to-one situation. On the other hand, individual interviews would allow a more detailed understanding of a particular person to emerge.

This activity can also be used as part of an evaluation of a programme, as well as finding out about individual attitudes to reading.

Rationale

We can develop as teachers through developing a greater understanding of our learners, including the approaches they use to learning what they value.

12.2 Action research – reading activities

Outline	Teachers engage in a piece of action research, either individually or with colleagues.
Level	Any
Time	Open-ended
Focus	Researching reading tasks
Preparation	Read as much as possible about the different reading activity types that are frequently used in language teaching and the rationales put forward for them. For example, some task types may integrate reading with other skills, while others may focus solely on reading. Some activities may focus largely on vocabulary (*Find a word which means …*) while others may focus on overall meaning. Some might encourage the learners to express a personal reaction to the text.

Procedure

Plan

1 Use what you have read to evaluate the activities in the material you are using. Could they be made more effective?

2 If so, plan adaptations to the activities, or design different ones for a series of lessons. Keep in mind what you want to achieve through the changes you make. You could focus on just one area, e.g. increasing affective engagement with the texts, or make broader changes.

Act

3 Teach the lessons using the adapted/newly written activities. As you teach, try to observe the effect that the changes have. You may like to invite learners to give feedback on these sections of the lessons, or ask an observer to your lesson so that you get a more objective view.

Plan more

4 In the light of the data you find, consider whether the changes were successful, or if further changes would be beneficial. Be prepared to repeat the cycle of planning and acting.

Reflect

5 Reflect on what you have learned and the process through which you learned it.

6 Consider sharing your findings and the implications of them with other teachers, perhaps through providing a workshop, writing for publication or presenting at a conference.

Notes

One of the biggest barriers to teachers conducting research is the time commitment required. Teachers should be prepared for this before they start the activity.

This activity suggests researching different types of reading activity. However, the same model could be used to investigate other aspects of teaching reading, or indeed teaching more generally. In terms of reading, for example, you could also read about different text types (such as authentic material as opposed to that which is specifically written, or compare fictional and factual texts, or print and online, and so on). The information gained could then inform classroom action, as described above.

As well as reading about activity (or text) types, you could discuss these topics with colleagues to gain their views and insights.

You could work with other teachers on the project so that you gather more data and share ideas.

Rationale

Teachers are often characterized as the consumers of knowledge produced by researchers. However, this type of action research gives teachers the opportunity to produce local, situated research, relevant to their teaching context.

12.3 Analyzing pre-reading tasks

Outline	Teachers analyze the materials they use and specifically the pre-reading tasks.
Level	Any
Time	Open-ended
Focus	Analyzing pre-reading tasks
Preparation	None

Procedure

1 Focusing on the material you use to teach reading, look at a number of texts and identify the pre-reading tasks associated with them.

2 Complete a table (see *Example*) for each text, remembering that a single task may give support in more than one area. You can tick and also add comments, as appropriate.

3 Consider the following questions:
   • Using the data from your tables, do any patterns emerge?
   • Are some types of preparation more prevalent than others?
   • Is the preparation about right for your learners? Or do they need more, or less?

Example

Title of the text	
Number of pre-reading tasks	
Do any of the tasks activate background knowledge of the topic?	
Is background text type knowledge activated?	
Are learners likely to be affectively engaged?	
Is there vocabulary support?	
Is there a clear goal for reading?	
Are learners likely to be motivated to read?	

Notes
A similar technique of analysis could be followed for other lesson stages, such as while-reading tasks, or post-reading tasks.

Rationale

It is very easy for teachers to accept the material presented in the coursebook without much question. However, careful analysis can sometimes reveal productive ways in which the material could be beneficially adapted for particular groups of learners.

12.4 Materials evaluation

Outline	Teachers evaluate the reading materials that they use.
Level	Any
Time	Minimum of 30 minutes
Focus	Evaluating reading material
Preparation	None

Procedure

1 Select the reading materials to be evaluated. These may be the reading component of a coursebook you are using, or going to use. Alternatively, the material may be a collection of texts from other sources.

2 Decide on the criteria you will use for the evaluation (see *Example*). You could add or delete criteria, as appropriate for your purposes.

3 Decide on whether you want to evaluate each reading lesson and text separately, or whether you will come to a general, overall understanding. (Evaluating each separately will give a more precise outcome but is likely to take much longer.)

4 Complete the evaluation.

5 Consider the implications this has for the teaching of reading. Do you need to supplement the texts, or tasks, for example? Do you need to offer more/less support than that already provided for the learners?

Example
The form opposite may be used or adapted for the evaluation of reading materials.

Notes
The criteria given in the example could be used either before the lessons are taught, when the evaluation will be predictive, or after the lesson, when more reliable data will be available (for example, whether the learners actually found the text and tasks easy or difficult).

You may decide that not all the criteria are equally important.

Giving a score for each criterion may appear objective, but in reality the numbers are only a way for the evaluator to see trends and where they may want to focus their attention in adapting the material.

Rationale
The reading material will play a big part in the success or otherwise of the lessons taught. It is therefore entirely appropriate to analyze it. In some contexts there are very limited opportunities to change (or even adapt) the material, but an awareness of strengths and weaknesses can still help a teacher to exploit the material to its maximum potential.

Materials evaluation form

Reading materials evaluation

Give the materials a score of 0–5 for each question below. Make any notes that you think would be useful to explain your reasoning.

1 Are the texts intrinsically interesting?   0 1 2 3 4 5

_____

2 Are the materials at an appropriate level?   0 1 2 3 4 5

_____

3 Are the materials realistic (i.e. are they of recognizable genres and do they have the   0 1 2 3 4 5

    features associated with that genre?)

_____

4 Are the reading tasks realistic (i.e. do they ask learners to use or react to the   0 1 2 3 4 5

    text as they would outside the classroom?)

_____

5 Are the texts and tasks similar to those that your learners do/will encounter   0 1 2 3 4 5

    outside the classroom?

_____

6 Is there an appropriate range of text types?   0 1 2 3 4 5

_____

7 Are the materials presented in an appealing manner?   0 1 2 3 4 5

_____

8 Is there support for the learners before reading?   0 1 2 3 4 5

_____

9 Are there appropriate post reading tasks?   0 1 2 3 4 5

_____

10 Do the materials teach reading strategies?   0 1 2 3 4 5

_____

12.5 Peer observations

Outline	Teachers observe each other teaching reading lessons.
Level	Any
Time	Lesson observation + 30 minutes for pre- and post-lesson discussion
Focus	Understanding practice through observation
Preparation	None

Procedure

1 Work with a fellow teacher you trust and respect. Arrange to observe each other teaching a reading lesson.

2 Before the observations, agree on what you will each look out for. The observer's role should be to gather data, rather than being judgemental (see *Example* for some areas of possible observation).

3 After the observed lesson, arrange a time to meet in order to discuss it. The observer should be supportive and the teacher observed should try to be as open as possible, with a view to learning from the experience.

Example

This is not an exhaustive list of potential observation points. Add or delete as you see fit. It is not designed to be used as a checklist, but as a basis for discussion.

- *Was the text appropriate for the learners? (consider level of difficulty, length, text type etc.)*
- *Was the text interesting to the learners? (perhaps try to plot a graph of learner engagement over time, based on body language and participation)*

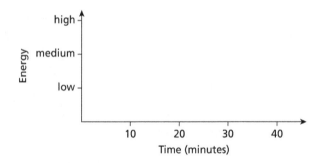

- *How many minutes of the lesson were actually spent with the learners reading? Was the balance successful?*
- *If published material was used, were any changes made? If so, how successful were they? With hindsight, would any changes have been desirable?*
- *Was there a lead-in to the text? What purpose did it serve? (e.g. to build interest, to support with vocabulary)*
- *Were the learners clear on what was expected of them?*
- *What techniques were used when learners' reported back on tasks? (e.g. peer checking, the teacher nominating individuals)*

- *To what extent was the practice of other skills (speaking, listening or writing) embedded in the lesson? What were the advantages of the approach taken?*
- *Was there any additional support for weak readers? Would such support have been possible, useful or desirable?*
- *Was there a focus on reading strategies? Would such a focus have been possible, useful or desirable?*
- *Was the text used as an object of study after initial readings, e.g. was it used to teach grammar or vocabulary? Would such a focus have been possible, useful or desirable?*

Rationale

A teacher is necessarily bound up in the teaching of the lesson as it unfolds. This can make it very difficult to find a critical distance from the lesson and learn as much as possible from it. An observer will be able to devote their full attention to the agreed points, perhaps seeing details that would be hard for a teacher to pick up on.

In this case, both participants get feedback on their teaching and watch another practitioner. There are opportunities to learn about teaching in both roles.

If you can develop expertise in a particular field, it may be that you will be asked to observe the lessons of other teachers. It remains useful to be observed yourself, not least because you remember that observations can feel threatening and judgemental if they are not conducted sensitively.

12.6 Team teaching

Outline	Teachers plan, teach and then discuss a reading lesson together.
Level	Any
Time	The length of the lesson + 30 minutes planning and follow-up discussion
Focus	Understanding the teaching of reading through collaborative practice
Preparation	Work with a colleague and plan a reading lesson together. Try to discuss options as fully as possible and weigh up which ones would work best for the learners concerned. Once the lesson has been planned, decide who will teach each section. One person could teach half the lesson straight through, or you could split the lesson into shorter sections.

Procedure

1 Team teach the lesson. Act as a non-judgemental observer as your partner teaches.

2 Arrange a time to discuss the lesson. Try to be as mutually supportive as possible. Think through the planning decisions that were made and consider any alternatives that with hindsight may have been more effective.

Notes

If the lesson is long and has several different sections, it is not necessary to plan and teach the whole sequence together. You could choose to focus exclusively on the sections that deal with reading.

Rationale

The joint planning means that responsibility is shared for the lesson. Planning usually involves considering options and making principled choices, and therefore gives a very good insight into how someone else views teaching. For that reason, this procedure is very useful with less experienced teachers as it gives an insight into their current state of thinking and allows more experienced colleagues to support them in what they need to focus on to develop.

This is a variation on a lesson observation in that each person will act as teacher and observer in the same lesson. This has the effect of balancing power and reducing the potential for any one person to feel judged.

12.7 Reading group

Outline	A small group of teachers get together to discuss a previously read text.
Level	Any
Time	45 minutes approximately
Focus	Developing understanding and practice through reading and discussion
Preparation	Work with a small group of colleagues. Select a text that deals with the learning and/or the teaching of reading. This could be taken from a teaching manual or be more research-oriented (see *Example*). Distribute the text to members of the group a few days before the meeting.

Procedure

1 Try to structure the discussion in some way, at least at the beginning. This could be achieved by asking questions such as *What did you think about …?*, or *Do you agree with …?*.

2 Try to relate the article and discussion to your learners and teaching context. This can be achieved with questions such as *Is this relevant to our learners?* or *How does this apply to our situation?*.

3 If the discussion proves useful, agree another subject to read about and then discuss at another meeting.

Example

There are many texts that could be used to inform a discussion, with many teaching manuals having specifically designated chapters. Here are some examples of texts that could be used:

Anderson, N. (2012) 'Reading instruction' in A. Burns and J. C. Richards (eds.) *The Cambridge Guide to Pedagogy and Practice in Second Language Teaching*, pp. 218–215, New York: Cambridge University Press.

Carrell, P. and Grabe, W. (2010) 'Reading' in N. Schmitt (ed.) *An Introduction to Applied Linguistics*, pp.215–231, Abingdon: Taylor & Francis.

Paran, A. (2003) 'Intensive reading', *English Teaching Professional*, 28.

Thornbury, S. (1999) *How to Teach Grammar*, Chapter 5, Harlow: Pearson.

Watkins, P. (2011) 'Making the most of it', *English Teaching Professional*, 74.

Williams, R. (1986) '"Top ten" principles for teaching reading', *ELT Journal*, 40(1) pp. 42–45.

Wallace, C. (2001) 'Reading' in R. Carter and D. Nunan (eds.), *The Cambridge Guide to Teaching English to Speakers of Other Languages*, pp. 21–27, Cambridge: Cambridge University Press.

Notes

In order to structure the discussion, Activity 2.1: *Using symbols* could be used.

A discussion group such as this does not have to take place physically but could be done online and with colleagues in other countries. Remember though that the insights from one context may not be directly transferable to learners in a very different context.

Rationale

Reading about teaching and learning is an excellent way to support the process of linking our practical knowledge to theory. Working in a group allows even tentative ideas to be slowly developed and built on. If the group is formed of teachers working in the same context, their ideas will apply to the local, immediate situation in which the teaching takes place.

12.8 Giving a workshop on reading

Outline	Teachers prepare and deliver a workshop on reading for colleagues.
Level	Any
Time	45 minutes
Focus	Sharing good practice
Preparation	Choose some issues related to reading that you think would be relevant to your colleagues. Capture these in simple statements that teachers can discuss (see *Example*). Choose four or five reading activities that you have used and you think may not be familiar to your colleagues. These could come from this book or from some other source. Choose a text that will allow you to demonstrate the reading activities (or at least some of them). Copy the statements and any other materials you need.

Procedure

1 Ask teachers to discuss the statements you have chosen in small groups. Explain any statements if necessary. In an open group, invite the participants to report back on each statement. Be prepared to contribute your own thoughts and observations.

2 When appropriate, introduce the activities. You could choose an appropriate text (such as *M is for Mindset* on page 274) and demonstrate the activities for the teachers.

3 Invite teachers to comment on the activities. You could guide this towards discussing their relevance and usefulness to the learners you teach.

4 In small groups ask the teachers to discuss how they teach reading, e.g. the activity types they find particularly useful, and in particular the needs of the learners in your particular context. Again, invite participants to report back.

Example

The statements chosen could be largely theoretical (example 1), or focus more on practical issues (example 5). You could add a Likert scale to show scale of agreement (as in example 1).

1 L1 reading skills will determine L2 reading proficiency.

   strongly agree   agree   neutral   disagree   strongly disagree

2 The texts we use with learners should be authentic.

3 Reading aloud has no place in the classroom.

4 Learners should always work with texts that challenge them.

5 We cannot really teach reading but we can give practice.

6 Learners find reading lessons boring and they could do the reading at home.

Notes

If you have not given a workshop for colleagues before, it can seem daunting. However, you will almost certainly find that colleagues are both supportive and keen to hear your ideas and share theirs.

Of course, workshops can also be jointly presented and if you work with a colleague the responsibility will be shared.

This is just one possible outline for a workshop. There are many other possibilities that could be explored.

Rationale

Giving a workshop is a great way to support other colleagues because the people attending are likely to teach very similar learners as each other and therefore share similar triumphs and frustrations. This is not only an opportunity to share ideas and learn from each other but also can build camaraderie amongst teaching staff.

Text bank

⬉ An unusual meeting

An unusual meeting

Paris, 1936, and bright lights flickered in the night from the Café des Deux Magots, a popular meeting place for intellectuals and artists. A woman was sitting alone at a table. She was wearing black gloves, embroidered with roses. She spread her left hand on the table.

In her right hand she held a small penknife and repeatedly stabbed it into the table between her fingers. Sometimes she missed and traces of blood could be seen soaking through the gloves and onto the tablecloth.

A man watched her, transfixed. He was unable to take his eyes off the woman. Eventually, he spoke to her, using French. She looked at him, paused, and replied in perfect Spanish before driving the penknife one more time between her spread fingers.

They immediately fell in love and soon began a stormy, passionate relationship. He kept the bloodstained gloves as a reminder of the occasion for the rest of his life.

She was a brilliant woman and successful photographer and he was one of the greatest artists in history. Her name was Dora Maar and his was Picasso.

From *Teaching and Developing Reading Skills* © Cambridge University Press 2017   PHOTOCOPIABLE

▶ It's Time to Accept That Elephants, Like Us, Are Empathetic Beings

It's Time to Accept That Elephants, Like Us, Are Empathetic Beings

Elephants help each other in distress, grieve for their dead, and feel the same emotions as each other – just like us.

An African elephant spends time with a young one at Maasai Mara National Reserve in Kenya

Elephants, we all know, are in peril. We humans are waging what amounts to a war against them because they have something we want and cannot make on our own: ivory.

The West African country of Gabon holds most of Africa's remaining forest elephants. Their main stronghold, Minkebe National Park and its surrounding buffer zone, was home to an estimated 28,500 elephants in 2004. By 2012 the number had plummeted to about 7,000 – a loss of 20,000 or more elephants.

People are shooting, poisoning, and spearing the animals at such a rate across the continent that some scientists already consider them 'ecologically extinct.' There are now fewer than 500,000 wild African elephants – maybe no more than half that number – and barely 32,000 Asian elephants.

They cannot fight against us; they cannot win this battle.

And the horror of what is happening to them is surely compounded in their minds by the empathy they feel for one another – an emotion that scientists have at last been able to demonstrate experimentally in elephants.

Elephant Empathy: One Example After Another

But why did it take an experiment? Research on elephants is full of examples of the animals apparently behaving empathetically – recognizing and responding to another elephant's pain or problem. Often, they even make heroic efforts to assist one another.

In Kenya, researchers have watched mother elephants and other adult females help baby elephants climb up muddy banks and out of holes, find a safe path into a swamp, or break through electrified fences.

Scientists have spotted elephants assisting others that are injured, plucking out tranquilizing darts from their fellows, and spraying dust on others' wounds.

A two-year-old African elephant baby climbs on the back of his mother

And on at least one occasion, researchers have watched an elephant struggle to help a dying friend, lifting her with her tusks and trunk, while calling out in distress.

Aren't such accounts sufficient for scientists to say unequivocally that elephants, like us, are empathetic beings?

Sadly, no. For various reasons – some scientific, some philosophical, some religious, some economic – we have set the bar exceedingly high for recognizing emotions (other than anger and fear) in other animals.

Saying absolutely that elephants (or other animals) are empathetic requires an experiment, something that is difficult to do in the wild. Experiments mean that these are not chance observations – the results are repeatable.

To show that elephants experience the same emotions another is feeling, scientists watched captive Asian elephants in a park in Thailand. They noted when one elephant was upset by something, such as by a snake in the grass, and they recorded her behaviors to see if there was a pattern. There was. In response to a stressful event, an elephant flares out her ears, erects her tail, and sometimes makes a low rumble. Scientists watching elephants in the wild have reported the same behaviors.

Emotional Contagion

Both in the wild and in this captive study, researchers have watched other, nearby elephants react to the other elephant's distress by acting in exactly the same way. Scientists call this 'emotional contagion'.

www.nationalgeographic.com

The elephants also ran to stand beside their friend, touched her with their trunks to soothe her, and made soft chirping sounds. Sometimes one would even put her trunk inside the other's mouth, a behavior elephants find particularly comforting, the researchers say.

We do something very similar when watching a scary movie with a friend. When the main character is threatened, we feel his fear. Our hearts race, we may tremble, and for reassurance, we reach for our friend's hand.

The researchers also recorded what the elephants did when they were in the same locations with their same friends nearby, but nothing stressful occurred. In those moments, none of the elephants acted in an empathetic way.

By comparing the two types of events – stressful versus nonstressful – the scientists were able to say that 'emotional contagion' occurs only when an elephant sees another in distress.

Some scientists may still argue that this is not sufficient evidence for true empathy, that the experiment doesn't reveal what's going on in an elephant's mind when she rushes to aid a friend or worries over a dying companion.

But the fact that elephants make any effort at all on another elephant's behalf suggests that they are at the very least highly aware and emotional beings, concerned in some manner for each other.

Do They Know We're Destroying Them?

We cannot know for certain if African elephants know that they're under attack, that we're wiping them out across the continent. There are few, if any, survivors from most poaching events, and those that do make it can't tell us of their trauma. We'll never know what elephants may have witnessed or heard in the forest while their friends and relatives in other families were being slaughtered.

We have some idea, though, because in South Africa in the late 20th century, wildlife officials authorized the killing of entire elephant families in some fenced parks, such as Kruger. The officials worried that if a fenced elephant population grew too large, the animals would consume all the vegetation – so they culled the elephants.

Somehow, other elephant families in the park knew this was happening. Perhaps it was the cries of terror as the animals were shot. Or perhaps those being killed were able to emit low rumbles that carried the news for miles.

Immediately after a culling operation – and even after rangers cleaned up the area, removing all the bodies – other elephant families would come to the scene. They inspected the ground and smelled the earth, and then the visiting elephants left, never to return.

Observers say that even when the area where a culling took place was good habitat for elephants, the animals chose not to live there.

What happens now where poachers kill elephant families and herds? Do the animals, filled with empathy for what the others suffered, come to investigate the killing fields? Do they abandon those awful precincts forever?

Those studies have yet to be made. But in the meantime, can we put our empathy to use in finding a way to help the elephants? Can we put an end at last to the poaching?

A true story

A true story

It all happened about fifteen years ago when I was in Kenya, staying with a friend of mine from boarding school. Her family ran a lodge in the middle of one of Kenya's national game reserves called the Masai Mara. It's famous for its safaris and was one of the most beautiful places I'd ever seen. The spectacular wildlife, endless views and magical scenery were all just incredible. The holiday was a wonderful experience overall but there is one day that has stuck in my mind for all the wrong reasons.

We were in the grounds of the lodge and it was a lovely day with a clear blue sky and a wonderful warm sun. We were lying on towels on the grass, reading books and dozing – it was blissful. After a couple of hours, I was lying on my front and I was starting to fall asleep when suddenly I felt something crawl over my leg. I was about to brush it away but for some reason I decided not to and instead I turned round to see what it was. I looked round just in time to see a long green creature slither over my leg and go under my towel. I leapt up in a second, shouted and told my friend what had just happened. To my surprise, however, she looked neither shocked nor worried and instead told me calmly that I must have seen a lizard and confused it with a snake. She didn't believe me! She thought I was overreacting, that I was new to her country and didn't know what I was talking about! She thought I just had an overactive imagination! Again, I tried to convince her I had seen a snake and pleaded with her to check under the towel.

She looked bored but finally she picked up a stick and with a sigh went over to the towel to check what was there. Gently, she hooked the stick under the towel and lifted it out of the way. And sure enough, there on the grass, under the towel, was a green snake coiled up. We got a clear view for just a few seconds and then in a flash it shot off into longer grass.

I was quite pleased with myself at this point, satisfied that I had been right and that I had indeed seen a snake. I turned around to my friend to say 'I told you so!' but was surprised by her expression. The calm face from earlier was replaced by a quite different one. 'What is it?' I asked. She was silent and shaking, and then she told me in a quiet voice that the snake that had been under my towel was one of the most poisonous snakes in Africa. One bite and you start to bleed out of your eyes, your mouth, your ears … If you don't get to hospital within a couple of hours, you bleed to death. We were in the middle of the game reserve. There was no hospital or even airstrip anywhere near us. In sum, if it had bitten me, I would have died there in the Lodge.

From *Teaching and Developing Reading Skills* © Cambridge University Press 2017   PHOTOCOPIABLE

M is for mindset

www.learningtoteachenglishblog-m-is-for-mindset

M is for Mindset

The term 'mindset' is most associated with Carol Dweck and it attempts to capture the 'implicit theories' we hold about phenomena such as intelligence and learning. Dweck and her colleagues' research has become increasingly influential in recent years, not least because it has clear relevance to classrooms. The impact has also been enhanced by the accessible writing style adopted in some of her work, such as her 2006 book, which has resulted in a huge readership for her work.

Dweck says that it is possible to see the 'world from two perspectives' (Dweck, Chiu and Hong, 1995). One of those perspectives is characterized as a 'fixed mindset', where we view intelligence and learning ability as something we are born with, something essentially 'fixed' and predetermined. The second perspective is that of the 'growth mindset'. People with this orientation are more likely to think that hard work and perseverance are more important to eventual success than natural ability.

Differences in the two mindset perspectives become most notable when a learner is faced with challenges and the evidence is clear that learners with a growth mindset orientation do better (Petty, 2011). This may not be surprising because those with a growth mindset believe that their effort will be rewarded and the challenge will eventually be overcome. This is in contrast to those with a fixed mindset, who may be inclined to give up quicker when faced with a challenge because they are not sure of eventual success. Therefore mindset orientation has a direct impact on learners' motivation.

Individuals do not necessarily have a single mindset. Instead, they may have different mindset orientations in different situations. For example, a person might believe that extensive practice will result in success in learning to play tennis (so displaying a growth mindset) but also believe that being able to play guitar to a high level relies essentially on having been born with a gift for music (a fixed mindset).

Mercer and Ryan (2010) investigated mindsets in language learning and found that even within that one sphere learners might have different mindset orientations for different subskills. So, a learner might believe that proficiency in listening could be improved through practice, while believing that a high level of pronunciation was better explained by having a natural ear for the language.

Discussion of growth and fixed mindsets tends to lead to the assumption of a binary distinction between the two but this is a simplification. In reality, the two orientations are extreme positions on a continuum, with most of us locating somewhere along the line, but with a tendency to one or the other.

The good news for teachers is that growth mindsets, the orientation that seems to promote more successful learning, can be taught, at least to some extent. As mindsets deal with implicit beliefs, learners might not even be aware of them and therefore a discussion of mindsets can help learners to develop an awareness of their own orientations and this in itself can bring about beneficial change. Another teaching strategy, particularly for young learners, is to highlight stories that demonstrate success being the result of hard work and perseverance, hence modelling growth mindsets. Teachers can also praise the effort applied to a task (I can see you worked really hard on this – well done) rather than the result (you got everything right – well done).

From *Teaching and Developing Reading Skills* © Cambridge University Press 2017   PHOTOCOPIABLE

However, Dweck herself has argued that effort is not sufficient for success. She argues that effort is only one factor and that learners may also need help in developing and applying efficient learning strategies (Dweck, 2014). It is the combination of effort and knowing how to learn that is likely to lead to success.

Mindset orientation is certainly an important individual learning variable and it can be influenced by schools and teachers to give learners a better chance of success. However, we should remember that there are also social factors that influence eventual learning outcomes and such factors are beyond the reach of an individual teacher, or, indeed, learner.

Dweck, C. (2014) 'The power of believing that you can improve'. Available online at: https://www.ted.com/talks/carol_dweck_the_power_of_believing_that_you_can_improve?lanlanla=en. [Last accessed 5 August 2017]

Dweck, C. (2006) *Mindset: The new psychology of success*, New York: Ballantine Books.

Dweck, C., Chiu, C. and Hong, Y. (1995) 'Implicit Theories and Their Role in Judgments and Reactions: A World From Two Perspectives', *Psychological inquiry* 6(4), pp. 267–285.

Mercer, S. and Ryan, S. (2010) 'A mindset for EFL: learners' beliefs about the role of natural talent', *ELT Journal*, 64(4), pp. 436–444.

Petty, G. (2011). 'Dweck's theory of motivation'. Available online at: http://teacherstoolbox.co.uk/T_Dweck.html. [Last accessed 5 August 2017]

▶ An email of complaint

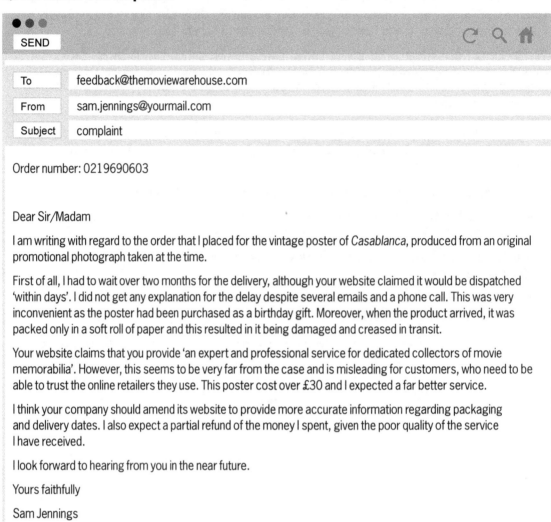

SEND

To	feedback@themoviewarehouse.com
From	sam.jennings@yourmail.com
Subject	complaint

Order number: 0219690603

Dear Sir/Madam

I am writing with regard to the order that I placed for the vintage poster of *Casablanca*, produced from an original promotional photograph taken at the time.

First of all, I had to wait over two months for the delivery, although your website claimed it would be dispatched 'within days'. I did not get any explanation for the delay despite several emails and a phone call. This was very inconvenient as the poster had been purchased as a birthday gift. Moreover, when the product arrived, it was packed only in a soft roll of paper and this resulted in it being damaged and creased in transit.

Your website claims that you provide 'an expert and professional service for dedicated collectors of movie memorabilia'. However, this seems to be very far from the case and is misleading for customers, who need to be able to trust the online retailers they use. This poster cost over £30 and I expected a far better service.

I think your company should amend its website to provide more accurate information regarding packaging and delivery dates. I also expect a partial refund of the money I spent, given the poor quality of the service I have received.

I look forward to hearing from you in the near future.

Yours faithfully

Sam Jennings

From *Teaching and Developing Reading Skills* © Cambridge University Press 2017   PHOTOCOPIABLE

⟐ SueZe Lashes

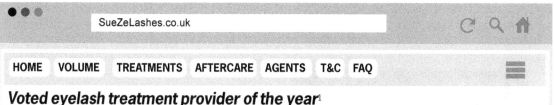

SueZeLashes.co.uk

| HOME | VOLUME | TREATMENTS | AFTERCARE | AGENTS | T&C | FAQ |

Voted eyelash treatment provider of the year[1]

SueZe LASHES

The perfect treat. The perfect treatment.

Here at SueZe Lashes we always want to share our good news – and we think this is very good news.

As the leading experts in volume technology, we are pleased to announce that our all new 3D eyelash extensions, featuring eProSynth+ are now available. Our unique eProSynth+ formula is scientifically proven to keep lashes separate for longer – leaving you to enjoy perfect eyelashes 24/7. No fuss, no curlers and no need for mascara.

Just perfect lashes. Always.

Each lash extension coated with eProSynth+ is added individually to your own lashes* and creates the natural luscious look you want. All your natural beauty – extended. And simply irresistibly attractive lashes.

Feel the confidence of perfect lashes.

To book an appointment with one of our expert advisers, click here.

Be the you that you want to be.

[1] As voted by readers of EyelashHome.com

* All our bonding agents are manufactured to EU safety standards.

From *Teaching and Developing Reading Skills* © Cambridge University Press 2017   PHOTOCOPIABLE

⟰ Football conversation

Two friends are each watching a game of football between Portugal and Poland. They are in different countries and chatting to each other on a real time messenger app as the game happens. Peter is from the UK. Monika is from Poland.

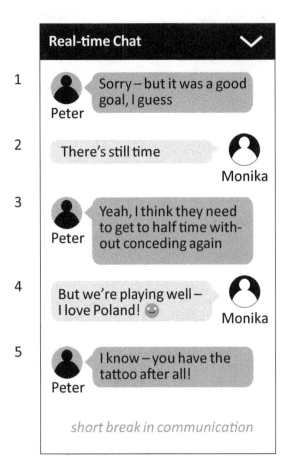

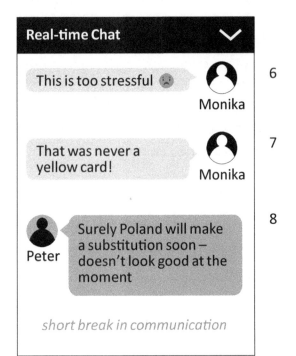

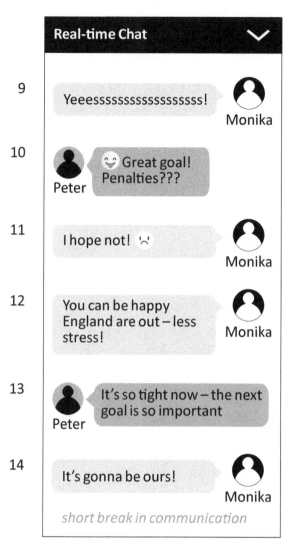

9 Yeeesssssssssssssssssss! — Monika

10 Peter — 😀 Great goal! Penalties???

11 I hope not! ☹ — Monika

12 You can be happy England are out – less stress! — Monika

13 Peter — It's so tight now – the next goal is so important

14 It's gonna be ours! — Monika

short break in communication

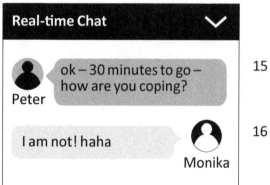

15 Peter — ok – 30 minutes to go – how are you coping?

16 I am not! haha — Monika

PHOTOCOPIABLE

Index

Activity names are in **bold**. Locators in *italics* refer to figures and tables.